P9-DNZ-434

PLAY THERAPY TECHNIQUES

edited by
**Charles E. Schaefer, Ph.D.
and Donna M. Cangelosi, Psy. D.**

JASON ARONSON INC.
Northvale, New Jersey
London

This book was set in 11 point Cheltenham by Lind Graphics of Upper Saddle River, New Jersey

1997 Printing

Copyright © 1993 by Jason Aronson Inc.

10 9 8

All rights reserved. Printed in the United States of America. No part of this book may be used or reproduced in any manner whatsoever without written permission from Jason Aronson Inc. except in the case of brief quotations in reviews for inclusion in a magazine, newspaper, or broadcast.

Library of Congress Cataloging-in-Publication Data

Schaefer, Charles E.
  Play therapy techniques / by Charles E. Schaefer and Donna M.
Cangelosi.
    p. cm.
  Includes bibliographical references and index.
  ISBN 0-87668-176-3 (pbk.)
  1. Play therapy—Methodology. I. Cangelosi, Donna M. II. Title.
  [DNLM: 1. Play Therapy—in infancy & childhood. 2. Play Therapy—
methods.   WS 350.2 S294p]
RJ505.P6S27 1993
618.92′89165—dc20
DNLM/DLC
for Library of Congress   92-49535

Manufactured in the United States of America. Jason Aronson Inc. offers books and cassettes. For information and catalog write to Jason Aronson Inc., 230 Livingston Street, Northvale, New Jersey 07647.

Contents

Preface

Regardless of school or theory, all play therapy plans involve the use of specific techniques or strategies to implement the treatment. Many useful writings on play techniques have appeared as articles in our literature over the past fifty years but they are located in widely scattered journals and are very difficult for clinicians to access. The purpose of this volume is to provide, for the first time, a convenient sourcebook of practical techniques in play therapy.

In selecting articles for the book we were guided by three main criteria: first, to offer as wide a variety of play techniques as possible, including art, puppet, sand, dramatic, water, doll, costume, and game play. Second, we wanted to include both classic and more recent approaches. Third, we sought articles that contained explicit "how to" procedures to guide both novice and experienced play therapists.

Since this book is intended as an orientation in the field of play therapy, the selections are mainly concerned with the individual treatment of children. Future volumes are planned to cover strategies for family and group play therapies.

This book is intended as an aid for doing play therapy with children. Of course, to become proficient as a play therapist, one must combine book knowledge with formal courses, professional supervision, and extensive clinical experience. The present volume is intended for students and practitioners of child therapy and counseling, including psychologists, psychiatrists, social workers, caseworkers, nurses, and child life and occupational therapists.

We wish to express our appreciation to all the authors who agreed to allow their writings to be reproduced and to the publishers for granting permission to do so.

Charles E. Schaefer
Donna M. Cangelosi
October, 1992

1

Introduction

The interest of psychologists in children and their play activities dates back to the latter part of the nineteenth century. Early studies were mainly concerned with the observation, categorization, and classification of play activities and their forms and structure.

Historically, the first author to attempt to understand the psychology of children through observations of play was Rousseau. Many years later, Sigmund Freud described child's play as "poetic creation." Freud theorized that play allows the child to transpose passive experiences into active ones, thereby allowing the child to gain mastery over conflictual experiences. At about the same time, Hertha von Hug-Hellmuth, an Austrian psychiatrist, observed and played with children in their homes in order to become familiar with their daily environment. Historically, she is credited as being the first clinician to use observations of play behavior as a method for treating children suffering from psychological difficulties.

The English School of Psychoanalysis, led by Melanie Klein, and the Vienna School of Psychoanalysis, led by Anna Freud, grew out of the work of Hug-Hellmuth. Both schools used the play technique as a partial substitution for the more verbal methods of child treatment. Since these beginnings in the second and third decades of this century, play investigation and play therapy have developed as important and by now indispensable methods in child psychiatry and psychology.

The first child guidance clinics opened in the early 1920s and beginning with them, the use of play in child psychotherapy has become widespread. This movement initiated the development and introduction of structured play techniques.

It was not until 1939, nearly twenty years after Hug-Hellmuth's initial introduction of play as a treatment modality, that specific, structured play techniques were introduced. David Levy (1939) was among the first child clinicians to introduce a structured play therapy technique that he called *Release Therapy*. Levy believed that the therapist, aware of the child's specific difficulty, could arrange dolls and play materials in a specific way to promote catharsis and insight through symbolic play. He believed that catharsis and subsequent relearning, vis-à-vis the therapist's interventions, are important for restructuring areas of development that have been blocked.

Jacob Conn's description of the *Play Interview* and Gove Hambridge's *Structured Play Therapy*, which are included in this volume, are elaborations of Levy's technique. Each of these procedures focuses on specific situations that are believed to be the cause of the child's difficulty. Likewise, Linda Kuhli's chapter describing the use of two houses in play therapy provides a specific application of the technique for use with children who have experienced loss, withdrawal, or rejection.

Levy's introduction of *Release Therapy* in 1939 coincided with Margaret Lowenfeld's introduction of what later became known as *The World Technique*. Buhler expanded and brought this projective sand technique to the United States in 1951. The technique uses a sandbox in which the child is asked to make a world from a wide variety of miniature toys. The toys chosen and the world created are seen as symbolic representations of the child's inner world.

While Levy's approach is much more structured and specific than Lowenfeld's *World Technique*, the two have in common a focus on symbolic play. Through the years, many play therapy techniques using puppets, masks, costumes, and the like have been introduced with the same intent—to foster symbolic play, thereby allowing children to reveal their emotional lives through play materials.

In 1938, Shaw discovered that finger painting provided cathartic and therapeutic functions for her young students. Several years later, in 1946, Jacob Arlow and Asja Kadis elaborated Shaw's ideas regarding the therapeutic properties of finger painting. They introduced this modality as a form of projective play and a vehicle for the expression of fantasies and free associations. Interestingly, Arlow and Kadis described finger painting as a socially sanctioned form of playing with mud. However, eight years later, Adolf Woltmann promoted the direct use of the more natural mediums of mud and clay as therapeutic materials for children involved in play therapy.

Woltmann noted that both mud and clay are neutral media through which the child can project meaning. In a 1954 paper, he credited Lauretta Bender for the insight that play therapy can be done with children of all countries by using sand, stones, palm leaves, snow, or pieces of ice—provided that such natural materials have meaning to the child. Consistent with this observation, the use of water, sand, and other natural media such as food have been cited over the years as having therapeutic value in the treatment of children.

Still another play therapy technique was introduced by D. W. Winnicott in 1968. This play procedure, which Winnicott called *the squiggle game,* was developed as a means for developing a relationship with his young patients and as a projective tool. Winnicott would draw a squiggle that the child could turn into something else. Following the child's elaboration of the squiggle, the child would draw another squiggle that the therapist could turn into a drawing of something that could, in turn, foster the discussion of important issues.

Several years later, Richard Gardner introduced a storytelling technique to elicit concerns and conflicts. Gardner's *Mutual Story Telling* technique involves asking the child to make up a story. The therapist, having interpreted the story psychodynamically, then takes a turn to tell a story using the child's language as well and the same setting and characters. However, the therapist introduces healthier adaptations and resolutions to difficulties with the goal of imparting insight, values, and coping skills. It is believed that the use of the child's language fosters the child's understanding.

Variations of Gardner's storytelling technique have been introduced over the years. For example, Robert Brooks (1981 this volume, Chapter 18) introduced a much more structured storytelling procedure that he calls *Creative Characters.* Like Levy, Brooks applies background information regarding the child's presenting problem but instead of using dolls, creates a story using animals as main characters to reflect the child's situation or difficulty. The child is then asked to elaborate on the story.

While storytelling techniques allow the therapist to steer the treatment and focus in on specific issues, other verbal play techniques, such as role-playing, allow for the child's spontaneous expression vis-à-vis the taking on of another person's role or identity. The idea of making believe, which is seen actively in doll play and other symbolic play procedures, is the basis of role-playing techniques that are used with children. Historically, role-playing techniques were used by adult therapists involved in psychodrama as well as Gestalt and behavioral therapies. Their application in the treatment of children has included both costume play and verbal role-playing approaches. Irwin Marcus (1966) noted that role-playing techniques are especially helpful in the treatment of latency age children who are often less willing to engage in doll play and other forms of imaginative play.

Unlike the young child who is primarily interested in symbolic games, the latency age child is interested in games with rules. This understanding of the needs of children at various developmental stages has led to the use of board games, which provide a vehicle for the latency child's need to develop a sense of achievement, competence, mastery of the environment, and self-esteem. Gardner in 1969 was among the first child therapists to describe the use of checkers as a diagnostic and therapeutic instrument. The competitive component of this game is seen as having value in that it provides an opportunity for the child to gain a sense of mastery and competence and for the therapist to gain a better understanding of the child's intrapsychic dynamics and interpersonal style.

Gardner's development of the *Talking, Feeling and Doing Game* several years later stirred what has now become an industry of noncompetitive therapeutic board games. Child therapists from a wide variety of theoretical backgrounds have developed games to promote communication, insight, and cognitive understandings, and to address the needs of specific populations such as abused children, children from divorced families, and children with special educational or social needs.

More recently, computer games and electronic techniques have been introduced as tools for play therapy. As an adjunct to the more traditional play techniques they are seen as a vehicle to engage children in treatment and can be used to help children develop problem solving skills, improved ways of channeling aggression, higher level thinking skills, cooperation, and other interpersonal values and skills.

In the past seventy years since the observations of Freud and von Hug-Hellmuth, the practice of play therapy has become the most widely used modality of child psychotherapy. Despite a wide variety of theoretical orientations that now exist within the field, the basic premise that play is the child's preferred and natural medium of expression has been integrated into the work of child therapists. A recently developed international association marks the fact that play therapy is, in fact, a specialized field within the mental health profession.

This book is intended as a resource for child therapists engaged in the practice of play therapy. It is organized in six major sections. While there is significant overlap in terms of the categorization of play therapy techniques, the primary attribute of each was considered in organizing them into sections. Following is a brief synopsis of each general section.

Section I outlines symbolic play techniques beginning with the early works of Conn and Hambridge and spanning thirty years to include various uses of dolls, puppets, masks, telephones, and blocks.

Section II outlines play techniques using natural media such as sand, water, food, mud, and clay.

Section III includes drawing and art techniques used in play therapy. A variation of Winnicott's squiggle game, as well as finger painting and the use of specific techniques, is included.

Section IV combines storytelling, role-playing, and relaxation/ imagery techniques for children. These were grouped together because each uses verbal communication to achieve therapeutic gains.

Section V describes specific uses of classic board games in doing play therapy with latency age children.

Section VI describes the use of computer games and electronic games, two innovative approaches in the field of play therapy.

References

Levy, D. M. (1939). Release therapy. *American Journal of Orthopsychiatry* 9:713–736.

Lowenfeld, M. (1939). The world pictures of children. *British Journal of Medical Psychology* 18:65–101.

Marcus, I. M. (1966). Costume play therapy: the exploration of a method for stimulating imaginative play in older children. *Journal of the American Academy of Child Psychiatry* 5:441–452.

Winnicott, D. W. (1968). The squiggle game. *Voices* Spring, 140–151.

PART I
Symbolic Play Techniques

2

The Play-Interview

JACOB H. CONN

The child who is brought to the psychiatrist is ill at ease, apprehensive and wondering what is going to happen next. He is aware that he has aroused the fears of his parents and that he has become a nuisance to those in his environment.

Parents are given an opportunity to present their side of the story in great detail. An interested physician makes it his business to listen respectfully and helps to relieve the parents of the burden of excessive self-criticism or unjust accusation. In this manner they may ease their tension and redistribute the responsibility for the child's behavior in keeping with their own emotional needs and intellectual convictions.

How can the psychiatrist get the child to present his side of the story? What is bothering him? What are his complaints, dissatisfactions and interests? What has *he* contributed to the fears which have developed at home or at play, and to what degree have others made him unhappy?

I have had the opportunity of working with children at the Children's Psychiatric Service (conducted by Dr. Leo Kanner) of the Harriet Lane Home, Johns Hopkins Hospital, and in private practice. The methods which have been developed since 1932 have been included as part of the general personality survey of the child. In each case the home and school situation is reviewed and physical, psychometric and other special studies are made in accordance with the needs of the individual child. Social service aid is often enlisted, school adjustments are recommended and the attitudes of the parents are investigated in conjunction with the play-interview of the child. Thus in a previous paper, (Conn 1939), I stated that "The play method is included in this plan of treatment as one of many procedures. It serves to supplement other methods and contributes material which deals with the personal, emotional and imaginative aspects of the child's behavior. During each play-interview the child is treated as an equal, whose opinions are respected and listened to attentively. The child's responses are accepted at their face value. No preliminary attempt is made to bind the child to the physician by ties of gratitude for favors granted or the need for adult protection. In each case the child's complaints are made the focus of the therapeutic situation. The child comes to the physician because he is frightened, car sick or enuretic. How can he best be helped and be taught to help himself? How much has *he* contributed to his personal discomfort? The question of personal responsibility and the acknowledgment by the child of the role which he, himself, plays in the total situation comes up repeatedly in this method. The physician assumes the part of the friendly, informed adult, who is naturally curious to know *why* the child makes the doll do and say what it does when it does. The procedure provides a number of opportunities for the child to express his feelings and thoughts through the medium of the dolls, as if they were responsible for all that was said and done. Thus the child, as an impartial spectator, can view objectively what is going on, at the same time that he is actively participating in an intimate discussion of his own attitudes. It is not the child himself, but the doll, who is afraid of the dark. It is not he who is jealous or hates, but the doll-character; therefore, he can give an account of the motives and imaginations which may explain the doll's behavior, and consequently his own. Toy furniture and dolls representing various characters (parents, teachers, siblings, etc.) are used during the play-session, and various 'sets' are arranged by the physician as upon a miniature stage."

The child is given an opportunity to play freely with the dolls, but the emphasis in this procedure is placed upon planned play-situations which may be repeated as frequently as desirable. Such problems as car sickness, fear states, stuttering, sibling jealousies, reactions to parental under- or over-solicitude and more recently, the sex attitudes and sex awareness of the child have been studied by giving him an opportunity to express himself in a series of play-interviews.

Clinical Presentations

The first case is that of Ruth, aged 10 years, 11 months (I.Q. 110), the youngest of four children, brought to the clinic by her mother, a slovenly woman, who was living with a man to whom she was not married. The home was described as being neglected and filthy; the parents had quarreled frequently. The father was out of the home and was working as a laborer. He had been in a state hospital at one time. Ruth had failed the fourth grade during the past year. In this setting this frail looking, timid child had developed fears of the dark, fidgetiness, facial tics, nail biting, head jerking and frequent throat clearing.

During the first contact Ruth stated that she was afraid to stay home alone, reported frequent dreams of falling off cliffs, and spoke of her fear of dark stairs. She added: "When I hear a fire engine, I hope it isn't my mother. I run home. I remember to see if she is safe." She also was unable to play away from home for any length of time without returning home to learn if anything had happened to her mother.

In addition to working with the home situation, it was decided to work with the child through the medium of play-interviews. Ruth was told to select any of the dolls and to play whatever game she wished. She chose a mother, father, little girl and boy dolls and began to re-enact a domestic scene. After playing for a while, she put the baby girl to bed with a lullaby. During this phase of her play-interest, suggestive questions were of no value in getting her to speak of her fears. Ruth had said:

They (the parents) go to bed. The children sleep at the bottom of the bed.

Q: Does anything happen during the night? A: No.
Q: Do the children sleep all night? A: Yes.

She continued her spontaneous play, awakening the parents, serving breakfast; then the father was sent off to work. The mother and the little girl were taken out for a walk, and on the way the mother met a friend and walked off with her, leaving the little girl alone.

Q: How does she feel? A: She don't feel so happy. The little girl feels frightened. She is afraid of strangers. They might take her away. They might kidnap or kill her.

She continued:

The mother calls the brother, and they return home. She is always afraid. She sticks around her brother.

Q: Of what is she afraid? A: That someone might pick her up and kidnap her.

The third play-interview took place a week later. After a preliminary play-introduction, the psychiatrist set up a toy house and said:

This little girl (doll) walks up the steps. How does she feel?

A: She is real careful. She keeps close to the wall. Somebody might throw a knife down from up on the third floor (she had seen this occur in the movies).

Q: Why does she get scared? A: Because it's real dark and real spooky. She thinks somebody is going to come down the steps and kill her.

Q: Who might kill her? A: It might be a stranger, a rough looking boy. (She picks out a male doll.) I was coming up the steps. He (the male doll) might be on the third floor and throw a knife. He might take her money and run away. (The male doll was arranged to face the girl doll).

Q: What does she see? A: She sees a gangster-looking guy.

Q: Can she recognize him? A: She must recognize him.

Q: Whom does he look like? A: Like a boy (who lives) downstairs. He is real tall, gawky-looking.

Q: What do you think he might do? A: He steals.

Ruth recalled that he once stole his brother's jewelry and said, "I get scared every time I see him." She added that she really thinks that this boy might jump out at her and take away her grocery money, and then threaten to kill her if she told.

During the fourth session, two weeks later she was asked:

Q: What things did you begin to learn about? A: Why the doll was scared to stay alone. She was afraid because somebody would kidnap her.

Q: Whom shall we play with? A: The same dolls.

The patient selected a little girl and a boy. She set up a bedroom and a kitchen. She described how the children are in bed, the father has his breakfast, kisses his wife goodbye and goes to work. The children are awakened and have their breakfast.

Q: Now we soon are going to see why the little girl is scared.

A: The mother finishes cleaning the home, then goes to town, coming home in time to prepare dinner. The children come in together.

Q: Why? A: The brother is afraid that someone might kidnap her (if he leaves her alone). The brother runs off to school (after dinner). The little girl cries. She starts to school alone. A man jumps out of the alley and grabs her. He binds her. He learns that she wasn't in school. The family start searching and can't find her. They telephone the police. The mother sits around and cries. When the father goes out to look for her, he passes a "spooky house." He hears a little cry. "Why, that's Dorothy." He sees her all tied up and takes her out. He picks up a club, then ties up the hands of the kidnapper, whom he finds asleep, and brings them both home. When the kidnapper wakes up, the father socks him one with his fist. He says, "If the cops couldn't take you to the police station, I'd kill you." Then the cops come and take him away, and they live happily ever after.

Q: Why was she kidnapped? A: I don't know.

Q: What does she have to know in order not to be afraid of kidnappers?

A: She has to know why they want to kidnap her. She hasn't any money—why should they want her?

Q: Now take the kidnapper—place the little girl in front of him. Let her look at him. (The patient does this.) She is looking at him. What does she see?

A: She sees her kidnapper.

Q: What does he look like? A: Like her father.

Q: Why does he look like her father? A: They look rough and cruel.

Q: And her father looks? A: Rough and cruel, in his eyes like.

Q: And *your* father looks? A: Rough and cruel.

Q: Now let this little girl go into the house alone.

A: She is afraid of the dark. Somebody might jump out.

Q: Who? A: The kidnapper. He is like her father. He looks rough and cruel.

Q: How can this help you? A: It can help my nerves. Help me be more brave. I used to be scared of darkness, but now when I think of it I am not scared in darkness. I think it's imagination.

Q: What did you learn today? A: Today I learned this little girl was kidnapped. The man looked just like her father.

Q: What does that mean? A: Maybe it could have been her father that kidnapped her or someone who looked like him. Maybe it's imagination, that she wants to be kidnapped.

Q: All those ideas are? A: Her own. It means she wants to be kidnapped.

Q: If she is kidnapped? A: She'll be with her father.

Q: What good can that do for *you?* A: It can make my nervousness stop. I want to be kidnapped. I want to be with my father.

Q: Do you *really?* A: Yes. But I don't want to leave my mother to be with my father.

The fifth play interview occurred one week later. The patient was asked,

Q: How are you feeling? A: All right.

Q: What did you learn last time? A: I learned not to be afraid that somebody is going to kidnap me.

Q: Did it make any difference? A: I am not scared any more going up steps.

Q: Really? A: Yes, I am not scared. Nobody is going to kidnap me. I haven't anything. It was my father; he wanted to get me away from my mother. He wanted me around him some time.

Q: Whose idea was that? A: Mine. I'd like to be kidnapped—because it was my father who was going to kidnap me.

Q: Why did you like it? A: Because I'd be with my father.

Q: In other words, you were really scared of whom? A: Of myself, of my imagination.

Q: Let's make out this is a country place, and this little girl (doll) came there. She is not with her mother or father. What does she think?

A: She is lonesome, she wants to go home.

Q: What is she thinking? A: That something might happen to her mother.

Q: Let's see what could happen at home. Put the girl doll here on this side, and let her imagine what can happen at home, while you play it out.

Ruth began:

Mother is fixing breakfast for her husband. He kisses her goodbye and goes to work, and the (older) sister goes to school. The mother is left alone. She lies down to rest. She is not feeling well. (The older girl helps with the dinner.) The husband calls a doctor who says, "She is very, very ill and should go to a hospital right away" She is taken to a hospital. The little girl is thinking of whether her mother is going to die, but she doesn't; she gets well.

Q: You knew what I meant by the country, didn't you?

A: Yes, Happy Hills. (This is the convalescent home where Ruth had been for several days, three months previously. She had made her mother promise to think of her every evening at six o'clock and apparently had done the same. After one week she ran away and, when caught, threatened to kill herself if she was not sent home to her mother. Ruth was held by the police until her mother came for her on that day.)

Q: What were your imaginations? A: Maybe my mother was sick and she might die.

Q: The kidnappers were whose imaginations? A: The little girl's.

Q: So are what other imaginations? A: The mother being sick.

Q: What does the little girl think? A: Her mother often gets sick with indigestion. She might get sick and die.

Q: It's whose idea? A: The little girl's.

Q: What kind of an imagination is this one? A: The mother will get sick and die. The little girl will have her father. She's still got her father and she feels all right.

Q: Now this little girl's father and mother live apart? A: Yes, but they ought to live together. That's what the little girl wants.

Q: She has only one or the other. What imagination can she have? A: That her mother might die.

Q: Why? A: She'd be by her father, if he would take her.

Q: Does she really want to be with her father? A: Yes, sir.

Q: How much? A: A whole lot, 'cause she likes her father too.

Q: How can this help *you* in any way? A: It helps me from being afraid that my mother might die.

Q: What can it do for you? A: It can stop me from being afraid.

Q: Before when you played on the street, how did you feel? A: Frightened.

Q: Why? A: I used to imagine somebody might kidnap me. I used to rush home to see if my mother is all right.

Q: Now? A: I know it's imagination.

Q: Whose? A: The little girl's.

Q: Whose is that? A: Mine.

Q: How can this help you? A: It'll help my nerves. I won't run home to see if my mother is all right. I know it's just imagination.

Q: Whose? A: Mine.

The patient did not keep the next two appointments, but returned two months later for the sixth play-interview.

Q: How are you? A: I feel all right. I feel fine.

Q: Is there any difference now from the way that you used to feel? A: I used to feel nervous; now since I came here, I am not afraid to go up our steps, stay in the dark and stay by myself.

Q: What else? A: I am not afraid any more of getting kidnapped.

Q: Have you any complaints? A: No, sir. Q: Any dreams? A: No, sir.

Q: Any scared or funny experiences? A: No, sir.

Q: Do you mean that you can go up and down your dark stairs and not be afraid? A: Yes, sir.

Q: How is that? A: I know no one would want to kidnap me or hurt me. I haven't anything to give them.

Q: How did you get the idea? A: Just had the feeling.

Q: Why? Because? A: It meant to get me away from my mother. Once somebody grabbed my sister in an alley. She got away. (This occurred about one year ago.)

Q: Has she been scared of kidnappers? A: No, sir.

Q: But you were scared of them? A: 'Cause I read of so many kidnappers in the papers.

Q: Why did you make so much of all that? A: I wanted to be kidnapped.

Q: Why? What would happen? A: I would just go with my father.

Q: What about the running in from play scared and being worried about your mother? A: I don't have to worry. I know it's my imagination, and my mother is O.K.

Q: How do you explain that? A: I used to think that something might happen to her. She might cut herself or hurt herself, or get indigestion. She often gets indigestion and she has no one with her.

Q: What might happen? A: She might die. She had two operations already. Now I don't run home. I know she is all right.

Q: Why did you have these imaginations? A: My mother would die, and I'd go with my father.

Q: That's the same as what other imaginations? A: The kidnapping imaginations.

Q: Why couldn't you stay at Happy Hills (the convalescent home)? A: I wanted to be home. Something might happen to my mother while I was out there.

Q: Why? A: 'Cause my mother would die, and I'd go with my father.

The seventh play-interview took place two weeks later. Ruth was asked:

Q: How about the dark? A: I am not scared of the dark any more. My mother puts out the lights to keep the mosquitoes out. I stay in the kitchen alone.

Q: Before? A: I used to go in with my mother and lay down alongside of her. (Ruth also said that she was not afraid of walking down the stairs.)

Ruth was seen for the eighth and last time after an interval of two years and two months. The seven play-interviews had been distributed over a period of four months. During this last interview the patient (age 13) stated that she was no longer afraid of the dark and that she was able to cross dark alleys without being apprehensive. She said that she no longer ran home to see if her mother might be ill and added: "I know she can take care of herself. If anything did happen, I would be notified right away, and if I was home, it would happen anyway." She vaguely recalled being afraid of kidnappers, but she could not remember whom the kidnapper had resembled.

The above material illustrates the method of working directly with the child and the emphasis which is placed upon *the concrete difficulties which have arisen at a specific time in this child's life-situation.* No claim is made that this method will provide a "cure all" for all of the problems which may arise in the future. Neither can it be stated that the personality of this child has been so altered that she will not be involved in other difficulties. Thus, four months after the above interview, Ruth and a boyfriend were picked up in the park late at night by the police and referred to the Juvenile Court.

Ruth had utilized her freedom from her fears of the dark by staying out late with boys. The influence of the neglected home, where the mother is living with a man to whom she is not married, cannot be minimized in planning for the care of this patient. In addition to the personal and emotional issues, which have been studied and treated by the method of the play-interview, the family and social factors must be taken into consideration by the physician and the community agencies who are interested in this girl's future welfare.

Henry, 10 years, 8 months of age (I.Q. 96), the oldest of three children, had been referred to the Children's Psychiatric Service, Harriet Lane Home, because of his failure to progress in school. He was described by his mother as being "nervous all the time" and wetting the bed, biting his nails and having temper tantrums during which he struck at his mother. Henry had experienced breathholding spells in early childhood which were treated by dashing cold water upon him. Despite these complaints, the mother added that Henry was "unselfish" and "generally admitted that he had done wrong, although he knew that he would get punished" and that he had many loyal friends among the troop of Cub Scouts to which he belonged.

His parents had been divorced when he was 7 years of age, four years before his first visit to the clinic. The mother, who had been deserted after discovering that the father was carrying on an extra-marital affair, was remarried two years later to an uncongenial older man. The step-father is said to have paid little attention to the patient.

During the first contact Henry complained:

My head aches. I get it when I go sleigh riding. The last time was yesterday afternoon. I am dizzy. I can't do my work. I am nervous. I can't study. I can't get my mind to it. I don't get to sleep until twelve o'clock, and in the morning I wake up real early and just lay there. When I wake up, my legs hurt me and I am tired.

Q: Are you afraid of anything? A: I am afraid of colored people. I am afraid in the dark, but I am getting out of that. The street cars get me dizzy and scared. On a slippery day I am scared. I think a machine will slide and hit it, or it will run off the track.

Q: Do you dream much? A: About my father, that he will come back some day. He is in Florida. He is working there. I seen him the last time (two years previously). He sees me once a year. He left me when I was seven years old. I forgive him 'cause he treats us nice, he sends us money. I think he left for his health.

The boy's attitude to his step-father:

He says bad things about me. He curses and tells dirty jokes around me. He fusses a lot when the house ain't warm. He treats all of us good. He goes out almost every night, plays cards.

His attitude to his two sisters:

We fuss a lot. One of them is just like me. She is nervous, skinny and underweight. That's Nancy (age 9). But Kingsley (age 7) is fat like an elephant. She can take hard cracks, but Nancy can't. She cries every time she falls down.

His attitude to the school situation:

The first two years was swell. Then in the third grade it began. I got nervous—plenty nervous. Some of the work was hard.

Q: Especially? A: Spelling. I can't get along with spelling. The best is history (P), English (M or P) and geography (M or P). I get P in reading and D (failure) in spelling.

After this complaint statement was made by the patient, a boy doll was placed in a toy bed. Henry was asked:

Q: What does he think of before he falls asleep? A: Of his mother, what she has done for him. I say my prayers.

Q: What might happen? A: There is one thing I am scared of, it's that furnace down there. The flames in the morning come up and might catch the house on fire. We have cotton on the chairs. Cloth burns good and it would set the furniture on fire. I think about my mother and father. I pray a lot. I pray to God to make my father come back and make him well.

Q: Let's imagine he falls asleep and dreams. A: I dream about my mother and father, that they will get me new things. I dream he will bring me a dog. He promised it to me. But my step-father don't like animals.

A toy street car with a female doll, two girl dolls and a boy doll in it was placed before the patient:

Q: How does the boy feel? A: He feels like he is dizzy. When he rides on a street car long, he gets dizzy and he gets scared.

Q: In which way? A: Like a car would skid and hit the streetcar and bump it off the track. In the summer time nothing gets me dizzy 'cause there is nothing to worry about. Nothing can skid.

Q: You can begin to see that it's not the streetcar that makes you sick. A: It's me, it's the boy, what he really thinks.

Q: What will happen if it turns over? A: People will get hurt naturally. The boy will think he will get hurt and die.

Q: And what else? A: His parents might get hurt. He rides with his mother. His mother is taller. She can fall over him and get hurt worst, and the boy wouldn't get hurt hardly. The boy has nothing to worry about; he would be put into a home.

Q: What else? A: He might live with his father. If he lives with his father, he would have nothing to worry about.

Q: What is the point of all this? A: The boy don't have nothing to worry about. It's the way the boy thinks of bad things. He thinks of the car turning over and hurting his mother.

Q: So that? A: So that he will have to live with his father instead of his mother.

Q: And that? A: Is what he should do.

Q: All this is whose idea? A: His, the boy's.

Q: Who is that? A: Me.

Q: Here is a boy (doll) in bed. What does he think? A: He thinks about the fire. He shouldn't, 'cause it ain't going to happen.

Q: Now suppose there is a fire? A: It's going to spread. It will set the whole house on fire. Maybe his mother or step-father or sister will get hurt.

Q: And then? A: He ain't got nothing to worry, 'cause his real father will take care of him.

Q: In other words? A: It's the same thing as the streetcar.

Q: In which way? A: The streetcar ain't going to turn over, and the house is not going to catch afire. The boy worries a lot.

Q: But the boy uses these ideas in which way? A: He worries about them, he is afraid they will happen; then he goes to live with his father, when his mother is dead.

The patient was seen on two occasions two weeks apart, and came for a follow-up examination nine months later. At this time he reported that his step-father had deserted the family. Four months later, Henry and his two sisters were placed in a home for dependent children. He had been free from car sickness and fears of fire since the second play session.

When Henry was seen again for the last interview (seven months after the first contact) he spoke of his streetcar sickness as follows:

That's all gone. I don't have any more troubles with the streetcar. I used to think that a car would hit the streetcar. We (I and my mother) would be a goner.

Q: What about the fears of the fire? A: I thought the house would catch on fire and burn us, my mother and I and my sister.

Q: Then? A: I'd go to my father.

The patient said that he had no fear of fire at this time.

Henry had hoped that he would be sent to his father when he went to the children's home. He spoke of his sleep as being "swell." He had been placed in a special class for children of limited intelligence, where he stated that he had "picked up a lot" and was doing better in his studies.

This material indicates that the behavior disturbances of this child are definitely related to his life situation. The play-procedure gave him an opportunity to express his feelings, hopes and fears in a sympathetic setting. It was one of several aids (school adjustment, children's home placement) and the desertion of the step-father which helped to re-establish his security, following which his fears of fire, car sickness, insomnia and other evidences of uneasiness disappeared.

The problem of anxiety and hypochondriasis is illustrated by Barbara, a 6-year-old, self assertive, red-headed child of above average intelligence (I.Q. 116). This child was referred because she was keeping the family awake by screaming that she had an earache. Two weeks before the onset of the "pains," the patient had a tonsillectomy, and two days later the crying spells began. Several physical examinations contributed nothing to explain why she was upset.

Barbara was the daughter of an oversolicitous mother and doting father. She had been the center of attention until the baby came, ten months previously. The patient had been irritated by the attention paid to her baby sister. She had been heard to say, "You don't pay attention to me, only to the baby."

Thus we have all the factors for a jealousy and attention-getting reaction in a spoiled, self-assertive youngster. But is this what the child is thinking?

A toy bed with a girl doll in it was set before the patient. Barbara was asked:

Q: What happens? A: Her throat hurts her. It really did at first. Now she gets up and cries every night.

Q: Why does she cry? A: She wants her mother to come in.

Q: If this girl cries, what is going to happen? A: She wants her mother to stay with her.

Q: Why does she cry? A: She wants to make her mother sick and die. She'll go to Heaven.

Q: Then? A: She'll have no mother.

Q: Does her throat hurt her bad? A: No.

Q: Then she is hollering for nothing? A: Yes. She wants to worry her mother.

Q: Now you know that the little girl is trying to have her own way. A: You're right. I am not going to cry.

Q: Are you going to sleep alone? A: Yes.

Three days later the mother reported that Barbara had slept alone without screaming for the first time in two weeks. She had referred to her earache only when she had been left out of the conversation.

During the second session, the patient spontaneously said, "You know what I did? I slept alone."

Q: Why? A: 'Cause I wanted to. My throat didn't hurt at all.

The problem of Barbara's contrariness in eating and dressing was taken up in this session. A little girl doll was seated at a toy table upon which were placed several toy dishes:

Q: How does this little girl eat? A: She doesn't care. She takes her fingers and puts it in her mouth and licks them, then walks away from the table. She tells her little sister not to eat anything.

Q: Why does she do that? A: She wants to show her mother and father how bad she wants to be.

Q: Why? A: She is trying to worry her mother.

Q: Why? A: So her mother (who has partially grey hair) will get gray hair and go to Heaven. So she won't have a mother. Her father will have to get a nurse. You know my grandfather died of pneumonia.

Q: Now you know why you don't eat with a fork? A: I want to worry my mother sometimes. She says she will go to Heaven if I keep on worrying her—so I try to worry her.

A mother doll is placed alongside of a little girl doll. The patient speaks for each doll by saying: "Doesn't our daughter eat terrible?" "You are right, she does eat terrible. We got to go down and watch the children how they eat. . . . Now she doesn't eat with her fingers. She doesn't want to be a bad girl."

Q: Here is a mother and her little girl. The mother gives her a dress to wear. A: The mother wants her to wear a brown dress. She says, "No, I want to wear my green dress." She is trying to worry her mother sick. She wants to let her mother go to Heaven; then her daddy will have to get a nurse.

Q: Now this girl can be a good girl. She knows why she wants another dress. Now you are going to be a good girl. A: 'Cause I don't worry my mother sick. I don't want my mother to go to Heaven.

Q: Why were *you* bad? A: I wanted my mother to go to Heaven.

Q: What is Heaven? A: Where they keep all dead people.

Q: And dead means? A: Their eyes are shut and don't open.

The next week, during the third session, the mother reported that Barbara had accepted whatever dress the mother had given her and had stopped annoying the baby. There had been no further complaints of earache. The patient reported that she was "all right."

Q: Why have you been so nice? A: 'Cause I want to.

Q: What did you learn here? A: If I didn't do what she (the mother) told me, she'd go to Heaven, and I wouldn't have any mother. And a nurse would have to do all the work.

Q: So? A: I'll be good I don't want that.

The child who becomes fearful is reacting to a particular life situation. It is not sufficient to state that the patient is an emotionally unstable child who has been subjected to a scary situation. In each individual case there are two important questions which must be answered. First, why has this specific fear state been elaborated out of a number of available fear patterns to which the child has been exposed at home, in the neighborhood and in the movies? Second, how does this fear state help the child out of a difficult life situation? The function of the fear, which is accepted and strongly reacted to, must be considered in every case.

Rita is a 10-year-old child of low-normal intelligence. She is the daughter of a dull, nagging mother, who is constantly complaining of diffuse aches and pains. The child is a whiny, scared, thin little girl who eats poorly, is afraid of the dark, has many somatic complaints, and has a marked fear of being kidnapped. The mother says that, "I always tell her not to go with strangers and to holler for help if a man would attack her."

Here apparently, is the source of the fear of being attacked and kidnapped. But why has this particular pattern of fear been accepted by this timid, apprehensive child?

The answer to these questions lies in the life situation of the child. Rita is the older of two children. Her younger sister, Gloria, aged 8, is the father's favorite child. She is called "smarter" and "prettier" than the patient. Rita is obviously at a disadvantage in this family setting. How can these facts explain why the fear of kidnapping plays such a significant role in her life? The child furnished the necessary connecting links in an experimental play setting.

Rita had placed two dolls, each in its own toy bed:

Q: These babies are? A: Asleep.

Q: Let's see what happens. A: The little one woke up. She sat on the floor. The other one woke up. They started to call their mother.

Q: Why? A: She (the older one) wanted something to eat.

Q: Why? A: She wanted the little one to go down stairs.

Q: Why? A: Somebody might come up and grab her (the younger sister).

Q: Why? A: Because her mother all the time tells her stories, and they believe it—about a baby who was sleeping in bed and a kidnapper came in and kidnapped her.

Q: Who? A: The baby. They started to believe it and thought it was true.

Q: Why? A: Because she (the older girl) thought that her sister was going to be kidnapped. . . .

Q: How does she feel? A: Not so good. She thinks the kidnapper will get her, and she makes out she takes up for the youngest one if the kidnappers would kidnap her (the younger sister).

Q: Then she'd feel? A: Better. . . .

Q: Why will she feel better? A: She isn't so smart as the other.

Q: And? A: She wants to stay home and play herself.

Q: Why? A: She'd get more—she'd get all the clothes. . . .

Q: Now what does she understand? A: About the kidnapping. When somebody tries to kidnap her sister, she won't let them. . . .

Q: Before? A: She'd feel glad. Now she don't, now she remembers she ought to feel bad about it.

Q: Whose idea was it? A: The oldest one. She won't be frightened because she understands a little. . . .

Q: What? A: She said, "How would she feel if she got kidnapped?" She began to think and then she said, "She wouldn't like it to have her sister kidnapped."

Q: Whose idea is it, the kidnapping? A: The older one's.

Q: What does that explain to *you?* A: That I won't be afraid of the kidnappers.

In this manner Rita was desensitized to her fear of kidnappers. She began to play less apprehensively and for the first time was able to sleep without a light in her bedroom.

The inter-relationships of jealousy, fear and hate and their disorganizing effects upon the behavior of the child are illustrated by the following material.

Eva is a 16-year-old, aggressive, emotionally unstable girl, who had run away from several foster homes, was known to drink, smoke excessively, and to have had sex relations. Her parents consented to have her placed in a state school for delinquent girls because of her spite reactions and constant quarreling with her younger sister and her mother.

As a child, Eva had demonstrated the capacity for prolonged temper tantrums, petty stealing from her mother, and truancy. She was finally expelled from school. She had failed twice in the seventh grade, despite the fact that she had achieved average intelligence scores on two psychometric tests.

There is an older brother and a younger sister in this home, who have made a fairly good adjustment. The father is a self-assertive, industrious working man, who is a stern disciplinarian. The mother is an oversolicitous, emotionally unstable woman of limited intelligence.

After Eva had been away for six months, the parents petitioned the court to permit her to return home. Eva was paroled with the understanding that she would undertake private psychiatric treatment and remain under the supervision of the Juvenile Court probation officer.

A lead to some of the personal sources of these emotional outbursts was obtained when Eva became fearful that she was ill with meningitis. A girl friend had recently died of this disease, and the patient had dreamed of her death. Eva had awakened frightened, and had felt as if she was suffering from the same illness. She would frequently tap her knee and feel her neck in order to know if it were becoming stiff.

Eva went on to say that she was afraid to see a dead person. She said, "It even makes me sick to hear about it." When she was 8 years old, Eva had been told that someone had died in the house where they were living. She became frightened, and now says, "I hated to stay in the house. I was afraid they might kill me or strangle me." It is of significance that Eva always imagined that it was a woman who lay in the coffin whenever she heard of, or dreamed of, a dead person. This was the case even if she had been told that it was a man who had died.

There had been similar episodes of terror, during which Eva had been unable to sleep at home whenever any member of the family had died. In an attempt to determine what attitudes were associated with these fears, the patient was asked to act out these imaginations by means of a doll. A girl doll was placed alongside of an adult female doll, who was supposed to represent a dead body.

Q: What does she (the girl doll) think? A: Someone might strangle her. She is afraid and she thinks she has done something. She's afraid of death and afraid of being attacked. When I saw the movie *San Francisco*, I became afraid of earthquakes. I'm afraid I'll be killed. She acts as if she killed the dead person, as if she murdered the corpse.

Two girl dolls were placed side by side, and the patient continued: The big girl is jealous of this little girl because she is the baby. The mother was more affectionate for the baby. She (the older girl) develops a jealousy, and then a hate of her sister.

Q: How does she show this hate? A: Fighting with the sister, taking things away.

Q: And? A: She hit her at night. Once I took a pan of boiling water and threw it on her leg. She acted like she don't like me and that made me hate her more. I tried to kill her. It used to burn me up.

Q: Who is the corpse? A: It's my sister. This girl thinks her sister will pay her back for the way she treated her. She (the older girl) wished the sister were dead. I wished that she would go away and never come back, and in the dream she comes back to repay me.

Eva was reassured concerning her fears of death and meningitis, and went on to discuss her desire to be a boy. She related how she had wanted to play football and climb fences. She thought of other girls as "sissies." Eva said, "If I could only be a boy and play rough games and go hiking. My father and brother were like pals."

The patient began to realize that her desires to be a boy were tied up with her interest in securing her father's affection. Her alcoholism and smoking belonged to the same group of motivations. She was acting "tough, like a boy." She supplemented the above statements by saying.

"It would mean everything to have my father love me so I could get as much freedom as my brother."

The aggressive, self-assertive child, his feeling of rejection and his need for self-expression is illustrated by the case of Silvio, age 9 years, 7 months, I.Q. 91. This boy is the second of three brothers. The father had fits of temper during which he would beat his wife, and finally he deserted the family when Silvio was 3 years of age. The mother is a tense, apprehensive woman who finds herself unable to cope with the financial strain of the family situation and Silvio's behavior. Her complaint was that "He won't do what I tell him and answers me back. He picks on the other children (age 8 and 11) all the time. He is a scared child who is afraid to stay alone. . . . He is always hitting other children. He hit a little girl the other day. He breaks bottles and upsets garbage cans. I am afraid that he will hurt somebody. He is sent home from school nearly every other day. I am a nervous wreck from him. He gets on my nerves. When I tell him to do something, he won't do it."

Direct conversation (in a previous interview) had resulted in the following record:

Q: How are you? A: All right.
Q: Why did you come to the hospital? A: For being restless in school.
Q: How do you like your teacher? A: I like her. She's nice sometimes.
Q: Do you have to fight much? A: No, sir.
Q: Do you like your studies? A: Yes, all right.
Q: How does your mother treat you? A: All right. I'm always good at home most of the time. Sometimes I throw stones.

Since the method of direct questioning had revealed very little concerning Silvio's attitudes, he was given an opportunity to express himself through the medium of several dolls representing children and adults. He was told, "Here are some boys and girls and some grown people. Let's see what is going to happen." Silvio chose a boy doll and began: "He is always bad when he wasn't supposed to be bad. He fights." (At this point Silvio banged the two boy dolls together.)

Q: Then what? A: Then he goes up to his teacher and kicks her. Then he goes over to this boy and pulls his hair. Then he walks out of the schoolhouse and kicks the janitor. Then he goes home to his mother, and his mother says, "Why ain't you in school?" He says, "I been fighting. She sent me home." He kicks his mother and runs out. He sees a boy walking along the street and hits him. . . .

The physician then pointed to the dolls alternatingly as Silvio replied for each one.

Boy doll: Why are you acting so tough?
Bad boy doll: It's none of your business.
Girl doll: You shouldn't show off.
Bad boy doll: Aw, I ain't showing off. I'm tough.
Q: The next girl says?
A: Second girl doll: You think you're somebody, hitting everybody.
Bad boy doll: I'm a tough guy around this block.

In a second play-interview Silvio was asked:

Q: What did we learn here last time? A: About the bad boy and the good one.

This one (pointed to a boy doll) didn't do what his mother told him. He shows off most of the time. He goes around picking fights. . . . He goes around with bad boys and breaks windows of houses and hops trucks. And he goes around tearing people's dresses. . . . And he takes his mother's eye-glasses and sets them on the ground. And he goes around hitting people with rulers. And he trips people. And he goes around at night hooking stuff and hopping trucks. And he goes around pulling people's hair. And he goes around the streets and sticks people with pins. And he goes around to people saying: "You want a cracker?" and they say, "Yeh," and he cracks them in the face. And he goes around throwing sand in people's faces. When he sees dogs and cats, he throws rocks at them. He takes B-B guns and shoots out windows. And when girls have bows on their hair, he pulls them off of them, and when he sees a boy with suspenders, he pulls them back and hurts him. And he takes pea shooters and shoots boys. And he goes around lifting girls' dresses up. And goes in a bathroom and pulls all the paper towels out. And he spits water all over the people. He pushes lights in an' out until his mother tells him to stop. He takes burned out bulbs and throws them down the alleys. And takes two bottles and ties strings around them, and when a car goes by, it will knock the bottles down and they'll break. And he takes ink and throws it on people's clean clothes. Around the house he is banging in the window and doors. He goes and pulls his mother's hair like it's a bell ringing. He takes off his shoe and hits people with it. He walks around the street and slaps kids right in the face. And he pulls people's neckties. And he scratches people's tables. And his mother tells him not to do it, (but) he fills the tub up to the top and turns the heater on full speed. He takes the screws out of the cellar doors. He goes around and pulls off girls' hats and throws them all around. He goes around and takes a hammer and bangs it on fire escapes. He yells in druggists' stores and rings doorbells and yells in there. He goes in druggists' stores and hooks something. He goes around and knocks chairs down and he breaks the legs of the chairs. . . .

Q: Two boys are talking about this. This boy asks: "Why do you do it? (The physician pointed from one doll to the other, the patient speaking for each doll.)

Q: Doll A: I just asked you.

Doll B: You don't have to ask me nothing.

Doll A: I don't care what you say. You ought to do what your mother says.

Doll B: My mother is a lot of phooey.

Doll A: You'd be sorry if you didn't have a mother.

Doll B: My mother ain't nobody. She acts too smart. I answer back and curse her.

Q: What is he trying to prove? A: He is trying to prove that he is bad. He likes it; he feels nice and strong.

Q: If he didn't do it? A: He'd be ashamed that he couldn't fight.

Q: What does he have to prove? A: That he is tough. . . .

Why did this boy feel as he did to his mother? Silvio's attitudes concerning his mother were studied in conjunction with his relationship to his siblings. The physician placed three boy dolls about a toy table. He pointed to the smallest boy doll, then to the others, indicating that Silvio was to reply for each doll character. Silvio began by speaking for the youngest boy doll:

Youngest boy doll: What are you always starting a fight for?

Second boy doll: Your mother gives you more things than I get.

Oldest boy doll: Oh, Mom don't give us more to eat than you.

Second boy doll: Oh yes, she does too, 'cause I see her.

Q: This boy always thinks? A: That they are getting more.

A: All this is whose idea? A: His.

Q: What does he really think? A: He thinks his mother wants to kick him out.

Q: And? A: That's why he always fights.

Q: That shows what? A: That he is scared that his mother will kick him out.

Q: Just like? A: Me.

Silvio's attitude to his aggressiveness was also studied. The physician asked:

Q: What does he (the boy doll) want to be when he grows up?

A: He'd like to be a gangster and go and murder anybody. He is afraid someone will get him someday.

Q: How does this boy feel? A: He is scared that a ghost might get him in the night when he is asleep. The next time he is afraid to sleep by himself.

Q: What else is he scared about? A: That a boy might beat him up someday.

Q: This boy is really? A: Scared.

Q: He has to show? A: He is tough and bad.

Q: Why? A: He is bad (and) scared and a sissy.

Q: The real reason that *you* try to be tough is that? A: I am a sissy and afraid.

Q: Afraid of? A: A ghost might get me.

Q: Now you can see what being tough is. A: Being bad and scared and not doing what you are told. . . .

The manner in which such a fear of ghosts is handled is illustrated in the next case, which presents the problem of enuresis associated with similar fears. George is a retarded 10-year-old boy (I.Q. 75). He is the third of four children of an emotionally unstable mother who has screaming and fainting spells and an easy-going father who barely makes a living. He had been enuretic and scared since he had meningitis complicated by one-sided deafness at the age of 6. About one year previous to the first play-interview he had been badly frightened by a boyfriend who was wrapped in a sheet.

His fears were studied by placing a boy doll in a toy bed and inquiring:

Q: What is he (the boy doll) thinking? A: Something is going to get him.

Q: (Another boy doll is added). This boy says: Who? A: A ghost is going to get him.

Q: Then? A: He wets the bed.

Q: Why? A: He is scared to get up.

Q: And? A: I don't get up to go to the bathroom.

Q: So? A: I wet the bed, I try not to be scared.

Q: What happens? A: I get scared anyhow.

Q: Who is doing the talking? A: Him, the boy.

Q: What does he think? A: The ghost is going to get him.

Q: It's not the? A: Ghost.

Q: It's? A: Him.

Q: Who is he? A: The boy.
Q: Who is the boy? A: Me.
Q: What did you learn? A: Not to be scared.
Q: How? A: That it was me thinking.
Q: Why won't *you* be scared? A: It's not a ghost. It's me thinking.
Q: So when you want to go to the bathroom? A: I'll get up and go.

Two weeks later the mother reported: "He used to wet the bed two or three times a week. During the past two weeks he has not wet the bed once. He gets up and goes to the bathroom. He used to be afraid of the dark and now he's not. He'll go upstairs by himself now and to the bathroom. Now he goes upstairs and lights the lamp himself. (Before?) He was afraid. (Why?) I don't know. (What made him better?) I don't know. He used to be afraid of dead people. He isn't afraid of the dark or dead people no more. His imagination isn't as great as it used to be."

George reported: "I don't wet the bed. I wasn't scared like I was before 'cause I know it was no ghost. (Before?) I thought it was a ghost. (Why?) The boy scared me. (Now you know?) It's my imagination. You're thinking about it. (Who is the ghost?) Yourself. (Who is that?) Me."

The patient was seen a month later. It was learned that during this interval he had wet the bed once. George recalled that the night he wet the bed it had rained and he "got scared of the ghost."

Q: Why? A: They generally come in the rainy time.
Q: What did you learn? A: There is no ghost.
Q: How about the rain? A: I was scared.
Q: And you thought? A: That the ghost comes.
Q: That means? A: I was scared. It's me thinking.

George was seen again three months later. On this occasion his mother said: "He is coming along fine. He ain't scared no more. I send him upstairs in the dark and he goes alone. He used to send his little brother upstairs first, then he'd go up behind him. Then he would come down first and make his brother (age 5) come down last. He doesn't wet the bed any more. He gets up at night and goes to the bathroom all by himself. He's real friendly with other children and he doesn't seem to be afraid of them."

George reported, "I am better. (Why?) There ain't no ghost. (Why?) I am only thinking about it." An attempt was made at this time to get George to understand why he sent his little brother upstairs ahead of him. A large boy doll was placed alongside of a small boy doll:

Q: This boy goes upstairs with his little brother. Whom does he want to go first? A: His little brother.

Q: Why? A: They will grab him.

Q: Why? A: He wants the little brother grabbed.

Q: Why? A: (Speaking for the boy doll) Because I have to give him all my toys.

Q: Whose idea is that? A: Mine.

Q: What did you learn today? What did you want to happen? A: Him to get grabbed.

Q: Why? A: I wanted to play with my toys by myself.

George was interviewed again after an interval of six months. There had been no return of his enuresis or his fears of the dark.

The personality changes that occur when a parent decides to alter the natural growth tendencies of a child are illustrated in the next in our series of case histories. What takes place when a mother makes up her mind that she wants a girl, and the child is a boy? What can the child do about a behavior pattern that has been forced upon him? The following material demonstrates what the child is thinking, while he apparently is accepting the desires of such a determined mother.

Charles, age 10 years, 4 months, was experiencing a serious behavior disorder when he was brought to the psychiatric clinic of the Harriet Lane Home. The mother gave the reasons for bringing him as follows:

"It's that scary disposition at night; in fact (even) during the day he is afraid to go from one room to the other or to go to the cellar. He is afraid there is something wrong; otherwise he wouldn't act this way. His favorite is playing with girls; he takes after his daddy that way. He bites his fingernails. I have painted them with iodine and mercurochrome. I told him if he swallowed the nails, they would lodge in his lungs, and he would have to be operated on. He still does it. When the doorbell rings, he runs back to where the crowd (family) is. I have taken him by the hand and showed him there was nothing to be afraid of, but it don't help. Street cars make him deathly sick ever since he has been in the world. I first noticed it at several months of age."

The present condition had begun insidiously during the preceding summer. Seven months before the first interview, Charles had become apprehensive and fearful while spending a vacation on an aunt's farm. He had failed in school for the first time (grade 4B) and had anticipated being sent back to the class of his former teacher. He had greatly disliked and feared this woman because of her "hollering" at the class and her rigid disciplinary methods.

His apprehensiveness had increased until he had become fearful every time the doorbell rang. He began to postpone going down into the cellar where the lavatory was until he not infrequently wet himself. He acted as if frightened when he had to pass from one room to another. He cried out and was restless during the night. Nevertheless, he had attended school regularly all during this period.

The mother had been disappointed when she had learned that she had given birth to another boy baby. She had wanted a girl baby during her first pregnancy and was doubly anxious for a girl before Charles was born. She immediately turned all her efforts to raising Charles as if he were a girl. She protected him against the "rough" boys of the neighborhood and kept him dressed as a girl until he was 3. Except for an occasional girl, Charles had no companions until he was sent to school.

He was called "sissy" by the boys, with whom he could never get along, but was a favorite with the girls. He reached the fourth grade before he failed. Achievement tests revealed that he was below grade in both reading and arithmetic. He had been given a group intelligence test and had scored a rating of dull-normal intelligence (I.Q. 91).

The teachers noted that he was afraid to play with boys because he might soil or tear his clothes. One teacher wrote: "He is tolerated by the girls and hated by the boys. He antagonizes the other children by tattling on them. He acts like a girl, even talks like a girl; he uses expressions like, 'Oh, my gracious!' "

Charles was so particular about his appearance that he would never wear his old clothes. He never fought when he could possibly avoid it. He washed his hands many times a day. He recently had put nail polish on his fingers. He had been car sick since early childhood. He had been fearful of being kidnapped for some time before he came to the clinic. During the time of the Lindberg kidnapping he had spoken of his fear of being kidnapped.

Charles was an affectionate child who liked to kiss and be kissed by both parents. For a long time he had demanded the first kiss after his father shaved in the morning, saying, "Don't let mother have it." He also wanted the last kiss before his father left home in the morning.

There was one sibling, four years older than the patient. He was described as a "regular boy" and very much interested in athletics. He teased the patient calling him "sissy." The mother had tried her best to make him also act like a girl, and, at the age of 6, he had had to outwit her (with the help of his father) in order to have his hair cut short.

The mother was a tall, energetic, asthenic woman. She was apprehensive and constantly worried that her husband might be injured at his work, which was inspecting gas tanks. When he was a few minutes late, she became upset. She was subject to car sickness and was also afraid of high places. The father had an easygoing disposition. He occasionally still had night terrors and recalled that as a boy he had liked to play with girls. There was no other evidence of either major or minor behavior disturbances in the family history.

The physical condition of the patient was normal except that he was slightly overweight, with a moderate degree of lumbar lordosis and chronically diseased tonsils with some cryptic exudate.

The mental status of Charles, when first observed, was as follows: He was a friendly, cooperative child, who entered the room with a cheery greeting. His mannerisms were girlish. He sucked his fingers, and his nails were closely bitten. He spoke with a slight lisp and was a mouth-breather. He readily discussed his "fears and nervousness." He spoke of running home "all scared" in order to see what might have happened to his mother, who he was afraid had been injured in an automobile accident or by falling from a window. At times he thought that his father might have been hurt in an accident.

He said that his hardest school subject was arithmetic and he read with many errors. "Civil" was read as "carnival," and "nerve" as "never."

Charles stated that he first had played with boys three months before the interview, but as they had built a bonfire and talked "dirty" he had left them and had never returned to play with them. He preferred the company of girls because they were not so "rough."

The patient was given his first opportunity to express his own ideas and feelings in a series of play interviews at weekly intervals. It was decided to begin with a study of the reasons for his nausea and vomiting on street cars.

A toy car with two chairs was set up to represent a street car, and a boy doll, a lady doll, and a motorman doll were placed in the car.

Q: Where are you going? A: Uptown. (Calling out) Baltimore Street! Anybody want to get off? Lexington Street! Johns Hopkins Hospital. . . . The lady says, "I want to meet my husband." While they are going, the motorman drops dead. The seats go over (throws the seats and dolls over).

Q: How did it happen? A: Somebody shot him, and the bullet went through the car and killed the lady.

Q: How does the little boy feel? A: He's happy. It wasn't him this time.

Q: What does the little boy expect to happen? A: He expects an accident. He's afraid he might get hurt—he'll get in an accident. He feels unpleasant. He's afraid it might happen to him. He don't want to ride on cars. He thinks he is going to be hurt. The car might turn over. He might go out in an auto—the auto might turn over.

Q: Afterward? A: He feels good after he gets off.

Q: He feels like, just like—

A: Like I do. I feel scared sometimes. I felt scared Saturday coming up here. I saw a horse and buggy almost hit the car. It might have killed my father and I—I was sick. . . .

Q: What might happen? A: I am scared of my mother and father, because they might get hurt.

Q: What are you afraid of most? A: My father. He's always climbing on the tank three hundred feet high.

Q: Why does the little boy vomit? A: He gets sick, same as I do.

Q: Now? A: I know I worry about my mother and father.

Q: Before? A: I used to think I ate something.

During the next three sessions, Charles played as if he were a girl. He discussed women's clothing, dancing, and frequently spoke of not liking boys.

The notes taken in the sixth play interview reveal the attitude of the patient toward boys:

Q: Whom does the little boy like to play with? A: Girls.

Q: Why? A: The boys are too rough.

Q: How? A: Smoking, cussing, getting dirty, running, playing ball.

Q: What would he like to do? A: Take walks (and) play with girls; skip with them; tell stories.

Q: Why? A: He thinks it's nice. The boys are too bad. . . .

Q: How does he play with the girls? A: He tells riddles. "You!" (speaking to doll). "What goes upstairs on eight legs and comes down on four?"

"A cow."

"No. You!"

"Two cats go up and one comes down."

Q: How does he play with the boys? A: (Putting a small boy doll in front of a group of boy dolls.) "Now we got you, haven't we?"

"Now, what have I done?"

"You know. You threw a brick at me."

He knows he didn't do it. She pulls this boy's hair. I mean he begins to fight. He has his feet around her. She has her—(he is using "he" and "she" interchangeably). I don't like it so well. It's rough.

Q: Why rough? A: He's tackling her; he is tearing his pants; he's mad. This little boy is beating this big boy. She's finished with; he's stamping on her.

Q: Who is she? A: It's a lie. (He makes the boy doll stamp on the female doll's head.) He scraps her around the street. He's trying to kill her. (He repeatedly bangs the doll's head on the floor. He becomes very noisy. He "wipes" the table with the female doll.)

After Charles had played out his fears of boys, and had repeatedly beaten the female doll, as reproduced in the notes of the sixth session, the mother reported in the seventh session a week later: "He is improving in going through the house and on staying home alone. He didn't look like my boy, his hands were so dirty last night. Before that he never had dirty hands. He really looked out of place."

At the same session the patient reported as follows: "Let me tell you something. My mother went out and I stayed home alone, all by myself.

Q: Previously? A: I'd be scared. I'd think I'd hear somebody at the front door, that somebody would come in and take something—money or something. I haven't been as scared as I was. Yesterday I did my homework all alone in the house.

The patient also reported that he had begun to play with a boy and had enjoyed this contact for the first time. He added: "The boys play better games than girls. Two months ago I played with girls. I speak to girls (now), but I don't play with them."

Nevertheless, the need to play out the killing, beating and choking of a female doll was present. The seventh and eighth sessions brought these demonstrations to a climax. There was a noticeable decline after this time in the boy's effeminate manner of expression and his interest in feminine topics of conversation.

Charles was getting to the point where he could identify the female doll, who had been mangled or killed by her falls and accidents, as his mother. By the tenth hour the car sickness had disappeared to the extent that the patient was able to come to the clinic, on the street cars, unaccompanied. The next three sessions still contained narratives in which women were being killed, slapped, or banged around.

The fourteenth session (three weeks later) was introduced by the mother with the statement: "He goes from room to room without any fear. He goes down in the cellar. He comes home pretty soiled. That's something unusual. He's playing more with boys. He didn't play with boys at all before."

It might be of interest at this point to inquire about the mother's attitude. How did she account for these changes? How much did she know concerning what was going on in the playroom? She was asked: "How do you explain these changes in his behavior?"

A: I don't know. We did everything, but it was of no use.

Q: Do you think he just outgrew it?

A: No. It must be something you people did here.

Q: Why? A: Because he couldn't outgrow it in such a little time. He is just as loving as ever. I get my kisses just the same. I am very well pleased. He comes over in the street cars. He doesn't come home and say he is sick over that.

During the sixteenth session, Charles related the following story, in which was described his emancipation from the feminine attitudes forced upon him by his mother and the sources of his fear of being kidnapped. He selected a toy house and a boy doll and spontaneously began: "There was a little boy. He came to a house. He opened both doors wide. If he saw anything, he'd run. He walks in this room; he don't see nothing. . . . He goes in this room. He sees a baby girl. He pulled the baby girl out and threw her out of the window."

Q: Why? A: He knew that his mother never had a baby girl. . . . The little boy goes into another room, the bedroom, where he found a little baby boy. He (the baby) was calling, "Mama!" He threw the baby out of the window. He knew that his mother had one boy. He was the only child. He looked out of the window and saw a lot of colored men, and a colored man ran home with the baby.

Q: That's a nice story. A: That ain't all yet. He shuts both doors. He hears something fall, the door opens. Do you know who it was? Guess who!

Q: You tell me. A: It was his father walking in his sleep. His father was down the cellar, and the father was walking in his sleep. And the boy thought it was a man.

Q: Who? A: A colored man, and it was his father. . . .

Q: Who was the little girl? She is just like . . . ?

A: I don't know.

Q: And the little boy is like?

A: He wasn't one foot tall. He was a baby boy. He was like me.

Q: And the baby girl? A: The baby girl is like me. Don't put it down. Don't write it down! (He gets up.)

Q: He threw the other boy out of the window so that . . . ?

A: He was the only child.

Q: Who was the one he threw out of the window?

A: The girl. His spirit! Don't write that down.

Q: What is "spirit"?

A: It's his shadow, his spirit. He knew that his mother never had another boy.

Q: And that little boy . . . ?

A: He was his cousin Hugo, his imaginary cousin.

Q: Who was the little boy?

A: He was his brother.

Q: And he (the brother) went out of the window . . . ?

A: So he could be the only boy.

It was reported at this time that Charles of his own accord had requested a separate bedroom. Before that he had slept with his brother. He went to bed alone and fell asleep without a light. He continued his play with boys and reported the "fun" he was having.

His improvement had been maintained when he was seen eight months later (nineteenth session). He spoke of enjoying "gym, soccer, and indoor baseball." He had played touch football.

Q: Do they play rough?

A: Not so rough. You block them in to keep from touching the ball.

Q: Do they knock you down?

A: Sure. You just get up and play over again.

Charles had passed and was doing fairly well in the sixth grade. He had repeated the fifth grade during the previous year. He had lost all of his girlish mannerisms, and he no longer confused "he" with "she," as he had formerly done. His stories were about "cowboys" and contained no references to dresses or ribbons as in former interviews. The patient refused to play with the dolls during this (the nineteenth) session, saying, "I don't like to play no more. They (the dolls) are girls' things."

The twentieth session took place after an interval of fourteen months. Charles had passed the sixth grade. He was boyish in all of his mannerisms. He announced that he remained at home "all by himself." His mother was afraid to stay at home alone. He had come unaccompanied to the clinic on a street car. His mother could not come as she was still subject to car sickness.

Charles was able to recall the complaints which had brought him to the clinic three years ago: "I used to get sick, but I don't any more."

Q: Why? A: You made me well so I wouldn't be scared any more. I learned that there was nothing to be afraid of. Before, I used to think my father would fall off a tank and used to be worried about my mother.

Q: What did you think of?

A: I used to think about my mother, of an accident—that if I was in an accident I might get killed and (also) the driver and my mother. I just wouldn't see my mother any more. It would be imagination. I used to think that my mother would fall out the window while washing the window.

Q: When did you have those thoughts?

A: When riding on the street car.

Q: What else?

A: Some automobile might bump into the street car. It would turn over and kill me and my mother.

Q: What was going on in your imaginings?

A: I was trying to be a girl. I used to let my imagination run away with me. I used to imagine my mother would die. She was trying to make a girl out of me. I didn't want to be a girl; I wanted to be a boy. I thought about my mother falling. It was only nonsense.

Q: Not exactly. That's the way you did what?

A: Turned into a boy. She used to treat me like a girl. I dropped her out of the window. She got hurt. She was killed and buried.

Q: Why? A: So I could be a boy. I had to kill her.

Q: Where? A: I dropped her out of the window on the street car.

Q: What happened? A: An accident.

Q: And all that . . . ?

A: That was to get rid of her.

Q: So? A: I could be a boy.

Charles was seen last after another interval of two years (four years and seven months after his first visit to the clinic). He reported that there were no complaints of car sickness or fears. He was in the eighth grade at the age of 14 years, 11 months. He said that he enjoyed playing ball with the boys and was getting along well with them. He had grown rapidly during the interval and was five feet, eleven inches tall and weighed one hundred and fifty-two pounds. At this time he was asked: "Do you remember what was the matter when I first saw you?"

A: I was scared of my mother, that something would happen to my mother. Now I have my own door key. I come in by myself, and I don't worry about my mother.

Q: Do you remember why you were upset?

A: I was always scared she'd fall and hurt herself.

Q: Do you recall why?

A: I don't remember.

Q: Your mother was anxious for a . . . ?

A: Girl.

Q: How did you feel about it? A: I used to play with the girls a lot. I wouldn't play with the boys.

Q: Why? A: I don't know.

This material illustrates the variety of factors that may be involved in the production of a fear state in a 10-year-old boy. There was the physical finding of infected tonsils and a history of school difficulties, which included a degree of reading disability, dull-normal intelligence and a domineering teacher. There was an emotionally unstable mother, who had determined to make her son think and act like a girl, and there was the personality makeup of the boy. In this psychobiological setting the patient developed a state of insecurity in which general apprehensiveness appeared; then fear of being alone and of being kidnapped, and imaginations that his mother might be injured at home and on street cars and that his father might be hurt in an accident while at work or while riding in a vehicle.

The play interviews provided an opportunity for the child to express himself. He utilized them by repeatedly punishing or killing his mother and by producing a dramatic account in which he disposed of "the baby girl that his mother never had" and of his older and more masculine brother. During the period of observation he became aware of and accepted the responsibility for the role he had played in his illness and began to behave like an average boy, free of his fears and secure in his family relationships.

These and similar experiences have demonstrated that children can reveal their attitudes and difficulties more effectively by re-enacting them in play and have led to the hope that the method of the play-interview might be of help in getting children to discuss their sex attitudes and sex knowledge without so much of the usual feeling of shame and embarrassment. After an introductory phase, during which the child learned to reply for each of a number of dolls as indicated by the physician, the play-interview was directed by degrees to the study of sex awareness.

The following material indicates how a 9-year-old girl brought together her attitudes concerning courtship and marriage and her concept of the origin of babies. Harriet was 8 years, 3 months of age when she observed her mother dressing a chicken and remarked, "Oh, the chicken has eggs in her." Her mother explained, "This is the egg bag, and it comes down this tube and out of the hiney boots (anus)." Nothing was said about babies at this time. Four months later Harriet asked her mother where babies come from. Her mother replied, "You have to have a lot of money, and then God sends the baby down, and the mother has to get the milk and feed the baby, so she goes to the hospital." Harriet then asked: "How do poor people get so many babies?" and was given an evasive reply. When she was 8 years, 10 months of age, a girl friend told her that the baby came from a seed in the mother's stomach and not from storks.

How did this 9-year-old girl synthesize this material?

The play-interview was started by placing a boy doll, a girl doll, a "mother" doll and a "father" doll before Harriet. She was asked:

Q: What does this girl say about her boy friend?

Harriet began an imaginary conversation, speaking for each of the dolls as it was pointed to by the physician. The questions of the physician and the replies of the child were recorded verbatim by a secretary, who was in an adjoining cubicle:

A: Girl doll: My boy friend is getting so much nicer, I'm going to marry him, I think, if he will let me.

Mother doll: You're too young. Wait until next year, you'll be 18. It's up to your father.

Girl doll: I forgot about him. He never lets me do anything.

Mother doll: I'll go talk to him and send your boy friend in here.

Girl doll: Sh-h-h, Darling (referring to her boy friend). Mother has gone in to tell Father about getting married.

Boy doll: That's swell.

Mother doll: Daddy, your daughter wants to get married.

Father doll: I'll talk to that heathen, (To girl doll) Why do you want to get married?

Girl doll: I love him. You don't understand because you're not a girl.

Father doll: No, wait until next year, and young man, you better keep your hands off my daughter.

The physician then spoke for the girl doll:

Q: She asks him: What do you mean by marriage? Why do people get married?

A: Father doll: To tell you the truth, you better talk it over with your mother. She'll know more about it.

Harriet: She goes to her mother.

Girl doll: Mother, look. Why do people get married?

Mother doll: My dear, that's a question, a real question. People get married because they want to have little babies, and you're in disgrace if you have one and are not married. If you want to get married for that reason, that's all right. If it ain't that reason, don't get married. Sometimes it's wrong to get married. (While listening to a radio program a short time previously, Harriet had heard about a baby being born to an unmarried mother.) The physician again spoke for the girl doll:

Q: What does the baby have to do with getting married?

A: Mother doll: When you have a baby, the baby is the important part about you. Babies don't come from storks. We have them ourselves. They're inside of us. Understand now?

Girl doll: Yes, Mother, but may I get married now?

Mother doll: All right, all right. . . .

Harriet: They dress her up for the wedding. Here's all the people. (Harriet arranges several boy dolls and girl dolls about the first girl doll and her "boyfriend.") These ladies and gentlemen want to see her get married.

Q: Why does the girl want all those people? A: They're going to see her get married.

Q: Why? A: She wants to have a big wedding.

Q: Why? A: Because she's getting married and this will only come once.

Q: So? A: Here they come. The wedding is over. Here's the doctor and nurse, and she is down in the hospital. This is her mother sitting down here talking to her.

Mother doll: See now, my dear child, you know what it is, getting married.

Girl doll: Yes, I do, but I still like the idea. . . .

Doctor doll: Nobody can see her now.

Girl doll: I can't see my own husband?

Mother doll: No, not until this is over.

Harriet: The doctor asks the girl:

Doctor doll: Do you know where babies come from?

Girl doll: No, I don't. Mother has never told me.

Doctor doll: I'll tell you because you're getting ready to have one. The baby comes from inside the woman, and a woman is made to have them. Now I think we'll take you upstairs.

Harriet: Then she'll have a baby upstairs.

Q: How? A: I'll show you. They're upstairs, the doctor and the nurse.

She is in bed and the doctor and the nurse stand around the bed. She is going to have it. Then the nurse walks in, and the other doctor walks in. There are two doctors at the foot and two nurses at the sides.

Doctor doll: The baby comes inside of you, and then out the baby comes. It's the way that you want it. The baby comes from the back part of your body, and in other words, your hiney, and your baby comes from there, and from then on it's in the hospital until you're ready to go home. . . .

Q: She would like to know how the baby got in there.

A: Doctor doll: That's easy. The baby is a seed inside of you, and seed gets larger and larger, forms head, body, then arms, legs and feet, and when it's ready to come, it goes from your stomach down through a special tube and comes out the back.

Q: She asks: What has the father to do with the coming of the baby?

A: I never heard that one.

Doctor doll: In the first place you have to have a father to take part in the baby.

Q: She asks: What does that mean?

A: Doctor doll: That means that the father has to take care of the baby. . . . The father takes more to it if it's a boy.

In this manner Harriet brought together what she had observed and learned at home with what she had heard from her friends and over the radio and synthesized this material into her present conception of how a baby is born. The formation of social attitudes, such as the interest in a "big" wedding and the attitude to the unmarried mother, is illustrated in this material. The manner in which sex instruction is given to a daughter by a mother and the origin and development of this child's concept of anal birth is elicited in a matter-of-fact manner.

The child's spontaneity was encouraged through the method of the play-interview. The questions of the physician and the replies of the child concerning these and other sex topics were recorded verbatim and can be compared with those of 200 other children, ranging in age from 4 to 12 years (Conn 1948, Conn and Kanner 1947).

Conclusion

A method has been described of working directly with the child through the medium of play-interviews. The emphasis in this procedure is placed upon the concrete difficulties which have arisen at a specific time in the child's life-situation. Illustrative clinical material dealing with car sickness, enuresis, sibling rivalries, parent-child relationships, fear states and the development of sex attitudes and sex awareness has been presented. The child was given an opportunity to play freely with dolls, but the emphasis in this procedure has been placed upon planned play-situations, which could be repeated as frequently as desirable. The play-interview was included as one of many procedures. It served to supplement other methods (social service aid, school adjustment, working with the parents, etc.) and contributed material which dealt with the personal and emotional aspects of the child's behavior.

The data collected in this manner seem to indicate that the attitudes, motives and imaginations of the child are closely associated with his life situation and actual experiences. Facts obtained in this manner are relatively free from the interpolation of adult interpretation and may help to contribute to a program of mental hygiene in childhood.

The life histories of these children demonstrate that there can be no royal road in the collection of facts which help to explain child behavior. *No one theory can account for all the facts in any one case.* There is the factor of the original endowment, and the developmental, physical and situation-determined facts to be evaluated. The attitudes of the parents, of the teacher, of the child's associates at home and in the neighborhood have to be studied as they affect him in his daily life. In the difficult, painstaking labor of collecting all of these significant items, there is one important fact, which too often is forgotten, namely that the child himself has something to contribute. The child, like the adult, has a biography, which includes important past experiences and a present life situation. In addition to the need of working with the family situation, the school and community problems, the emotions of the child must be taken into consideration.

The child has a need to express his dissatisfactions, fears, hopes in his own natural fashion through the medium of play. In this manner he can begin to understand what he has contributed to the total situation, and thus begin to accept his share of the responsibility for what is going on.

The procedure of the play-interview provides opportunities for the child to speak for each of a number of dolls. He learns to express his feelings and thoughts through the medium of these dolls as if they were responsible for all that was said and done. In this manner he first becomes aware of and soon accepts the fact that he has contributed to his own discomfort. The question of personal responsibility and the acknowledgment by the child of the role which he plays in the total situation come up repeatedly in this method. By bringing together hitherto unrelated experiences for the first time the child can view the whole story and see himself as others see him.

The emphasis is placed upon the child's finding and expressing himself in the presence of an appreciative adult, who can listen to the parent's complaints and yet continue to like the child and invite his confidence. No attempt is made during the play-interviews to arouse antagonistic or hostile tendencies. Guns, pistols, knives, soldiers, etc., are not included in the play materials. It is worthwhile to point out that under these conditions aggressive manifestations and anxiety situations occur very infrequently, and in no case has the physician been molested or attacked by the patient.

The termination of the play-interview is accomplished with the consent of the patient, who decides whether to return in one or two (or two or three) weeks in accordance with his individual needs. The interviews are continued until the child, himself, has no further use for them. *Improvement, when it does take place occurs as a rule following the first few sessions.*

The acceptance of a child for treatment is in itself a significant therapeutic fact. The much troubled parent finds someone to confide in who is willing to take over the responsibility for the care of her "fearful" or "nervous" child. This "calling off the dogs" or criticism and nagging is appreciated by both parent and child.

The value of a spontaneous parental account has been noted. Further study, as a rule, can only amplify these parental statements since they include fundamental descriptions of the activities of the child, each in its individual setting.

The psychiatrist does not "discover" new facts; he can only translate the observations which he has received into other terms and conclusions, and help to create experimental situations which put them to a test. The play-interview is such a test situation. The child is given the chance to verify or deny a parental statement or a theoretical possibility and, in doing so, not only learns what he has contributed to the total situation, but for the first time finds himself secure in a personal relationship. He can, therefore, begin to develop the courage that comes from self-criticism, a sense of freedom arising out of self-expression, and be helped in the direction of happy, healthy living.

References

Conn, J. H. (1939). The play-interview: a method of studying children's attitudes. *American Journal of Disabled Children* 58:1199–1214.

_____ (1948). Children's awareness of the origin of babies. *Journal of Child Psychiatry*, vol. 1.

Conn, J. H., and Kanner, L. (1947). Children's awareness of sex differences. *Journal of Child Psychiatry* 1:3–57.

3

Structured Play Therapy

GOVE HAMBRIDGE, JR.

During some thirty years of clinical practice, David M. Levy worked out a series of play forms which he found useful in the treatment of children. Essentially what he did was to devise a series of specific stimulus situations which the child could then freely play out. I have taken the liberty of calling the overall technique "structured play therapy." Levy was interested in the technique as a research method, as in his "Studies in Sibling Rivalry," and also as a psychotherapeutic procedure, as in "Release Therapy." It is, however, unfortunate for students of the art of psychotherapy that he has not written more extensively on the subject from the clinical point of view. The present chapter is a preliminary effort toward a systematic review of the use of structured play therapy in the larger framework of psychotherapy with children. My objectives are two: (1) to evaluate the technique critically in comparison with other techniques and (2) to stimulate trial of the technique by other therapists.

In the area of direct psychotherapy with children, the physician has at his disposal a number of techniques. In large measure, the differences between these techniques depend on the nature of the therapist's activity during the sessions with the child. For instance, the therapist acts to focus attention, to stimulate further activity, to give approval, to gain information, to interpret, or to set limits. Structuring the play situation is a form of activity which can serve any of these functions. As a consequence, the technique should be used selectively with different patients and at different times during the treatment of one patient. With some, it should not be used at all.

The structured play situation is used as a stimulus to facilitate the independent creative free play of the child in treatment. The patient should already be acquainted with the playroom, which should in turn be supplied with materials of proven value from a clinical point of view. The child will then have the opportunity to choose other play materials beyond those which are given him at the outset of structured play. Lack of adequate facilities may vitiate the advantages of using play therapy. Since the child's own selection is an important and significant element in treatment, play therapy should not be conducted with limited materials.

Types of Play Situations

New baby at mother's breast (sibling rivalry play). This is the standard stimulus situation used by Levy in his classic experiments on sibling rivalry and the hostile act. The therapist provides a mother doll, a baby doll (preferably readily destructible and replaceable), and a self-doll, called in the play brother or sister, depending on the sex of the patient. The therapist inquires of the child if he knows what breasts are for, simultaneously modeling a clay breast and placing it in position on the mother doll. If necessary, the child is told briefly of the milk-giving function of the breast. He is then asked to make, and place in position, the mother doll's other breast. Then, while placing the mother doll in the chair and the baby in her lap sucking at the breast, the therapist says, "This is the mother and this is the baby. The brother (or sister) comes in and sees the baby for the first time. He sees the baby nursing at his mother's breast. What happens?" A further stimulus to the expression of hostility can be added by saying, "He sees that bad, bad, baby nursing at his mother's breast." This play situation is useful not only to facilitate the abreaction and working through of sibling rivalry and dependency conflicts, but also to check on a patient's progress during treatment. Thus, for comparative purposes, it is advantageous to use it in the standard form, so that one may compare the patient's handling of this situation from time to time.

Balloon bursting. This type of play was devised by Levy for use in "release therapy." Its primary purpose is the activation of self-assertion in inhibited children through the release of suppressed or repressed aggression and hostility. In setting up this play, the therapist provides a large number of colored balloons of assorted sizes and shapes. He says, "Now we are going to play with balloons." He blows up a balloon and ties the end. It is very important that the first balloon be blown up only a little bit, so that when it breaks it does not make such a loud noise that the child is so frightened that he will not continue the play. Experience teaches that if the play is not introduced too early the child can usually be encouraged to break the first balloon. The therapist encourages the child to break balloons in any way he wishes. Stamping and jumping are most common. Special devices—nails, mallets, dart guns, and so forth—should be available to the child for the playing out of specific problems or impulses. As the play progresses, the balloons are inflated closer to the bursting point. Later, if the child is able, he should inflate and tie the balloons himself. With more anxious children, it may be necessary to precede the balloon play with less startling forms of noise making, such as paper-rattling, participating in calling, shouting, and so on.

Peer attack. This play may be useful for the resolution of conflicts involving a fear of retaliation, a guilt-born need to be punished, bullying behavior due to displaced hostility, or for the interruption of certain types of automatized patterns of social isolation. It may be presented in different ways, as illustrated by the following examples. With a self-doll and a peer doll of appropriate sex according to the historical context, the therapist says, "This boy meets another boy who walks up to him and, for no reason at all, hits him hard. What happens?" Or, "This boy for no reason at all says to the other one, 'You are no good.' What happens?"

Punishment or control by elders. These two forms of play facilitate the therapeutic handling of problems in relationship to authority. Each is taken from an appropriate situation in the child's history, past or present. For children who have not made an adequate differentiation of the two situations, they may be used in sequence. The most common sources are from life at home and at school.

Separation. This play is designed not only to offer an opportunity for the release and expressive mastery of separation anxiety and separation anger, but also to afford diagnostic information relative to the child's ability to orient himself in time. For this reason, separation for a definite time interval is specified. The therapist provides a mother doll and a self-doll and says to the patient, "The mother tells the boy (or girl) that she is going away and will be back this afternoon (or "tomorrow" or "next week," etc.). What happens?" Thus the child may play out a problem centering either about the idea "Will mother return?" or about uncertainty as to when mother will return.

Genital difference. In this scene, the therapist uses two dolls. These may be play therapy dolls constructed with genitalia. Or they may be more readily obtainable and cheaper dolls modified at the time with clay. Clay is superior, not only because of ease of removal and replacement, but also because in this area plastic representation of fantasy promotes fuller impulse modification and ego mastery. One doll, the self-doll, is of the same sex as the patient; the other doll is of the opposite sex. This play form is used rather late in treatment, when it will be less threatening to the child, and then only if there is direct indication for its use. The therapist says, "This boy sees a girl naked for the first time. What happens?" Variations on this play are important. For after the therapist has presented the situation as just outlined a number of times, he may recognize that the boy patient is not as afraid of the impulses represented to him by this play—or of punishment for these impulses—as he is afraid of the girl's jealous attack upon his organ. If under circumstances such as these, the child does not spontaneously reorient the play, the therapist can restructure it as follows: "This girl sees the boy naked for the first time. What happens?" To emphasize the girl's activity, he asks, "What does she do?" I find it helpful in this play to provide water, balloons, and baby bottles with nipples, so that the child can play out fantasies regarding the function of the genital organs. This play often facilitates the working through of genital difference problems in boys, such as castration fear, prudery, fear of the girl's jealousy of his organ, and tabooed exploration. In girls, rejection of femininity, envy and fear of the male genital, castration fear, and hostility toward males are some of the problems which are appropriate for this play form.

The invisible boy (or girl) in the bedroom of his parents. This type of play requires a mother doll, a father doll, and a self-doll; a bed for the parents may be used. I prefer not to introduce articles of furniture, but to leave this up to the child, who knows that they are available in the playroom. The therapist says, "Here is the boy, and here are his father and mother. They are asleep in their bedroom. The boy is invisible— nobody can see him. He goes into the bedroom. What happens?" Or, "What does he see?" "What does he hear?" "What does he do?" The therapist facilitates the unhindered play in whatever direction the child chooses, whether, for instance, this be primal scene play, competition with the parent of the same or opposite sex, or the elaboration of a fantasy of sexual activity as a battle between the parents.

Birth of a baby. This calls for a hollow rubber doll with a pelvic opening. The doll must be large enough so that a small celluloid baby doll can be passed through the opening and be inside the mother before the play is introduced. A self-doll is not included in the original structuring of the play. To start the play, the therapist says, "This is a mother doll. There is a baby inside who is going to be born. What happens?" There are several alternative procedures. For example, the physician may hand the prepared mother doll to the patient, asking if the patient knows what it is. Again, the physician may pick up the mother doll and insert the baby doll through the pelvic opening as a means of starting the play. In any case, it is important for the patient actually to perform with the dolls the act of birth. The child often will suggest further variations on the play as he indicates the primacy of certain fears. Levy has told me that in his experience there are three major fears, the most common of which is associated with the question, "How does the baby get out?" The other two are associated with the questions, "How did the baby get there?" and "How does the baby live (stay alive) there?"

Acting out dream. The handling of dream material or other fantasies brought in from the outside, as opposed to those produced in the therapeutic situation, can frequently be facilitated by the use of structured play. The therapist may select any part or all of the dream, as long as it does not become too complicated. For instance, a 10-year-old girl with a great deal of repressed rage at her mother reported in the third hour a long dream in a part of which a green witch captured her with the intent of killing her. At that point in treatment the basic conflict, of which this dream represented a graphic picture, was a major threat to this sensitive girl. Activation of this conflict purposely was delayed until the nineteenth hour, when the dream was set up as structured play. She immediately expressed overt hostility toward her mother and conflict about the feminine role. After this was worked through, the patient no longer saw adult women as witches and no longer felt that it might be preferable to be a boy.

Another use of structured play in relation to dreams is to externalize or make explicit the conflict implicit in a reality situation. The latter is portrayed verbally and the child is asked to show in action how the self-doll dreams about this situation.

Other individualized play. Innumerable conflict situations, as they present themselves either in the history or other sources of data about the child, can be presented in dramatic form for play therapy.

Testing play. The therapist may use structured play situations to test his hypotheses about the basis of some behavior, to test the accuracy of an interpretation before it is given and finally, to determine the significance of specific symbols which the child may produce in dreams, drawings, painting, modeling, or other creative activity.

Introducing Structured Play

Any new technique of treatment should result in increased economy of effort and closer approximation to the desired result. Structured play therapy increases the specificity of treatment method in direct psychotherapy with children. Simultaneously, it saves time by not indulging in hours of diffuse, therapeutically unremunerative activity. There can, therefore, be nothing pedantic or compulsive in the selection of play forms: The therapist uses only those forms of play which are indicated. He re-creates in dramatic play an event, situation, or conflict which, he suspects, precipitated or now maintains the child's illness. The patient is encouraged to show what happens—not just talk about it. The sources of information for this are primarily the history (as given by parents, patient, or others), the child's spontaneous (free) play, the child's changes of previously structured play, relationship material, and the mother's interim report on behavior since the last session. The therapist does not, simply out of a compulsion for thoroughness or fear of incompleteness, use forms of play manifestly unrelated to the patient's problem.

The therapist introduces structured play when the therapeutic relationship has developed to a point where there will be neither anxiety nor acting out to an extent disruptive to treatment. This means that the child should have developed enough security in the relationship with the therapist so that structured play does not precipitate overwhelming anxiety. However, the therapist who becomes anxious can contribute to such a result. Anyone who is to use structured play must either possess or develop self-assurance in his ability to handle this form of treatment. To step into the free play situation with deftness and surety in such a way as to facilitate rather than to interfere with the continuity of the child's communication and relationship with the therapist is a skill which, to be sure, comes only with repeated experience and practice.

Of the many variables the therapist should assess in introducing structured play, there are three that deserve particular mention. The first is the child's integrative capacity in the face of externalized affect, such as anxiety, anger, and the various need tensions; a higher integrative capacity gives more latitude in the use of structured play. *Flooding* (a term introduced by Levy to refer to a massive and uncontrolled release of all kinds of uncompleted acts from the past), accompanied by acute regressive and disintegrative states, should be avoided either during the treatment session or on the outside as a result of treatment. Second is the nature of the play; some play forms, such as sibling rivalry play, are generally less threatening, while others, such as genital difference play, are more threatening. Individual differences will make some children more sensitive to certain dramatic presentations than to others. The third variable to assess is the capacity of the people in the environment to handle realistically the patient's change in behavior in reaction to treatment. The family is informed of the expected increase in aggressiveness of the child as a result of treatment and is told to maintain the usual restraints at home. The therapist's task in this regard is to pace treatment so that the parents' ability to handle the child at home is not overtaxed.

The appropriate use of any therapeutic tool is a concern of the physician at all times. Since Levy's 1938 and 1939 papers on release therapy, in which he developed clear-cut criteria for the use of the technique in certain specific situations, some conflicting reports have appeared in the literature about the use of structured play therapy. Cameron (1940) recommended structured play techniques to less skilled therapists on the theory that the free play of the child is more threatening to the therapist. In 1941, Newell suggested a highly restricted use of structuring; namely, to start the play of the inhibited patient at the beginning of treatment. In 1948, Gerard said the technique was too limited, by virtue of inflexibility, to be of value. Most of these differences can probably be explained by the therapeutic predilections of the various authors. On the other hand, Kanner in 1948 indicated that many psychotherapists who work with children have incorporated a mixture of structured and free play techniques within the scope of their handling of patients. If it is true that this method is so widely used, and yet there is considerable difference of opinion about it, it behooves us to take a closer look at the characteristics and situations which could give rise to such differing experiences.

Therapeutic tools are used to aid the natural properties of growth and repair of the organism. If these proceed satisfactorily under more conservative measures, one does not use more radical ones. Consistent with this principle, although structured play is particularly suited to the release and mastery of repressed or developmentally by-passed and insufficiently lived-out affect, it is not used if the child makes adequate progress with the use of spontaneous play or verbal interaction. Just as the skilled surgeon knows when, where, how, and how much to use the scalpel for specific purposes, so must the medical psychotherapist know when, where, how, and how much to use structured play therapy. Thus the same instrument, when correctly used, is therapeutic; when it is incorrectly used, is harmful. The correction of misuse, however, is not to reject the instrument, but to perfect the necessary skills. While limited knowledge is available in this direction, the great part of it is still to be gained through clinical investigation and research.

Part of the answer to this problem may lie in knowing when to push structured play in the face of resistance by the patient, a situation which puts the careful therapist in an apparent dilemma. While many child patients take to structured play immediately and with gusto, others put up various types of resistance. It is a situation similar to that of the internist who must administer an antibiotic in spite of side actions of the drug, and attain a therapeutically effective drug level; a lower level is less effective and lengthens treatment. The parallel in structured play therapy may be more serious, because the psychotherapist, out of painful experience, may be so scared to push his patient that he infects the patient with the atmosphere of uncertainty and thus provides a breeding ground for an even greater unnecessary prolongation of treatment. The patient's resistance may arise from any of a number of factors, such as simple opposition, anger, fear of self-exposure, or the arousal of automatized defensive maneuvers. The therapist has different methods of handling each. In the face of slight opposition, he may repeat the phrase "Then what happens?" On the other hand, he may be more permissive and encouraging if the child is more frightened than oppositional. If the fear is of self-exposure from the idea of the reality of the play, the therapist may say, "It is just a game," or "It is not the real thing." When the patient starts the play gingerly, the fact that play has been started at all can be commended by exclaiming, "Fine! Good!" Other useful phrases are, "Let him (her) do anything he wants," "He can do anything he wants," "You can do anything you want." One can go even farther to facilitate the play of the more hesitant child who needs permission by example from the authority figure. The physician can say, "Now we will do it together," and act out the drama with the child the first time. The greatest facilitation is obtained if the therapist actually "does it first" for the child. This somewhat ticklish procedure is not used until other methods have failed. It is wise for the physician to wait until he is well versed in the vagaries of the use of structured play before he tries this last method.

Conducting Structured Play Therapy

This section of the chapter deals with different problems in the conduct of psychotherapy once structured play has been introduced.

The ideal of the play therapist is to facilitate play, not to enter into play. He is a shifter of scenes. The consequence which arises from breaking the rule of the passive role of the therapist is that he may be seduced into going too far. He should keep out of the play except in order to facilitate it, in spite of the fact that the child, for purposes of his own defenses, will try to draw him into it. The inevitable complexity of this apparently simple principle can be illustrated by the following example. A boy, aged 7, was already in treatment for multiple fears. On return from summer vacation, his mother reported, "He got anxious when he started back to school after vacation. He was upset by the air-raid drills. His appetite went, he could not eat. At one drill, the assistant principal said, 'If you don't hurry, you will all be killed.' He was terribly upset and would not go to school." The mother left the room and the boy came in, carrying with him a toy airplane and a wooden truck with wooden men in it. Structured play. At an appropriate point, the therapist crashed the plane into the truck. The patient took over without being told, and in vigorous play knocked men out of the truck, saying, "They are scared. One jumps out just in time and runs to his house, scared." He talked with the therapist about air-raid drills. Structured play. Therapist moved the toy plane through the air as if it were zooming, diving, bombing. As it approached the patient, he became briefly literally terrified, then very excited. Quickly his attitude changed and he shot at the plane with the dart gun. He said he was afraid of bombs. He shot the plane down out of the sky many times. At last, he was exultant, no longer fearful.

In this case, the activity of the therapist is an example of the overdetermination of his role. His activity represented facilitation in relation to the play of the child. It was, in addition, a test of the child's anxiety, as important for the latter as it was for the therapist. The therapist did not exceed the patient's integrative capacity in the face of anxiety. The structured activity focused or sharpened the patient's anxiety, thus, both literally and figuratively, giving him the target at which to shoot. Once anxiety has been reduced in treatment, there are times when it is therapeutically indicated to raise the anxiety for a specific purpose. In this illustration, the purpose was to strengthen ego mastery through an intense corrective emotional experience.

The question often arises, "How many plays must you use in the treatment of a particular child?" Or, "Should you not always see that such and such a play is used?" Let me repeat that the selection of structured play is not rigid. For example, if no problem arises about the birth of a baby, that play form is not used. As a matter of fact, no play form is introduced unless there is prior evidence that its use will have direct bearing upon the resolution of the problems for which the child's treatment was undertaken. While structuring is occasionally a useful adjunct in the psychoanalysis of children, this technique alone is not adapted to that goal of psychoanalysis which is concerned with the completeness of treatment; namely, the working through of every complex of the patient.

Structured play is always followed by the free play of the patient. I have consistently observed that this play must eventually show certain characteristics if the patient is to achieve a maximum of abreactive value, impulse modification, and ego mastery. These characteristics are (a) direct physical manipulation of the dolls, as differentiated from simply telling what they do; (b) relatively complete absorption in the play so that the patient is practically oblivious of his surroundings; (c) playing out the primary impulses involved, as opposed to stopping play before the defenses have been worked through. Other things being equal, the single most important factor in arriving at these aims is repetition of the play.

Once structured play has been introduced, there are three major sequences from which the therapist may choose for the conduct of treatment. These may be diagrammed like this:

1. Structured play—free play.
2. Structured play—free play—repeat same structured play.
3. Structured play—free play—new structured play.

Each of the sequences is independent. They are not interdependent, nor are they necessarily sequential. The therapist may choose from among them after each presentation of structured play.

In the first sequence, structured play is used as a stimulus to free play for the purpose of assuring the patient's continued productive activity in treatment. The aim is also the facilitation of free play, but with the specific intent of focusing activity upon a particular problem, selected because of its probably etiologic importance. In this method, the therapist follows the patient's play to an appropriate end point, then reintroduces the same play. The sequence "structured play—play to end point" is repeated until the child fully tires of this play. This may take a long time, with many repetitions over several hours, seemingly endless to the therapist. In general, the child's play is at first characterized by defensive maneuvers. As these drop out, the various derived and then primary impulses are played out. When these have been fully expressed, the child becomes bored with the play. It is the therapist's responsibility to recognize whether this is true satiation, or whether the boredom itself is a defense. The patient may avoid the play before full therapeutic benefit has been derived. If there is overt or covert anxiety of excessive intensity, it will be necessary to leave this play and to return to it later. The therapist must estimate what price he pays for continuing the play against resistance. It is often preferable to continue the play in spite of resistance, and to analyze or work through the resistance either concomitantly at the verbal level, or later at the verbal or play activity levels. In the third sequence, the aim is again the facilitation of free play. The therapist follows the lead of the child in order to make the stimulus to play more appropriate to the child's conflict. These changes in the structured stimulus are frequently selected from the child's play after a previous stimulus. For instance, in one case of a boy, 6 years old, the historical evidence pointed quite clearly to a problem of sibling rivalry. When the therapist introduced the new baby at the mother's breast situation, the boy quickly brought the father into the picture and demonstrated that his problem was an oedipal one. This lead was followed in subsequent structured play therapy.

Functional Significance of Structured Play

Psychotherapy today is more than an art. It is a clinical scientific procedure with ample room for personal experimentation. The need for quick, effective techniques is attested on all sides. Through psychoanalysis, we have learned to listen to patients and to recognize and utilize the latent content of their communication. We have passed through the exploratory phase when in our relative ignorance we had to track down every conflict a patient brought up. We leaven our ideal of the perfect therapeutic result with a recognition of the uncompromising limitations of reality. Our discipline has advanced to the point at which we can make explicit the problems of the patient entering treatment. The natural consequence of this is to focus our attention on these problems during treatment. Structuring of the play serves this function for the child patient. This enables patient and therapist to bring energy to bear where it will count, rather than to expend energy diffusely in random activity, which, although it may be highly informative for the therapist, is essentially doing little more than wasting the patient's time. It also serves the valuable function of requiring the therapist to arrive at a specific formulation and shows him quickly whether or not he is on the right track.

The functional significance, as well as certain aspects of the technique of the introduction and conduct of structured play therapy can best be illustrated by clinical material. The following is offered from this point of view.

Case 1.

This 10-year-old boy, the oldest of three siblings, was referred for treatment ostensibly because of school failure in the fourth grade, which he was repeating at the time of entering treatment. In addition, his mother, a quiet, friendly, self-assured woman, complained that he was afraid of needles and of going into an elevator alone, that he was too cautious, and that he was "too much of a mamma's boy." She said he would become panic-stricken if she were away from home. She said he was too fussy; he had to have clean underclothes and socks every day. On the other hand, she had to force him to wash his dirty hands before eating. She said he got along poorly with his siblings, being bossed and teased both by his sister, aged 7, and his brother, aged 5. He had few friends. He was poor in sports. He was shy and isolated. He played alone with his tricycle or with his toys at home. The boy's father, a heavy-set, blustery, impulsively aggressive man, who was sure he knew the answers and who made little effort to conceal his low regard for psychiatry, said the boy was nervous and afraid, especially of dogs. He said the boy had peculiar habits; for instance, he had to go back and turn the light off five times or more. He said the main trouble was the boy's lack of confidence.

The mother said that she had made many mistakes in raising this boy. He was her first child, and she conformed completely to the recommendations of the pediatrician. The boy was on a rigid feeding schedule as an infant, often screaming with hunger for half an hour before food. Toilet training began at 3 months and was a battle from then on. He was 3 when his sister was born, and he was not even allowed to touch the baby, at which time he acquired the habit of biting people, excepting only his mother. At the age of 5, he had a strep throat, immediately followed by the birth of his brother, and his being sent to kindergarten. Social withdrawal began at this time. At the age of 6 he entered first grade screaming because he could not see his mother. At the age of 8 he had weekly injections for six months for "allergy—asthmatic wheeze, angioneurotic edema, and sinusitis." Fear of needles began at this time. At the age of 10 he was very homesick at summer camp, lacked confidence, and was socially withdrawn. Two months later, he started to repeat fourth grade.

The patient was a well-developed, healthy, blond boy, shy, self-conscious, and very inhibited verbally. He did not know why he came for treatment. In the waiting room, his siblings were observed to be freely assertive and happy, and it was seen that they easily dominated the patient. He came on an average of twice a week; his mother was not in treatment. In the first seven hours, there was a gentle opening of release of affect by crayon drawing and finger painting. The patient was unable to make use of structured sibling rivalry play. (This is unusual and speaks for massive inhibition.) At the end of this period in treatment, he became "ornery" at home. During the subsequent twelve hours (eight through nineteen), balloon-bursting play almost exclusively dominated the picture. After a hesitant start in which the therapist blew up the balloons and tied them off, the patient became completely engrossed. Twice a week, for six weeks, he blew up balloons and filled them with air or water, then shot them or smashed them. Gradually, he personified the balloons, and then "killed them." Each hour, he would become oblivious of his surroundings, raging, stamping, jumping, giving orders, bursting balloon after balloon with a loud bang. At the end of this time, the mother reported that the patient was a lot more aggressive at home, primarily with her, but was still submissive to his younger sister, and still afraid of elevators. During the nineteenth hour, the patient looked very embarrassed when the subject of his mother's pregnancy came up. He said, "How can I tell if she is? I know—you can tell by the legs—no higher up." Therapist said, "By her tummy." After talking back and forth about the coming baby for a few minutes, the therapist introduced the baby doll into the situation as something that the patient could shoot at. He hesitated, and the therapist acted to give him an example, shooting the doll. The patient shouted, "You killed him!" He then went ahead and shot the baby doll himself. In a minute, he turned to balloons and wanted to insert things into them before inflating them. He put in pieces of paper; then he inflated some and shot them with excitement. He chose a large nail, named it "the soup," and threw it point first at the balloons. He rushed out at the end of the hour to see if he could ride down in the elevator alone. His younger brother shouted triumphantly, "He did it, he did it!"

The nineteenth hour has been presented in some detail because it represented a turning point in treatment. Up to this time, the patient had, with monotonous regularity, been playing the same game every hour ever since it had first been introduced by the therapist. Beginning with the nineteenth hour, the balloon play became less important to him.

In the twentieth hour, the patient for the first time did not reject the use of dolls to play out family battles. In the twenty-first hour, he started with balloons, but played mechanically, and in the twenty-second hour he stopped this play entirely in favor of dolls. In the twenty-fourth hour, the therapist reintroduced the standard sibling rivalry play. After some hesitation, the patient entered into vigorous play in which he introduced rivalry with the father. The parents were repeatedly killed. He announced in the twenty-sixth hour that his new baby sister had just been born. He expressed curiosity about how a baby is born. After the patient had talked about this for a while, the therapist again introduced sibling rivalry play. The patient represented some initial skirmishes among family members, in which the mother dropped the baby. He then said, "Now we will have a war." The big brother part was played by the patient, who treated the dolls as if they were his size and he were in the group, with fighting and yelling among all. Curiosity about the birth of a baby continued, and in the twenty-eighth hour, this structured play was introduced. He played through it several times, was encouraged by the therapist to continue, but stopped. (At this point in treatment, it was felt that it was too early to push the patient to complete this play against his reluctance.) The next time he came in, he very proudly announced that he was riding the elevator alone at home.

The final phase of treatment started in the thirtieth hour, when the patient related a dream of separation anxiety involving his mother, in which after his mother left him, he jumped off a boat into the water and was scared. In the next hour, he went through the birth of a baby play four times with vigorous participation. While playing it he said, "The baby is safe in Mommy's stomach. I wish I was in it. Somebody put an arrow in Mommy's back. The baby comes out by its side—it was a mistake." On the final repetition, he said that the baby was coming out by its head. He immediately started talking about swimming in water. He gradually lost interest. At this point, structured genital difference play was introduced. The patient's first response was that (1) the boy couldn't really believe that there was a genital difference and (2) the boy was punished by his parents for any interest in this area. Later (hour thirty-two), in reference to this new play form, he said, "I am going to keep up with this play until it is all over." He played it out repetitively over and over again. In the thirty-sixth hour he introduced oedipal material, following which (hour thirty-seven) the therapist brought in the invisible boy in the bedroom of his parents as well as the genital difference play. For seven sessions the patient played out a classical Oedipus situation and the concept of coitus as a fight.

Shortly after this, the patient's father reported that the boy's peculiar habits had ceased, that he was more self-confident, went out with children to play, and was no longer dominated by his siblings. The patient's mother concurred and added that it was much more troublesome to handle her son now that he was symptom free and self-assertive at home. Treatment was terminated at this time.

A year later, the mother reported that the patient had been slow in making new friends when the family moved to a new home. She complained that he tended to oppose her authority. His symptoms had not returned, and he was handling his siblings as well as he had at the termination of treatment. She complained of the boy's fear of criticism by his father and of the father's lack of understanding by being too hard on the boy. Two years after termination, the boy was seen. He had grown a lot. He was spontaneously friendly and made an easy relationship with the therapist. There was no evidence of return of symptoms. His relationships in the family and at school had remained improved.

Case 2.

This patient was referred for the treatment of persistent and intractable cardiospasm of three years' duration, which was by then threatening her very existence. She was a frail, wistful, ingratiating child of 11 years, physically little more than skin and bones. She had gained but seven pounds in the three years of her illness. She had always been a "good girl" who had been unable to cope with her two aggressive sisters, one older and the other younger. Her good behavior made her the favored child in the family. The diagnosis of cardiospasm was established radiographically two years before psychotherapy, a year after its onset at the time the child had had mumps. She had had only temporary relief at various times from sedatives, antispasmodics, and from a dilatation of the cardia one year previously. In the hospital, the physical and laboratory findings were all negative except for the esophagram. This showed a greatly dilated and moderately tortuous esophagus, spastic at the cardia. At the time she entered treatment, she felt hurt, lonely, different and was afraid of dying.

Eight sessions of interview therapy, carefully coordinated with a second surgical dilatation of the cardia, were held while the child was a bed patient in the hospital. These were pointed toward emotional evocation and the development of insight into the relationship between her personal experience of significant emotional stress and the simultaneous occurrence of her cardiospastic symptoms. This development was facilitated by the fact that interviews occurred at suppertime, and in talking about her feelings while eating the patient inevitably made the obvious connections. However, the patient did not work through the basic dependency and rivalry conflicts with their attendant reactions of fear and rage.

The second phase psychotherapy began after the patient was discharged from the hospital. The child came as an outpatient three times a week for five weeks and then twice a week until termination. She took easily to play with dolls. Structured play therapy was used repeatedly as a stimulus to play out conflicts centered about sibling rivalry and dependency in the oral context. Central to this aspect of her treatment was a burning hostility, resentment, and envy of the younger sister's being fed. Guilt was handled by direct interpretation in addition to the implied acceptance by the therapist of her feelings through the presentation of the structured play situations and his permissiveness and encouragement as she played them out in her own way.

The cardiospastic symptoms did not recur. After two months of treatment she was lively, smiling, happy, relaxed. She was put on a trial vacation from treatment for two weeks; treatment was then terminated. Eighteen months later, on follow-up interview, there had been no return of symptoms. Two and a half years after termination it was revealed that the child had occasional episodes of vomiting associated with emotional stress, but no regurgitation with cardiospasm. Follow-up esophagrams continued to show the same dilated and tortuous esophagus with slight retention at the cardia.

Termination

In conclusion, I should like to make a few remarks about termination. I have presented a technique of psychotherapy which is oriented toward the attainment of specific goals in treatment. Consistent with this aim is termination when these goals have been reached. The goals are determined by the therapist's clinical judgment of the treatment necessary to resolve the conflicts which produce the disordered behavior for which the patient was referred. This is checked empirically during the course of treatment, so that the patient is discharged at the point of optimum therapeutic benefit. A frequent temptation, however, is to continue treatment beyond this point so that it becomes relatively interminable. There are severe objections to this, among them being the fact that the treatment becomes uncontrolled. The patient may suffer from overtreatment, and the physician does not learn what his patient is capable of doing on his own after the original objectives have been reached. Finally, the value of the follow-up study is diluted by virtue of blurring of the end point and the loss of objective criteria for scientific control. In the long run, the proof of progress in our field comes from good follow-up studies. Therefore, we should take special care that what we observe subsequently can be clearly related to what went before in treatment, and that we do not confuse the issue by introducing intercurrent and uncontrolled variables through unnecessary nonspecific procedures carried out with the "hope" of producing a better result.

References

Cameron, W. M. (1940). The treatment of children in psychiatric clinics with particular reference to the use of play techniques. *Bulletin of the Menninger Clinic* 4:172–180.

Gerard, M. W. (1948). Direct treatment of the child. In *Orthopsychiatry, 1923–1948*, ed. L. G. Lowrey and V. Sloane, pp. 494–523. New York: American Orthopsychiatric Association.

Newell, H. Whitman (1941). Play therapy in child psychiatry. *American Journal of Orthopsychiatry* 12:42–49.

4

The Use of Two Houses
in Play Therapy

LINDA KUHLI

References in the literature on the use of houses in play therapy are relatively few. Erikson (1937) noted that the house is the only regularly occurring representation of the whole human form found in children's play. The house a child creates often reveals how he perceives his body and what he feels about it. Erikson also described house structures as symbolic expressions of a child's mental state (such as being caged) that can frequently be traced to early traumatic experiences. They can indicate the level of a child's object-relations, self-esteem, and identification within the family. Moustakas (1953) described play sessions in which a little girl verbally depicted two homes, one wild and one peaceful, indicating ambivalent feelings toward her home situation. Klein (1961) interpreted a boy's drawing of an old deserted house as his mother, whom he saw as unprotected and in danger of being injured.

In modern society, children face an increasing number of relocations, dissolutions, and family crises. Littner (1956) noted that the anxiety of children placed away from the family for day care or long term placement must be recognized and dealt with if they are to benefit from these experiences. Repression used as a defense against feelings of abandonment, helplessness, and anger can result in self-destructive behavior that damages a child's ability to be receptive to a new placement and sets him up for rejection by the new parenting figures. Fraiberg (1962) maintained that the ability to form new object relationships may be permanently impaired.

Clinicians in placement agencies are often faced with children who have moved through numerous placements without ever having worked through the initial separation process. Expanding the use of houses in therapy is suggested in this chapter as a tool for enhancing treatment of children working through separation trauma.

Case Example

An experience with a child in Lincoln Child Center's residential treatment facility for emotionally disturbed children will be described. The therapist's office contained a typical assortment of toys, including a large two-story house inhabited by several dolls. A box of blocks provided material for building another house.

Emily was the third of four siblings. Her home life was characterized by extreme neglect and reports of physical abuse. Her mother first noticed withdrawn unresponsive behavior when Emily was 4 months old. Developmental landmarks were described as late but normal. With the birth of her younger sister, Laura, when she was 3, Emily regressed further and became enuretic. Laura received the bulk of the mother's affection and protection, leaving Emily feeling worthless, unloved, and good only to the extent she could model herself after her younger sister. Emily's growth from that time was characterized by increasing conflict with her mother and peers, and with immature psychosocial development. She was excluded from the first grade due to extreme hyperactivity, distractibility, and refusal to follow directions in kindergarten. Sensory-integration and speech evaluation indicated poor form-recognition, a lack of focused and cohesive thought patterns, and a need to simplify incoming stimuli. Her IQ tested at 81. At the time of Emily's placement at age 7, Laura was the only other child not removed from the home.

Emily's ability to function in the new setting at Lincoln Child Center was considerably below age level. Her needs for attention and affection from staff took the form of excessive whining and clinging behavior. Rather than verbalizing her feelings, she threw tantrums or became withdrawn. She sought help with even the simplest tasks, such as bed-making, but staff felt that she was often more capable than she presented.

During Emily's first year and a half of weekly psychotherapy, she primarily focused on the doll house and the theme of trying to put order in an unorderly environment. She found everyone a place to sleep, regardless of how cramped the space. Her style of communication was one of endless questioning and perseverance, with a very flat and depressed affect and self-protection from challenge or over-stimulation.

Emily appeared to be struggling with her repression of a tremendous amount of rage, fear, and guilt over the inadequate mothering she and her siblings experienced. While physically she was in the latency stage, her doll play indicated a more primitive fixation and preoccupation with nurturing. She had a limited sense of control over her environment and her ability to assert her identity. Direction in therapy was focused on helping Emily conceptualize areas of conflict within the doll house in order to work through repressed fears and fantasies. It was felt that her severe organic impairments and difficulty hearing and responding to her therapist considerably limited her ability to use play therapy.

After a year and a half of placement another sensory integration evaluation concluded that all efforts should be made to simplify the types and degree of stimuli presented to Emily due to gross vestibular system deficits. Within the context of individual psychotherapy, it was suggested that her most commonly chosen media of play, the house, be made less complex.

Emily was encouraged to focus her attention on a more simply constructed doll house consisting of blocks to form an adult's and a child's room, with furniture suited to match large and small proportions. In time, it became evident that Emily began to attribute special meaning to this new structure and see it as a release from an anxiety-ridden situation which had had no solution within its own boundaries. Although this was originally designed to help construct order in her physical environment, it proved to fill a need on an emotional level. As the therapist realized this, she began using the two houses as the metaphoric symbols they represented to the child.

The process of problem-solving went through several definable stages and resulted in rejection of past parenting and identification with new standards of care offered in residence. First, movement of the family figures between the two houses enabled Emily to identify the dangers she saw within her home environment. The big play house represented her own home, where robbers entered through unlocked or broken windows to rape, steal, and kidnap children. Family pets proved to be monsters who tried to hurt people. Conflict and tension were at a continuous high level.

Once her fears were clearly portrayed, a guest entered the big home and served as a "good" mother who took care of the children, while the real mother stood by passively as a neutral figure. In other sessions, the family was put to bed safely in the second house, and when they became frightened the surrogate figure came to reassure and protect them. The warmly portrayed surrogate figure symbolized the counselors in Emily's unit.

At this point, Emily depicted a family meeting in her home at which a social worker said, "You have problems, little girl. You have to leave!" The doll was sent to another home where the children prepared for her coming by making up a special bed for her (an act of no small significance to Emily). For the first time in treatment, Emily had consciously identified her perception of herself as a "problem" to her family. Then, in a turn of fate, the introduction of the small play house seemed to open up to her the possibility of an alternative home where there could be order and caring. Her ability to play out her rejection was facilitated by her recognition that she had found something better. She tested the new home's dependability by asking if it was a place where kids could stay a long time. Her conception of an alternative home took months to incorporate as Emily continually moved herself and the family she left behind back and forth between the two houses.

Emily's use of two houses demonstrated a tentative trial in play toward a solution to the dilemma of splitting allegiance between two homes. As described by Greenacre (1959), repeatedly going over an experience makes it become more real and familiar to the child, allowing fears to give way to recognition. With this method, Emily had an opportunity to reverse her real life role as the receptor, and took on a position of power within the play.

With determination and no small feeling of guilt, Emily often tried to reestablish the family within the old house, only to feel overwhelmed by its size and lack of structure. She again began perseverative questioning about where everyone would sleep and how everyone would be warmly covered. Due to her frustration, she was gently encouraged to return to the second playhouse where things were less crowded and everyone had his own place. Gradually Emily worked through many of her feelings of rejection, and integrated the concept of a family being separated from itself and its home.

Meanwhile Emily began defining and asserting her own concept of a nurturing home environment, separate from her mother's. Having established a place of safety, she went back to the old doll house to master fears her mother instilled in her. She began to restore a sense of order to the old house as if to give it a new beginning. Broken windows had paper securely taped over them to keep the family safe and warm. Loose nails in walls were hammered in solidly. Dependence on mother for her frame of reference decreased.

Ten months after the introduction of the second play house, Emily's identification with the parenting she received at the child center became discernible. The little girl doll went to her doll mother and told her that the new home turned out to be a nice place after all where "the kids get help with their problems and get presents too!" A new self-esteem was evident in her attempts to make pretty things for the children to wear, and size furniture to their proportions. Constant references to her sister diminished. Contact with her family was maintained in play through pilgrimages to her first home to be reunited with the family for holidays.

Emily became increasingly capable of verbalizing her feelings about the poor parenting she received from her mother on visits. She preferred being with staff and children at the child center. She declined her mother's request to go home for her birthday and clearly laid out ground rules for her own protection when her sister asked to make a visit. How Emily wanted things done in her environment began taking priority over how others wanted them done.

The culmination of this growing confidence and assertiveness was her decision not to go on overnight visits with her mother when the circumstances of the visits frightened her (broken windows and being left at home alone with her younger sister at night). She began observing her mother's poor judgment and difficulty handling problems at home. She also talked of her younger sister's previously "perfect" behavior, which she now saw as inappropriate. Meanwhile, in therapy the release of energy hitherto bound in frustration enabled a gradual development of interest in cognitive tasks requiring frustration tolerance, concentration, and perceptual decoding abilities. A lifting of her depression was also apparent.

In the living unit, Emily evolved from using passive resistance as her only mode of control, and she became noticeably more assertive in situations. Staff observed improvement in her ability to see she could make choices in her life and get her needs met. She began to act much happier and began paying attention to her appearance. An increased use of humor and initiative contributed to her becoming the focus of more attention. There was also an increase in demanding, unreasonable behavior, characteristic of the "terrible two's" which was seen as a precursor to further growth.

Performance in school was the slowest area to change due to the feelings of failure it induced. At times she would be quite dull, lethargic, and unable to focus on tasks, while on other days she seemed brighter and more animated. Her teachers noticed that perseverative questioning was slowly decreasing and becoming more logical and directed. Sensory integration testing indicated very slow but steady growth.

On the occasional home visits, mother was pleased with Emily's increased responsiveness, cooperativeness, and inquisitive nature.

Implications

There are many traumatic situations children face that could be amenable to a two-house approach. Change in a family structure to accommodate stepparents and siblings is a common cause of stress among children. For a child in outpatient therapy, this approach could serve as a setting for testing out new family members, and expressing anger toward them in a safe environment. A child could also use two houses to deal with the birth of a new sibling by playing out the process of the infant's entry into the family and what he fears will be the ramifications.

This approach could also serve as a means of mourning the loss of loved ones due to death, divorce, or other circumstances. When a child experiences emotional withdrawal of a parent, intolerable stress within the larger home, or temporary loss due to traveling or hospitalization, he could use the second house as a retreat. Here he could define and direct the interaction with family members rather than feeling helpless.

A second house might portray the benefits of becoming invested in alternative support systems or caring people who are able to supplement the parenting a child is getting at home. Nurturing, sources of appropriate limits, and models for identification can be depicted. The second home provides the means for developing a child's sense of values, needs, and fantasies about what is desirable and possible. The child can take from the old that which is valued, and reject or rework that which is not. Changing how family members relate to each other and discharging feelings becomes possible within a less threatening context. Afterwards, the child has the choice of returning himself or his family to the "real" home.

The subtle variety of factors that could contribute to the usefulness of the two-house concept in play therapy suggests its value as standard equipment in the playroom.

References

Erikson, E. (1937). Configurations in play—clinical notes. *Psychoanalytic Quarterly* 6:139–213.

Fraiberg, S. (1962). A therapeutic approach to reactive ego disturbances in children in placement. *American Journal of Orthopsychiatry* 32:18–31.

Greenacre, P. (1959). Play in relation to creative imagination. *Psychoanalytic Study of the Child* 14:61–80. New York: International Universities Press.

Klein, M. (1961). *Narrative of a Child Analysis.* New York: Basic Books.

Littner, N. (1956). *Some Traumatic Effects of Separation and Placement.* New York: Child Welfare League of America.

Moustakas, C. (1953). *Children in Play Therapy.* New York: McGraw-Hill.

5

Using Puppets for Assessment

Use of Play in Assessment

Play, as Greenacre (1959) reminds us, is make-believe, not "real-reality." In make-believe, fresh versions of the not-real are created, as bits and pieces of past and present reality are glued together with the spirit of pretending. A collage of experiences is formed by the child, made up of feelings and imaginings, of inchoate wishes and fears. The child's emotional state and cognitive abilities, in combination with the inevitable distortion and decay of memory, coalesce to form a highly subjective picture of the world. It is this private inner world, as Frank (1948) has written, that is tapped by projective media and methods.

With such inevitable distortions of reality, one wonders why clinicians have historically trusted child play to reveal something of value about diagnosis or treatment. Why is play used, if it presents such a distorted picture of things as they were, or are, or as the child wishes/fears them to be? The trained clinician would answer that, imperfect and confusing as play may be, it still offers one of the best ways of learning about the psychic reality of the child, and his/her worries and wishes.

To gain a multidimensional picture of the personality through play, a variety of media has been used, including dolls, art materials, miniature life toys, blocks, games, sand play materials, and puppets (Bender 1952, Hartley et al. 1957, Haworth 1964, Lowenfeld 1939, Rabin and Haworth 1960, Rubin 1978, Schaefer 1976, Schaefer and O'Connor 1983). Among the most valuable yet, paradoxically, the least understood and utilized of these materials are puppets. A random assortment of puppets is generally included in most play-room supplies, but the clinician is usually left to learn about their use (and misuse) *in vivo,* and thus often fails to explore their rich potential.

Many therapists have written in an anecdotal fashion about the use of puppets in child therapy. One of the first to do so was Rambert (1949), a French analyst. She attempted to combine Piagetian concepts about intelligence with psychoanalytic insights, and thus spoke of stages (and ages) in the use of puppets, according to whether or not the child engaged in symbolic play. Much as Sarnoff (1976) has done recently, Rambert emphasized the importance of the defense of repression, suggesting that it was this factor that made it possible for the child to represent ideas and feelings symbolically, rather than acting them out directly.

Another early contributor to the puppet literature was Woltmann (1940, 1951, 1952, 1960) who explored ways of using play materials with seriously ill children at Bellevue Hospital in New York City. While he wrote about and filmed the use of marionettes in prepared shows, he also commented on the use of ready-made hand puppets in individual and group work.

While puppets have been used in assessment and treatment by many (e.g., Hawkey 1945, Howells and Townsend 1973, Irwin and Malloy 1975, Jenkins and Beckh 1942, Lyle and Holly 1941), the emergent data have rarely been critically examined in regard to the particular contributions made by the dramatic medium. Irwin and Shapiro (1975) devised a semistructured puppet interview to be used in assessment. Later, a rating form was used to assess the form and content dimensions of story data of hospitalized children facing surgery (Irwin and Kovacs 1979) and puppet data of abused youngsters and those injured in accidents. (Irwin et al. 1981). A follow-up study on "normal" latency children by Portner (1981) has provided opportunities to further test the usefulness of the puppet interview and rating scale and gather normative data. This chapter will present the puppet procedure and scale, along with case illustrations, in the hope that such material will provide a guide to clinicians who are interested in using puppets in diagnosis and treatment.

The Puppet Assessment Interview

Purpose

The puppet assessment interview is designed to give information in several areas:

Form and Content Dimensions

1. *Form Dimensions,* e.g., creativity; coherence and intelligibility; impulsivity. In assessing the process of the hour, one can also note the nonverbal communications as well as the overall level of (ego) control.

2. *Content Dimensions,* e.g., characters, setting, plot, and theme.

Diagnostic Data Derived from Form and Content

1. *Defenses and Coping Styles* that can be "read" from the material and child's responses in the post-puppet interview.

2. *Preoccupations and Conflicts,* expressed symbolically in the material as well as in the elaboration of the issues in the post-puppet interview.

Materials

In order to gain information about the child's ideas and feelings, a range of puppets must be provided for the child's selection. Fifteen to twenty puppets seem to be enough to provide an adequate selection, with a choice within categories. It is equally important for the puppets to represent a range of affects, including aggressive, friendly, and "neutral" puppets. The selection includes real and fantasy puppets, i.e., realistic family puppets, both black and white (man, woman, boy, girl); royalty family puppets (queen, king, princess, prince); occupational puppets (nurse, doctor, policeman, teacher); symbolic character types (ghost, witch, devil, skeleton, pirate, bum); animal puppets, both wild and tame (dog, bird, monkey, alligator/dragon). Animals should be included, inasmuch as they offer distance and a safe disguise, and are often ready objects for identification. The standardized interview includes the warm-up, the puppet show itself, and the post-puppet interview, including a final discussion of the child's feelings about the puppet session.

The Warm-Up

Generally it is helpful to ask a child initially what he or she was told about the purpose of the interview. One then gets a sense of how the child has (or has not) been prepared, and what the attendant fears/fantasies may be. Following this, the child can be told that the therapist is interested in what kids think about, and the stories they make up. In the session, the child will be asked to make up a puppet story with the therapist's help.

A basket of puppets is then emptied on the floor and both therapist and child sit on the floor together to examine them. The therapist attempts to be as unintrusive as possible, taking notes (mentally or unobtrusively in writing) on the child's reactions to the materials. Puppets that attract as well as those that are rejected are noted, as are the child's spontaneous comments and nonverbal behavior. It often seems that the story line is stimulated by the child's immediate visceral reactions as the puppets are examined and commented upon, verbally and nonverbally.

Following this inspection, the child is invited to select some puppets and to go behind a stage (or a table) in order to introduce the "characters" for a puppet show. As the child does this, the therapist may elect to talk to the puppets, asking open-ended questions if that seems to be indicated. Some children need help in the "willing suspension of disbelief" and seem to welcome the therapist's quiet permission to pretend. Most children, however, respond warmly to the appealing puppet task from the beginning and do not need the therapist's tacit permission or support to "make-believe."

The Puppet Show

Once the puppets are introduced, the story can begin. Most children have little difficulty getting started. They enjoy the fact that the therapist is the audience watching them; they seem pleased that the therapist is taking notes (or even tape recording) the session. If, however, the child is inhibited, the therapist may need to intervene to help the child to let go and play. In the warm-up, for example, the therapist can ask the puppet open-ended questions: e.g., "Oh, a witch! What *kind* of a witch might you be? . . . or, "Good day, Policeman. Can you tell me what it's like to be a policeman in this place?" If the child still seems to have difficulty, the essentials of a story can be focused upon: e.g., *characters* ("I wonder who could be in the story?"); *setting* ("And where might the story take place?"); *plot* ("And what could happen first?"). In this way, the child can be helped to think about the who, what, where, when, and later on, the why of the story.

On occasion it happens that a child wants and needs the therapist to participate. If so, it is important to stress that it is the child's story and she/he must say (in a stage whisper) how the story will go. The participating therapist needs to be sensitive to the child's nuances, follow his/her lead, being careful not to contaminate the story. It is usually a good idea for the therapist not to participate unless (and until) other ways of helping the child have been explored. The same child who initially requests help may be able to make up a story later on, unassisted.

Interview with the Puppets

Once the story is played out, the therapist can interview the puppet characters, thus extending the story line. By encouraging the child to stay in character with the story line suspended, the therapist can get added information about the child's thinking. Questions about who did what and why can be asked in a less intrusive way, without the action element, but still within the realm of make-believe.

Interview with the Child

Later, the child can be invited to come out from behind the stage and talk with the therapist directly about the story. One then has the opportunity to get a sense of the observing ego, defenses, and coping styles; to note whether the child can make distinctions between the pretending of the story and the reality of life, being reflective about what has just transpired. Whereas in the previous part of the session, action was stressed, in this part, the reflection process is emphasized. Words replace action; thinking replaces doing. This provides another chance to ask about themes, especially repetitive ones, and what might have stimulated them. One can inquire about the characters in the story, whether presented in a one-dimensional fashion, or as more complex human beings with diverse motivations. The child's identifications (e.g., self and object representations) become clearer with inquiry about the characters preferred/rejected in the story. Often it seems that characters who are loved *and* hated represent some aspect of the child's self-representations, the two dimensions being split as self-polarities. In this part of the interview one can make a rough determination of the child's linguistic and cognitive skills. The language used, concepts evoked, questions that are grappled with or avoided (for defensive or cognitive reasons) give clues to the child's strengths and weaknesses.

In this part of the interview the child can also be asked what part(s) of the story were most enjoyed and disliked; who in the story she/he would like to be and *not* like to be. The child can be asked for a make-believe title and a lesson or moral one could learn from it (Gardner 1971). This helps the therapist to understand what the child perceives as the problem, which is usually dynamically and symbolically related to conflicts experienced in reality.

Rating Scale

The emergent data can be examined for both form and content dimensions, the underlying preoccupations, and the defenses/coping mechanisms used to deal with them.

Content

The content tells what the story is about. It may be misleading, however, to assume direct correlation between story content and the child's actual reality experiences. Careful and sensitive questioning can often help find the linkages, when they exist, but the possibility remains that such material may reflect something the child has imagined, wished or feared. While this, in itself, gives valuable information about fantasy life, it is important to realize that the child's story has many determinants, only some of which may be actual experiences in reality.

Content dimensions that can give valuable clues include: title, setting, characters, plot, and themes.

Case Example 1: Billy

Eight-year-old Billy did a puppet play in his initial session, repeating the same story the next week. He was not able to finish his story in either session. He began his story while sitting on the floor; the beginning was the same in both sessions. One character, said to be the strongest, devoured all the other characters in the story. This was the case whether the main character was a wolf, a king, or a monster. The stories ended the same way—abruptly, as though the anxiety stimulated by the oral aggressive drives could no longer be contained. The moral, too, had a repetitive quality; "get him (the monster, wolf, etc.) before he gets you." And that indeed, seemed to be Billy's conflict, seen in his rivalrous interaction with his sister, father, and mother; as well as with constant battles with peers. Thus the therapeutic task was to help this troubled boy to understand and manage his intense aggression that was manifest in the talion principle of "kill or be killed."

Generally, the story has an overall affective tone which can give clues about the child's feelings. The therapist can make a judgment about the emotions expressed, whether more positive or negative in nature. Abused children participating in a follow-up study conducted by Elmer (1977) for example, had themes that were overwhelmingly depressive in content, reflecting despair, sadness and/or aggression, which seemed to be related to underlying object loss.

Discussion

While the content of the story may be vicious, brutal, or even reflect the "Goody-Two-Shoes" syndrome, one cannot live by content alone in assessing the mental health of the child. The form, however, can provide clues about the child's internal structure, the intactness or fragility of the ego; the superego and ego ideal; and the underlying conflict. The ability to maintain the "as if" stance, for example, may indicate an ability to contain the impulses/feelings within the story. Billy (case example 1), was unable to do that. He repetitively moved from what Ekstein (1966) calls "play acting" to "play action." Play acting is under the control of the ego; anxiety is mastered within the story. Play action signifies a regressive breakthrough of id impulses, resulting in play disruption (Erikson 1963). Such was the situation in a study (Irwin *et al.* 1981) with many physically abused children whose aggression rapidly escalated, as tiny infractions in the story led to catastrophic results, like a car careening downhill without brakes.

Form

Form qualities seen in child stories include creativity, coherence/intelligibility, and impulsivity. When one looks at the child's behavior over the course of the session, one can also assess the nonverbal communications as well as the overall level of ego-control.

Form dimensions are not nearly so visible in the ephemeral play, as Murphy (1956) points out, yet they often provide the most valuable clues about the child's state of well-being. A child's distress is mirrored in his/her play. This can be seen in constriction and rigidity, which often results in either an inability to play or stereotypic play; lack of flexibility in themes (e.g., repetitive themes of aggression, control, sexuality, etc.); inability to play in a way that makes sense, communicating ideas and feelings; or difficulty controlling the play or ending the story in a satisfying way.

Both form and content contribute to an understanding of the underlying conflict(s) and the child's defenses against them. Often it seems that the story presents a problem that the child tries to solve within the story boundaries. It is helpful, therefore, to look for the problem in the story as well as the proposed solution. Not surprisingly, the solution may reflect the same maladaptive thinking patterns that the child uses in reality. The problem, so to speak, reveals something of the child's preoccupations and conflicts, as well as the child's defenses and coping styles.

Often the disguise of the puppet play offers psychic protection; because it is "just a story," the child can safely pretend. In this way, anxiety and attendant defenses are by-passed and the play (as with dreams) continues. Nevertheless, the therapist may empathically feel the child's anxiety as certain themes are touched upon, even if anxiety is not so intense as to result in play disruption. Trying to puzzle out just what the child is anxious about leads the therapist back to the story content and the themes that emerge. The wishes that clamor for expression (e.g., to kill, love, devour, control, etc.) stimulate anxiety; defenses are set in motion to control the emerging impulses.

Defenses can be thought of in a general way, as those that are less mature (denial of reality, projection, somatization, acting out, and aggressive impulses that are directed against the self); those that are more commonly thought of as neurotic defenses (e.g., reaction formation, displacement, disavowal, repression, and intellectualization); and those that are more mature (e.g., altruism, humor, sublimation). Examination of the story material, especially the ways in which the child attempts to manage the feelings that emerge, give clues about the child's use of defenses, and aid in developing an assessment picture.

To portray ideas and feelings, the child makes use of a wide range of symbols within the story. Symbol formation is made possible by the child's intellectual development, as well as the ability to successfully use repression to keep unwanted ideas/impulses out of awareness. The symbols that the child uses are linked to underlying wishes/fears that have undergone repression (unconscious fantasies) and are allowed expression in a disguised fashion. Therapists who are able to decipher symbolic communication can often intuitively follow the child's story, feeling comfortable about decisions to intervene or keep silent, following hunches about the kinds of questions to be asked. In this regard, the therapist's knowledge of and degree of comfort with his/her own unconscious life is the most valuable guide.

Three case examples will illustrate the diagnostic data that can emerge from a puppet assessment interview.

Form: An Indicator of (Ego) Control

While therapists are naturally concerned about content (i.e., what the child plays out), the ability to control the play, seen in the form configurations, is diagnostically a more important indicator of psychopathology. Both Ronnie and Sheldon, whose diagnostic interviews are presented below, were very disturbed children who initially played in a chaotic out-of-control fashion. Whereas Ronnie was unable to organize a coherent story, Sheldon could do so, a more favorable diagnostic sign.

Case Example 2: Ronnie

The psychotic-like behavior of this abused 7-year-old is indicative of serious difficulty. This is seen in his inability to confine himself to the play sphere, the disorganization and impulsivity of the puppet play material as well as Ronnie's behavior throughout the session.

Eager to begin the session, Ronnie chose a boy and a girl (whose gender identities were repeatedly confused) and six additional puppets. The plot of this chaotic story was hard to follow but seemed to revolve around a witch who repeatedly captured and killed the other characters. They, in turn, would come back to life and try to do the same to the witch. Almost as soon as the story began, Ronnie said that the therapist was really the witch who devoured, sucked, spat, and exploded the other characters. From time to time, therefore, Ronnie would dart out from behind the puppet stage and "attack" the therapist, who was sitting in front, taking notes. He would then quickly retreat to the safety of the stage and continue the story. Although he had a witch puppet which he was using in the story, he seemed unable to confine the play to interactions with the puppet . . . he felt compelled to act it out, so to speak, with the therapist.

Confusion between reality and fantasy was demonstrated by Ronnie midway through the story. He had given one of the characters in the story his own name, and then became confused about who was who. He asked, "Who is Ronnie? Where is Ronnie? Is he in the witch? In my pocket?" Recognizing his very real distress, the therapist stopped the play and made clear statements about the pretend and not-real aspects of the story. She helped him to get reoriented, to establish boundaries between fantasy and reality, puppets and people, thoughts and deeds. Ronnie then said he wanted to continue and he finished the story.

The theme of the story, he said, was of a "witch sucking the blood and killing." The title was "The Godfather and the Old Witch" and he said he would have liked to have been the Godfather in the story. He then began to talk of some frightening times when he had been abused by his mother, and how he prayed for his father to come home and stop her.

The content of the story centered around the aggressive wishes/fears toward the witch; the form of the story was marked by impulsivity, disorganization, confusion, lack of ego-control. Ronnie's anxiety was pronounced. He was unable to confine himself to playing (rather than "acting" with the therapist); he was confused and had a loss of boundaries about real/not-real dimensions, as well as identity confusions (personal and sexual).

Case Example 3: Sheldon

Eleven-year-old Sheldon was referred for aggressive behavior, which seemed to mask underlying depression. After saying emphatically that he was not doing "no dumb story," he became intrigued with the puppets and began to inspect them, showing strong affective reactions to the various animals and people. He told three stories in the fifty-minute interview. The first two were played out while still sitting on the floor; the third story was enacted from behind the puppet stage. This seemed to be a metaphor for his increasing sense of control as the session wore on. While he initially showed violent behavior with the puppets and poor form configurations, he became less anxious and more organized during the session and finally was able to talk about his own problem.

In the first story, Sheldon picked up the puppets one by one; each was viciously eaten by the wolf-dog. Saliva dripped from Sheldon's mouth; his body was rigid and tense. There was no dialogue, only aggression and killing. When he threw away the last victim, the therapist asked if he could say what the story was about and Sheldon replied, "The Dog Attacked the City." When the therapist wondered about the attack, Sheldon asked, "You wanna see it again?"

Elaborating the story, Sheldon enacted a second, similar theme, adding dialogue and a different ending. A pirate came and interrupted the killing; the pirate drew a long sword and killed the wolf-dog and was given a reward of $1,000 for saving the city. As Sheldon was being "interviewed" about the second story, he became interested in a female puppet, undressed her and asked a series of questions about her (did she have tits; was she streaking, etc.). The therapist said it seemed he was curious about these things; he could make up a story about what he thought. Sheldon thereupon went behind the stage and enacted a story of a courtship, marriage, and two babies being born. ("They're coming out, right now.") The title was "The Naked Girl" and it was about a "good family with good kids." He said he would like to be one of the kids in the family and went on to talk about differences between good and bad kids. Asked how he'd characterize himself, he said he was "bad" because he always "got mad" and talked of some of the things that made him so mad and got him into trouble.

The themes of Sheldon's play reflected loss of control episodes (the wolf-dog puppet tried to bite the therapist's nose, bit the carpet, etc.), but the play became more controlled over time and the form improved. There was a shift from nonverbal to verbal explanations of behavior, from animals to people. The play was confined to the play sphere, being contained both behind the stage and within the "as if" pretend situation. There was less chaos and psychodynamically the play themes were at different levels of development.

An important diagnostic consideration was the shift in Sheldon's interaction with the therapist. Initially he kept her at bay with hostile words and aggressive acts; later, more controlled, he allowed more relating to take place. Overall, the story enactment seemed to suggest that Sheldon could benefit from structured intervention and he was capable of greater control than was first apparent.

Preoccupations and Defenses

The core of thematic play reflects the conflict that is enacted in the story. In playing this out, the child's defenses relax somewhat, ideas and feelings emerge; some are acceptable to the child's conscience; others stimulate anxiety and need to be defended against. As the story unfolds, one can see how the child tries to cope with the emergent conflict and the attendant ideas and feelings.

Case Example 4: George

An undersized, sickly 5-year-old, George was eager for the adult's attention, ready for interaction. He had been placed in a shelter after having been found hungry, in an unkempt, unheated house, alone for several days.

Shown the puppets, George chose two very large "parent" puppets and a daughter, Edith. In the story, the parents went away and left Edith without food. She said, "Poor me . . . they go out . . . I'm so hungry. They hogged up the food and left me with only a teensy bit."

As the story evolved, a friend (magically) appeared, gave Edith a banana and told her she could have a raffle ticket to win $1,000. Edith did so, then decided to share the money with her mother. "We can hire a housekeeper and then buy lots of food." The mother said she was sorry and wouldn't leave Edith without food again. The title of the story would be "Stop her, stop her, stop her" and George said he would like to be the friend who had magic. The lesson was "Don't let your mother go out."

In the post-puppet interview, Edith, the daughter, was asked how she felt being left in a dirty house with no food. George exchanged the Edith puppet for the skeleton puppet, who, he said, was Edith's ghost who was returning to get revenge on the mother. The skeleton then killed mother and stabbed Edith. When the therapist wondered what happened, George said, "It's because she was bad . . . if she gets mad, then she gets killed . . . you're not supposed to get mad." Asked if he ever felt mad that way, George said he did but tried not to, "cause you don't know . . . it's bad. Somethin' might happen to you or somebody might get killed." The therapist then wondered if there were other times Edith was angry with her mother. This theme was then explored in another story.

Examination of the story theme reveals the underlying conflict. George both needs and wants his mother to reform and be a good mother; simultaneously, he is full of rage and wants to kill her. He strongly defends against awareness of such anger, however; the wish to kill is projected, he feels *he* will be killed if he is angry. Defenses are primitive (denial in fantasy, and projection) but at the same time, he shows strengths in being able to use the play experience. His good intelligence and verbal abilities are manifest as he talks about his thoughts and worries, as well as his ability to accept the therapist's help, all the while staying within the play sphere.

References

Bender, L., ed. (1952). *Child Psychiatric Techniques.* Springfield, IL: Charles C Thomas.

Ekstein, R. (1966). *Children of Time and Space, of Action and Impulse.* New York: Meredith.

Elmer, E. (1977). *Fragile Families, Troubled Children: The Aftermath of Infant Trauma.* Pittsburgh: University of Pittsburgh Press.

Erikson, E. H. (1963). *Childhood and Society.* New York: W. W. Norton.

Frank, L. K. (1948). *Projective Methods.* Springfield, IL: Charles C Thomas.

Gardner, R. (1971). *Therapeutic Communication with Children: The Mutual Storytelling Technique.* New York: Science House.

Greenacre, P. (1959). Play in relation to creative imagination. *Psychoanalytic Study of the Child.* New York: International Universities Press.

Hartley, R., Frank, L., and Goldenson, R. (1957). *Understanding Children's Play.* New York: Columbia University Press.

Hawkey, L. (1945). Play analysis case study of a nine-year-old girl. *British Journal of Medical Psychiatry* 20:236–243.

Haworth, M. R. (1964). *Child Psychotherapy.* New York: Basic Books.

Howells, J. G., and Townsend, D. (1973). Puppetry as a medium for play diagnosis. *Child Psychiatry Quarterly* 6:9–14.

Irwin, E., and Kovacs, A. (1979). Analysis of children's drawings and stories. *Journal of the Association for the Care of Children in Hospitals* 8:39–45.

Irwin, E., and Malloy, E. (1975). Family puppet interview. *Family Process* 14:179–191.

Irwin, E., and Shapiro, M. (1975). Puppetry as a diagnostic and therapeutic technique. In *Psychiatry and Art*, vol. 4, ed. I. Jakab. Basel, Switzerland: Karger.

Irwin, E., Portner, E. S., Elmer, E., and Petti, T. (1981). Joyless children: a study of the effects of abuse of time. In *The Personality of the Therapist: Proceedings of the 1981 International Congress of the American Society of the Psychopathology of Expression*, ed. I. Jakab. Basel, Switzerland: Karger.

Jenkins, R. L., and Beckh, E. (1942). Finger puppets and mask-making as a media for work with children. *American Journal of Orthopsychiatry* 12:294–300.

Lowenfeld, M. (1939). The world pictures of children. *British Journal of Medical Psychology*, vol. 18.

Lyle, J., and Holly, S. B. (1941). The therapeutic value of puppets. *Bulletin of the Menninger Clinic* 5:223–226.

Murphy, L. (1956). *Methods for the Study of Personality in Young Children*. Vol. 1. New York: Basic Books.

Portner, E. (1981). A normative study of the spontaneous puppet stories of eight-year-old children. Ph.D. dissertation. University of Pittsburgh, Pittsburgh.

Rabin, A. E., and Haworth, M. R. (1960). *Projective Techniques with Children*. New York: Grune & Stratton.

Rambert, M. (1949). *Children in Conflict*. New York: International Universities Press.

Rubin, J. (1978). *Child Art Therapy*. New York: Van Nostrand Reinhold.

Sarnoff, R. (1976). *Latency*. New York: Jason Aronson.

Schaefer, C. (1976). *Therapeutic Use of Child's Play*. New York: Jason Aronson.

Schaefer, C., and O'Connor, K. (1983). *Handbook of Play Therapy*. New York: Wiley.

Woltmann, A. G. (1940). The use of puppets in understanding children. *Mental Hygiene* 24:445–458.

_____ (1951). The use of puppetry as a projective method in therapy. In *An Introduction to Projective Techniques*, ed. H. H. Anderson and G. L. Anderson. New York: Prentice Hall.

_____ (1952). Puppet shows as a psychotherapeutic method. In *Child Psychiatric Techniques*, ed. L. Bender. Springfield, IL: Charles C Thomas.

_____ (1960). Spontaneous puppetry by children as a projective method. In *Projective Techniques with Children*, ed. A. E. Rabin, and M. R. Haworth. New York: Grune & Stratton.

6

Finger Puppets and Mask Making

R. L. JENKINS AND ERICA BECKH

Finger Puppets

The purpose of this chapter is not to present finished results of a research study, but to stimulate some further realization of the possibilities of two media for work with children.

Dr. Lauretta Bender and Mr. Adolf G. Woltmann introduced puppetry in psychotherapy at Bellevue Hospital in 1935. Anyone who has witnessed the puppet shows on the children's ward at the Psychiatric Division of Bellevue Hospital has had ample opportunity to observe how vital and dynamic they are. Anyone who has talked at length with the children about them will realize that the material in these puppet plays strikes some of the deeper emotional chords and conflicts which are common in children and brings out the resonance and dissonance of the child with the self-assertion, resentment, dependence, affection and remorse of the child Caspar of the puppet stage.

These plays are not primarily spectacles but, in the tradition of the puppet stage, embody an active and dramatically intense interplay between puppet characters and child audience.

It was an interest in investigating the usefulness of puppetry in individual treatment work as contrasted with its use for groups that led to work here reported. This is not to imply that no individual use was made at Bellevue, for discussion of the plays with individual children was usual, and individual work on puppets was encouraged. However, the puppet play was a performance before a group.

Since we wanted the children to use the puppets themselves, the utmost simplicity of operation was essential. Hand puppets, such as

Caspar, are vigorous and expressive but are a little more complicated and require more skill than do finger puppets, the simplest of all the puppet family.

Finger puppets may be simply made from rubber balls. A hole is cut to admit the index finger. This is done by drawing a circle the size of the fingertip on the ball, cutting free the circumference by a series of knife stabs and tearing out the plug so formed. The forefinger slips into the hole. The ball is the puppet's head. The sponge rubber grips the forefinger which forms the neck. Features are cut from sponge rubber and fastened to the head with rubber cement or painted directly on the rubber. It is most satisfactory to mix on a tin plate or palette a little artist's oil colors in a clear, flexible vehicle which will adhere to rubber and not crack, such as a good bakelite base enamel. Balls so painted may be repeatedly bounced without cracking the paint.

The ball is the puppet's head. The thumb and middle finger are the arms. The ring and little fingers are usually the legs. This, of course, means the puppets are asymmetrical, a fact which troubles the children not a whit. If, from time to time, the third and fourth fingers jump out of character and join the thumb and middle finger as extra arms, or if the thumb and middle finger become additional legs, the children mind not at all. A wide variety of characters may be simply created. While the index finger becomes the neck, the other fingers of the hand are free for the manipulation which the puppet must undertake. Even 3-year-olds have little difficulty in keeping the puppet's head up on the index finger and carrying out some manipulation of stage activity with the other fingers. A variety of small articles, such as may be cheaply obtained at a dime store or a favor store or are available in the home, add interest as stage properties. Discrepancies of size cause no problem. Medicine may be given with a normal size spoon. Indeed, this adds an element of the humor of exaggeration. A letter may be written with a normal size pencil. A small crescent of paper pinned to a mother's forehead transforms her into a nurse, a feather stuck in the top of the puppet's head makes him an Indian. A fold of cardboard becomes a boat, a spoon an oar, a keycase a broncho, an aluminum doll kettle a basin or a helmet. A spring curling iron set in sponge rubber can make a formidable dragon.

These simple puppets attract children immediately and intensely. They are at once anxious to play with them and eagerly watch any performance by the therapist. In no case has there been any problem in establishing rapport when using puppets. After the first session, the children are eager to return to play with them again. The fact that they can be manipulated with sufficient effectiveness without practice means that they can immediately be utilized by the child for effective expression. They are more vivid, more alive, more unusual and more intriguing than are dolls.

Since the puppets are in fact the hands of the puppet player, these hands have for purposes of the play ceased to be a part of the child and are the bodies of the puppets. Aggressive or other tabooed actions undertaken by these hands are therefore, for purposes of the play, not the actions of the child manipulating the puppet but the actions of the puppet. If the puppet does wrong, it is the puppet, not the child, that is to be censured or punished. This gives the child license in the play to express tabooed actions while the responsibility rests on the puppet. Often the child will punish the puppet. This also makes it possible for the child and the puppeteer to discuss the child's problem impersonally, by presenting it upon the puppet stage as though related solely to characters there. Similarly, it is possible for the therapist, through the puppets, to bring to the attention of the child another point of view without assuming the onus of endorsing it. The therapist may even carry on a discussion between two puppets, one of which maintains a sharply critical and depreciatory attitude toward the child while the other defends the child.

The resources of puppetry lie in the flexibility and dynamic types of dramatization made possible and the way in which problems and discussions of problems may be made on an impersonal basis, yet may be personalized by the therapist at any time this seems desirable.

The following case exemplifies the use of puppets in therapy. Joe, 9 years old, was referred by his mother for disobedience, unmanageability and temper tantrums with screaming spells. The initial investigation revealed that Joe was jealous of his younger brother and intensely jealous of his 6-year-old nephew, the son of an older sister who lived in the home. In the second interview, the therapist suggested that Joe dramatize a dispute over toys between two brothers.

There appeared on the stage "Squeejump" and "Bill," Squeejump's younger brother. Squeejump complained that Bill took his toys. To the inquiry of the therapist Squeejump stated that Bill had toys of his own but they were "baby toys." Squeejump and Bill fought and Squeejump knocked off Bill's head. Interest by the therapist in the attitude of the boys' parents brought a scene between the father and a cousin. The father decided to break up all the toys because the boys fought over them. The cousin broke up and threw away the toys.

In the next scene, which was in no way suggested by the therapist, Squeejump and Bill reappeared. Bill had a new hat which his father had bought him. It fell down the sewer. Bill went after it; he drowned.

Squeejump proclaimed that he had warned Bill not to go, although he had not. Squeejump went to save Bill; Squeejump drowned. The mother reappeared and was informed by the therapist of what had happened to her sons. She was distressed, called a policeman, who rescued the two boys, who proved to be alive.

It requires no flight of fancy to see in this some expression of hostility toward the younger brother and nephew, in that Squeejump knocked off Bill's head. There appears a protest against more favored treatment of a younger child in Bill's parading the hat the father had given only him. Further hostility is expressed in that Bill drowned in the sewer. Then some repentance and Squeejump went to save Bill. Self-punishment appeared in that Squeejump drowned and, finally, the happy ending when the policeman saved both boys.

In conversation after the puppet play, Joe told of a time when his nephew was playing noisily with his (Joe's) toy cars. The father threatened to break the cars, whereat Joe grabbed them and ran downstairs. To some extent Joe was able in this interview to express in words his resentment toward his small nephew. He admitted he would frequently scream wildly when the nephew took his toys.

At the third session the mother reported some improvement of our patient in his relationship with his nephew and younger brother during the week.

The first scene Joe presented concerned Squeejump and Jack. Jack immediately was replaced by a fierce fantastic beast, the Blue Woofus, which was killed by Squeejump. In response to a question as to who the Woofus was, Joe readily replied, "My brother and other people." (This was the first time any direct suggestion had been given the boy that the puppets could be identified with any special people.) Most of the play this day concerned various people being beheaded by being run over by a castor which Joe picked up and used to represent a cow. He finally lined up a large number of puppet heads on the screen and knocked them off.

Joe was again reluctant in interview. In response to a question, he admitted sometimes feeling that people liked his nephew better than they liked him. He was able for the first time to express his feelings that his nephew did not belong in the same household, but added that he would not mind if the nephew did not break up so many of his (Joe's) toys. He came back again and again to this complaint.

After some time there was considerable improvement in the relation of this patient to his younger brother and his nephew, and the puppet plays reflected the change. It is hoped that enough has been related to illustrate the possibility of reaching the child's conflicts through puppets.

In short, puppetry is one road to releasing the spontaneity of a child's life. Children who stutter badly in an interview may play puppets without stuttering at all. On the other hand, at times too much spontaneity may be released, as when a boy of 10 became so excited on making the dragon attack a puppet that he urinated in his clothing.

With respect to the ages at which puppetry is useful, although children as young as 3 may play with them, they have been found most suitable for the age range of about 5 to 11.

The use of puppets does not commit one to any school of psychiatric thought or interpretation. It is possible to operate within or without any of the present so-called psychiatric schools and make use of puppetry. The interpretation and focus of therapists of different schools will doubtless differ somewhat, but all should find in puppetry a vital, dynamic and flexible medium for work with children. Puppetry is only a tool, and a tool can accomplish nothing except as it is handled. However, he who will make an effort to master this tool will find it has great power, wide adaptability, yet the most delicate subtlety. It takes children at their level and in their language. It gives them the opportunity to release in dramatic action those things they feel but cannot or will not express in words.

Mask Making

The making of masks provides another possible outlet for emotional expression. Among primitive peoples mask making has often been one of the most expressive and dynamic arts, and in our experience it may be so with children.

The process of mask making is simple and inexpensive. The face is first modeled in clay. Children frequently respond more freely to modeling than to drawing. The properties of clay and the physical activity it provides seem to stimulate the child. He is not inhibited by the fear that an error will be fatal. He quickly realizes that he can form and reform the medium at will. After the clay model is finished, it should be allowed to dry for several days. When hard, it is coated with vaseline and then covered with one inch strips or scraps of newspaper soaked in a thin paste of flour and water. These strips, slightly overlapping, are laid over the face from forehead to chin. They must be carefully molded over all details of the clay form. Four to five complete layers are necessary. After the papier-maché mold so formed is dry, the clay is removed. The mask can then be painted with poster paints. A final coat of varnish will increase the durability and decorative effect.

Mask making was used at the New York State Training School for Boys in connection with an experimental use of art work with delinquent boys. The boys received only technical instruction in the process of mask making. The creative concepts and their translation into clay and paint were entirely the work of the boys. Cases may be cited as examples.

One mask is a highly decorative version of a Chinese mandarin. The flesh color is bright red. The deep set, slanting eyes, open mouth and skull cap are a brilliant yellow. There is a flowing rope-like mustache and pointed black beard. The creator of the mask, Cortez, is a lively little 13-year-old boy. He has a record of thefts and truancy, but is more a neglected than a delinquent child. There has been some doubt as to his mental ability. Psychometric tests have indicated borderline intelligence. His conversation was vague, disconnected and confused, with digressions into fantasy. However, he would alternate confusion and ignorance with strikingly keen and independent common sense observation and practical action. In both drawing and modeling Cortez completed each unit in a project separately. It would seem that this boy of limited mental ability simplified a problem for himself by dividing it into separate and very simplified tasks with which he could cope one at a time. In modeling he became fascinated by the physical properties of the medium. He would begin to sing and whistle and rhythmically pound the clay. He became obsessed with the craftsmanship of each stage and seemed temporarily to forget the total project. He began with an oval mound and became absorbed with smoothing and resmoothing the surface, in spite of a suggestion that he would ultimately destroy it in making features. He added a wedge for the nose and again became lost in smoothing and perfecting its form. Later he dug out the mouth and eyes. The latter were framed by a ridge and he became fascinated with the form of the eye as a design in itself. The simplification and schematic stylization so conspicuous in this mask seem a result of this method of attack. One is struck by the lack of the emotional expressiveness in the mask that one would have expected from an imaginative child with tendencies to fantasy. Probably his method of work has prevented the embodiment of fantasy in the clay modeling. The highly decorative and original, unrealistic use of color, however, is a clear expression of the imaginative aspects of his personality.

There is an obvious danger that the art instructor, in interpreting the masks, will read in concepts and motivations that he has actually discovered by the personal contact with the boy. One check on this is the reactions of others, who have no previous knowledge of the boy, when confronted with the mask. In the case of the mask by Edward, the interpretations were variously expressed as "Bewilderment"—"He wants to know what it's all about anyway"—"Lost and at sea."

Edward is a tall boy of 14, the fourth of five children. His father is irresponsible and indifferent. The mother now lavishes her attention upon the baby and rejects Edward. His older brothers neglect him. He has a record for truancy, desertion, unmanageability at home, and activity as a gang leader. He is aware of the neglect by his family and is almost desperate because he has repeatedly written home and received no answer. He reveals insecurity in his art work, never takes initiative. He clings to mechanical and repetitious tasks, and is quickly put off by difficulties or errors. His mask seems to reveal his bafflement and despair. It is somber gray. The eyes, blue dots in white circles, are surprised and frightened. The mouth is open and helpless. Edward needed constant encouragement to continue and complete the first modeling of the mask. He had difficulty in physically coping with the clay and coercing it into definite, clear-cut forms. The final version had a strangely formless and amorphous quality. There was a conspicuous inability to delineate features sharply at any point. The nose flowed into the cheeks. In this case the mask becomes a vivid expression of a boy's inner state.

Keith is a tall, well-developed black boy of 13. He was committed to the Training School for stealing, truancy, and being involved in the passive role in pederasty with two adults. There is conflict in the home, the mother having forced his father to leave. The boy is upset at the conflict and feels guilt toward his mother. He claimed he stole out of fear of his father.

Keith has betrayed intense emotions and drives. He can react to others with quick hostility or strong attachment. He once fought another boy in resentment at a slur upon his sponsor. He immediately formed a strong attachment for the art instructor. This he revealed with the rather romantic and dramatic means to which an adolescent boy is apt to resort in the case of a "crush." There was an ardent and idealistic letter, signed by the "Black Ace." One day Keith modeled an ace of spades in clay, but refused to acknowledge the authorship of the anonymous letter, instead declaring he "knew the fellow who wrote it." It was during the subsequent discussion, initiated by the instructor, in which the inevitable limitations of the relationship were explained, that the boy began to model his mask.

This mask is a very striking and expressive version of a devil's face. It is bright red with green eyes and flowing black mustache and brows. It is modeled very vigorously, bold in relief, asymmetrical and mobile in character. It was executed with determination and hectic speed, almost slashed out at fever pitch. The intensity of the boy's reactions to the immediate situation gave a violence and force to his modeling that had previously been lacking in his delicate and precise drawings. The resulting mask was vividly expressive of conflict and turbulent emotion.

Salvatore is a muscular, powerful boy who moves and acts with swaggering aggressiveness. He has a record of automobile thefts, incorrigibility, and home desertion. At 16 he has roamed thousands of miles as hobo and thief. He is egocentric, egotistical, disillusioned, and cynical. In contact with others he will usually swagger, threaten, or seek to impress with casual accounts of his exploits and toughness. There is little if any evidence of a sense of guilt. Instead, he betrays innumerable hostilities.

Outstanding in this boy's personality is his need to dramatize himself. The mask, like Salvatore, is distinguished by its dramatic skill. It is, above all, spectacular. There is something of Salvatore's violent and cynical attitudes in its cruel, bestial scarlet mouth gaping against the blue flesh tone. Almost incongruous was the delicacy and sensitivity of the boy's actual modeling technique, combined with patience and diligence. His final success was a source of considerable pride which he tried to cover up with a wisecrack. In the shadowed sockets without eyes, and in some indefinable overtone there is, combined with the brutality, an intensely tragic, bewildered note, a confused, inarticulate, almost animal-like seeking for something not to be found. It is interesting that Salvatore's tough front may weaken when it fails to intimidate an adult and be replaced by a certain positive, if still graceless, response to normal social acceptance. And there is a stated seeking for reality, a satisfaction in something because "It's real," which seems to hint in verbal terms at the groping mirrored in the mask.

We are not ready, on the basis of limited experience, to present broad generalizations, except that this ancient art clearly offers possibilities of contributing to understanding the emotional life of problem children.

7

Costume Play Therapy

IRWIN M. MARCUS

During the years of development and maturation, there are changes in the child's motivations, dynamics, and methods of play. A number of excellent papers have been concerned with various aspects of the theory of play; among them are those of Sigmund Freud (1920, 1923), Anna Freud (1936, 1946), Anna Freud and Burlingham (1944), Erikson (1937), Waelder (1933), Ernst Kris (1934), Piaget (1945), and Peller (1954).

Fantasy life underlies all human activities and retains its basic themes, although during the course of healthy development reality issues will have a stronger influence upon the individual. Whereas the younger child can express his fantasies spontaneously with whatever material is available, the older child is less free in this respect. The latter may show initiative and creativity on an independent basis, yet he tends to require the cooperation of others for role playing and support in his more formalized imaginative games. Thus, the older child prefers real materials and more true to life situations, or stories he has seen or experienced in other ways. The limitations placed upon the type of communication an older child will permit, either in play or directly, is a reflection of his defenses and his fears of the fantasy content.

Experienced and skillful therapists are able to work with the various disguised manifestations of underlying mother–child or child–father and sibling relationships and conflicts. The transformations are seen in the child's sports, hobbies, secret clubs, and his intense feelings over winning and losing the great variety of structured popular games. Play behavior in the latency period is characterized by defenses that veer toward games which lack spontaneity, and tends to be conventional and competitive, with relatively little emotional content. The older child is gradually moving away from the disappointments and frustrations of his earlier dependency upon his family. With developmental changes, he is ready to seek the pleasures and security of new object relations through identifications with peer group and parentlike figures. The desire of an older child to play the usual games considered appropriate for his age helps him to defend against his earlier family conflicts by clinging to impersonal activity and shifting his competitive feelings toward his peers. However, this quality of ego development can be a real barrier to communication between a child and therapist when the child dedicates himself to concealing his feeling and is ashamed of his daydreams. Furthermore, the latency period is the time when adults expect the child to conform, to accept limitations, to develop good learning and study habits, skills, and group behavior. Thus, his anxieties are often met with reassurance, logical arguments, or ridicule which fosters the child's defenses against communication of his fantasies.

Utilizing the knowledge of play theory, this project explores *the possibility of deliberately stimulating a more spontaneous play pattern in older children.* The intent was to revive the imaginative play of the earlier years in a manner that would diminish the defensive embarrassment frequently produced by the usual play materials. Play patterns of the younger child allow vivid communication and the participation of others, but the grade school child *prefers props to support his role in the fantasy.* Therefore, costumes were provided in abundance for the purpose of setting the stage for dramatic play. In turn, this reopened an avenue that was once so pleasurable and useful for expressing emotional and conflictual experiences. Thus, the costume technique is designed to combine the advantages of the situational method and free play. Children who are disturbed because they have had to endure experiences of a traumatic magnitude can work toward mastery through playful repetition of more digestible portions of these events. By changing roles, children who were passive victims can become active aggressors. Their feelings of painful helplessness can be reexperienced with a happier, stronger, and successful conclusion. Although play is usually not complete abandon, there is sufficient relief from both reality and the conscience to allow for a display of the child's fantasies about himself and others. Play enables the ego to deal with the external pressures of reality and with the intrapsychic impact of impulses and conscience. With more complete emotional involvement in the fantasies of play, the child has a greater outlet for his anxiety and can experience the pleasure of wish fulfillment.

A striking aspect of costume play therapy is the ease with which older children can act out vital unconscious material without sufficient awareness to intensify anxiety and thereby resistance. The complementary role assigned to the therapist by the child allows the therapist to engage in meaningful responses, which promotes further communication and fosters problem solving. If the child is suffering from a neurotic illness, the interpretive possibilities open to the therapist are well known to those with experience in the field. The fantasy play may be linked with the significant episodes and figures in the child's real life; or the therapist may call attention to resemblances between play situations and the real relationships in a manner that allows the defenses to be worked upon. Metaphoric interpretation may be used when the assessment of the child's ego strength suggests that a distance must be maintained between the fantasy and the conscious awareness of the child—although, of course, the therapist must eventually bring the known conflicts into consciousness. When regressions are already present or easily evoked, as in the borderline and psychotic states, tenuous object relations can at least be maintained by confining interpretations to the patient's own regressed language (Ekstein and Wallerstein, 1956). Repetitious play on the regressed level, as long as the contact remains, provides a foundation for later, more mature identifications and the emergence of secondary-process thinking.

In therapy, the traumatic experience, conflict, and anxiety must be externalized and brought into the child–therapist relationship. As Anna Freud (1946) noted, fruitful work in child therapy requires a "positive attachment." Since the specific play roles become the chief avenue for communication, the context of the emotion is more readily recognized and handled, thus permitting the therapist to sustain his position as the child's ally. *A trusting and meaningful relationship evolves from the ability to communicate understanding* to the child, rather than from friendly playful activities as such. Costume play therapy allows the therapist to communicate with the child on whatever level the child presents. Playing out fantasies, feelings, and traumatizing situations through make-believe emphasizes the demarcation between reality and fantasy while bridging the gap with communication and understanding. Thus, the therapeutic nature of the costume play is promoted through sharing the disguised experience and mood, through closeness, mutuality, good communication, and understanding of the specific anxieties which accompany the fantasies. In all the techniques of play therapy, varying roles are explicitly or, more often, implicitly assigned to the therapist and assumed by the patient, depending upon the child's needs at the time. However, part of the difficulty in practicing and teaching play

therapy is precisely the problem of understanding the child's communications through play. Unfortunately, this factor may impart in the minds
of parents, student therapists, and others a mystical and esoteric quality
to the direct treatment of children. Costumes as a stimulus for imaginative play clarify the explicit nature of the role and utilize the child's need
for motility, activity, and defensive disguise.

Anyone who wishes to relate to children must know how to play or
converse with them. Therapists are at times "kept in the dark" and at a
considerable distance in the relationship because a child may reject
playing with dolls or puppets and would rather play a game or color a
picture than paint freely or play with clay. Costumes are natural equipment within the current experiences of both the child and the therapist.
The therapist at varying times throughout his life will "dress up" for
costume parties or events as a not infrequent experience in social "fun"
activities.[1] In costume play therapy the therapist does not dress up, nor,
in my experience, does the child require this. The costumes are for the
patients. The therapist remains an adult with his responses geared to the
reality of therapy, and he should not slip into acting out his own unresolved or revived conflicts. However, the ability of a therapist to be an
adult who can understand and still be with the child in his fantasy play is
a unique and essential quality of child therapy. The basic principles are
no different with the costume play therapy technique. The child's need
for the therapist to accept a role is more dependent upon the therapist's
response than the latter's appearance in a costume. The therapist's
anxiety about "what does this mean?" when viewing certain other play
activities is diminished and replaced with the increased security of
feeling a sense of mastery through improved contact and communication
with the child.

Although dress-up games are part of oedipal period play, its anlage

---

[1]The basic premise of this chapter is easily observed among adults in New Orleans
during Mardi Gras. I have analyzed a married woman who has a frigidity problem. She
reported that prior to therapy she dressed as a baby, her regression from the oedipal
conflicts. In a later phase, she spontaneously selected the role of a flapper. A patient who
had to fashion a costume for his date at a party created a nun's outfit for her, and in
analysis recalled he once heard someone say she was promiscuous, but he rejected the
idea because of his affection for her. Another woman, with sexual frustration as one of her
problems, repeatedly dressed in skin-tight leotards as a devil. A homosexual man once
dressed as a bum, but with a very large nose, whereas another homosexual patient could
never decide what he wanted to wear, reflecting his identity problem. A Jewish man in
conflict with his religious identity selected an Arab costume. Finally, there are always a
number of adults who dress as the opposite sex whenever costumes are permitted for an
occasion, an obvious revelation of unresolved conflicts.

may be seen in the early imitation and identification activities, when the child experiences the pleasure of closeness with mother and father through clumping around the house in their shoes and decorating himself with any other item of apparel he can snatch from the household. The popularity of the box of old hats sometimes included in a nursery school setting is an example of the natural attraction of children to dress-up games. It is an activity which is permissible at times in all ages, and thus resistance to this play is less likely to occur. The mutual pleasure of costume play enhances the likelihood of the child's returning to the same materials for more consistent working through of disturbed feelings and conflicts. In contrast, the anxiety or hostility displayed in activities of play where there is less pleasure and the therapist's role is more vague in the child's mind may contribute to the disruption of play.

The study was initiated with three children, a girl and a boy both 10 years old, and an 11-year-old boy. All three were photographed in black and white 16 mm. movie sound film during the early phase of their individual therapy. The introduction to costume play and samples of the technique and interaction during therapy were edited in a twenty-minute reel. The camera and professional observers were concealed in another room and viewed the therapy through a one-way mirror. Sessions were conducted weekly, for about forty-five to fifty minutes, with the author as therapist. The costumes included the following: those appropriate for a baby, mother, father, doctor, superman, witch, devil, clown, skeleton, ballerina, and three large pieces of colored cloth for a self-designed outfit.

The method is illustrated in the following example: Evan, aged almost 10, was referred by the Welfare Department because he was a slow learner and about two years behind in schoolwork. He seemed confused and incapable of following directions. Teachers complained of his daydreaming and inability to concentrate. He was effeminate in his mannerisms and submissive in his relationship to his fraternal twin brother. His constant and pervasive lying included serious distortions about his teachers, friends, and other adults. He stole, but accused others when objects were missing and later found to be in his possession.

In psychological testing Evan achieved an I.Q. on the Verbal Scale of 94, on Performance 92, and on the Full Scale of 92. It was difficult for the examiner to understand his stories on the Apperception Test, but one could grasp his sadness, feeling of loneliness, and fears that his mother would kill him. Both he and his brother showed ego disorganization. His schizophrenic mother had been hospitalized for several years, and since the age of 2 he had been in institutions and foster homes.

Treatment was initiated in May 1963 and terminated in December

1964. Evan was shy and reluctant about selecting a costume from the many hanging in open display and denied having any memories of play with costumes. In low, hushed tones he recalled various situations in which he was deprived of a variety of toys and play materials. His actions and communications were highly inhibited and constricted. He preferred to find a chair, sit down, and stare with a blank expression—a response that frequently causes therapists to become bored and frustrated. However, the therapist's sympathetic responses to Evan's past and present situations and continued encouragement to try making up a play with the costumes gradually succeeded. Evan cautiously examined each costume and finally selected the mother's outfit. He began playing the role of a teacher, asking the therapist to be the principal, and at other times the teacher's husband. He prepared large meals for the family, gave his children money for food, and in the school play he instructed the children, using a nearby blackboard, and assured them that they would pass.

The theme of a good mother who fed her children well prevailed for many sessions. The therapist commented on Evan's great concern that the children be fed. He responded by recollecting that others had told him his mother was sick and could not take care of him, and that he longed for his mother. In time the therapist mentioned that sometimes children are very angry about their mothers leaving them. Evan seemed to have a minimal response to this comment, but the sessions gradually shifted into a detective story. He reported a woman murdered because she murdered her children. However, the good woman who punished the bad mother would in turn be punished by the police. We talked about people being afraid to say their angry thoughts because of fear of being punished. The therapist interpreted that sometimes very sad children have very angry thoughts that frighten them, because they are afraid they will be punished by having to live away from their homes. During this phase of the play, Evan interjected thoughts about the fantasied cold weather in the play and of how he hated to be "out in the cold."

Evan later switched into the role of the ghost of the bad mother (stimulated by his selecting the skeleton costume during this phase) who had been murdered in previous sessions. There was much anxious and excited play about coffins and a ghost seeking revenge. In the end, the ghost was defeated by the therapist, who was assigned the role of policeman. Evan began to show overt warmth toward the therapist at this stage, being reluctant to leave at the end of the sessions, hugging the therapist upon leaving and arriving, and expressing eagerness about the next visit of his social worker who would transport him. He became more responsive and communicative with her during their time together. The sessions shifted to his playing the wife in a loving marriage. During this phase, among his many comments, he exclaimed, "Darling, darling, darling, hold me in your arms." In these periods we were able to talk about his fantasies about his father (who had deserted them), his wishes to have his father back, his fears about whether his father had hurt his mother, his fears about being hurt himself, and his fantasy that the only way a boy could be loved is to be like a girl. However, he had another solution to being loved which became apparent in the following sessions when he selected, for the first time, the baby costume. In the baby role, he arranged the chairs into a bed and curled into the fetal position, made goo-goo sounds, engaged in rocking motions, and sucked his thumb. The satisfaction and regression on this level of play were so intense that for a while he was inaccessible to contact. However, in coming out of the baby role, he was exuberant, smiled happily, and seemed much more relaxed.

The therapist did not appear to have any specific role during the foregoing, other than to allow Evan the gratification of his longing for the fantasied pleasures of being an infant again. This time he could imagine starting life with a new parent figure, the therapist. The therapist commented on how children who are unhappy wish to be a baby again and have new parents who will take care of them: to love and be loved. Evan responded very strongly with memories of a foster family he loved before he was shifted into the institution. I commented on his disappointments in the past and concern about trusting each new person in his life, including the therapist. His costume play then vacillated between the role of baby and that of a mother, re-enacting a cruel mother who hated her baby, whom he named for his brother. During these sessions he expressed a great deal of hostility toward his brother, and verbalized his feeling of being hated by his mother. With self-designed costumes from the pieces of colored cloth, he became a cruel queen and captured an explorer (the therapist) who had landed on "her" planet. The explorer was tortured in many ways, whipped, shot with ray guns, and made into a weak, submissive man.

His fantasy patterns showed marked sadomasochistic features. There were many variations of his fears of being injured, his self-image of being castrated, and his desire for and fear of inflicting destruction. His castration anxiety and sense of helplessness were translated into the fears of the explorer, and the resemblance of the cruel queen to a hated and feared mother were interpreted. His image of women as castrated, vindictive, dangerous torturers of men necessitated concealing his own masculinity. In response to the therapist's query about what made the queen so mad, he replied that "her face had been burned off by old men." He later remarked about women having to be cut open to take their babies out. Periods of decreased anxiety followed as the foregoing was repeatedly worked through. In later sessions he assigned the doctor role to the therapist to repair the damaged queen.

After several months of therapy, progress reports prepared by his social worker indicated that he had become more aggressive and defended himself in a physical encounter with another boy. His effeminate behavior diminished, and he showed improved ability to tolerate frustration, to accept discipline and disappointments. He became more demonstrative in expressing affection for the worker. After a year of therapy, his academic work began to show real improvement. His intense interest in the costumes gradually diminished, his communications became more direct, and he manifested a growing interest in typical organized boys' games.

The history of Evan was one of severe neglect early in life. His instinctual life could not be combined with the pleasurable sensory stimulation of good mothering. He experienced too much real deprivation and frustration which impaired the adequate development of his ego. Combining instinctual tensions with only fragmented perceptions causes a child to produce distorted fantasy perceptions of his environment. The result is a diminished attentiveness to the outside world, greater absorption in unconscious fantasies, gratifying daydreams, and impaired reality testing. With his ego organization thus disturbed, Evan's instinctual tensions were frequently relieved through primary processes resulting in "nonsense" and "silly" talk and behavior. His energies were dissipated by these conditions and a severe learning and behavior problem was inevitable. His hunger for a mothering relationship caused him to cling to primitive, distorted identifications with mother figures and to be submissive and dependent upon his brother and other boys.

Evan was very responsive to play opportunities provided by the costume technique. He quickly constructed a plot around a family setting, and, as expected, he played the mother role. Play forms may combine or merge with one another, and *preoedipal play,* with its preoccupation with mother, was present for a prolonged period. He dramatized the role of a mother figure, his teacher, and displayed his wishes for the good mother who would be loving to her children and husband. He presented a fusion of mother and teacher, playing both roles; in addition, he demonstrated his wish to be like her, to have her with him at all times, and to replace her in order to achieve closeness with father. During his preoedipal play he was characteristically very serious. His rage and anxiety in relation to mother gradually unfolded in the murder plot, as he tried to get rid of the bad mother and retain the good mother identifications and introjects.

Guilty reactions appeared in the punishment scenes wherein the police apprehended the good woman who killed the bad one. Fantasies of the magical power of bad mothers, corpses, and ghosts who can destroy their children reflected the delusional fear of the absent mother and provided opportunities for the therapist to play the policeman (institute-therapist-social workers, and benevolent conscience) who will protect him and diminish his fears and guilt. His rage and guilt were also felt toward his brother and were concealed behind a submissive reaction formation, but these feelings were ventilated in the baby-mother scenes. On the baby level he gratified and expressed his dependency needs and fantasies without having to defend against them with denial or repression. By the maintenance of the therapeutic relationship through the most regressive periods of the play, the primitive transferences became a bridge for reopening avenues of identificatory processes.

In later play he was more oedipal and assumed the role of the powerful omnipotent adult (queen) and happily controlled the therapist (child). During this play, he displayed his feelings about people who lied to him—the facts about his family and his own origin. On another level, he relieved his oedipal conflict by controlling father and (possessing) being mother. His castration anxiety was an important theme throughout this phase.

As the pressures of his intrapsychic conflicts were played out, his relationship to the therapist grew more positive and new identifications occurred, his attention to reality improved, as did his ego organization, and learning again became available to him. His ability to separate from mother attachments and develop his own individuality developed gradually and he became more assertive with his brother. Identifications with male figures became more acceptable and effeminate behavior diminished. The strengthening of the ego was also apparent in his increased tolerance for frustration and discipline.

Conclusion

Costumes are enjoyed upon occasion in all ages and are less likely to be considered too babyish by older children during therapy. Costume play therapy appears to be a worthwhile addition to child therapy, especially in older children who are less spontaneous in communication. The materials represent the only addition to the therapy. The therapeutic technique is essentially the same as we know it and interpretive work proceeds gradually to more mature levels. The goal likewise remains unchanged: to help the child understand reality in keeping with his developmental capacity.

References

Ekstein, R., and Wallerstein, J. (1956). Observations on the psychotherapy of borderline and psychotic children. *Psychoanalytic Study of the Child* 11:303–311. New York: International Universities Press.

Erikson, E. H. (1937). Configurations in play: clinical notes. *Psychoanalytic Quarterly* 6:139–214.

Freud, A. (1936). *The Ego and the Mechanisms of Defense.* New York: International Universities Press, 1946.

_____ (1946). *The Psychoanalytical Treatment of Children.* New York: International Universities Press, 1959.

Freud, A., and Burlingham, D. T. (1944). *Infants Without Families.* New York: International Universities Press.

Freud, S. (1920). Beyond the pleasure principle. *Standard Edition* 18:7–64, 1955.

_____ (1923). The ego and the id. *Standard Edition* 19:12–66, 1961.

Kris, E. (1934). The psychology of caricature. In *Psychoanalytic Explorations in Art.* New York: International Universities Press, 1952. pp. 173–188.

Peller, L. (1954). Libidinal phases, ego development and play. *Psychoanalytic Study of the Child* 9:178–197. New York: International Universities Press.

Piaget, J. (1945). *Play, Dreams and Imitation in Childhood.* New York: Norton, 1951.

Waelder, R. (1933). The psychoanalytic theory of play. *Psychoanalytic Quarterly* 2:208–224.

8

Use of the Telephone in Play Therapy

MOSHE H. SPERO

Play is a child's natural means of expression, reasoning, and communication. Fantasies verbalized in play can provide the therapist with vital information about a child and allow the child to achieve emotional growth, to satisfy certain developmental needs, and to obtain more integrated levels of ego structure and affect control (Erikson 1964, 1972). Toys implement a child's play, and various toys have been used in play therapy with children—clay and other art materials, toy furniture, dollhouses, doctor kits, dart guns, clothing, puppets. Some toys are preferred by different therapists because of different theoretical views on the expression of aggression and sexuality. Some toys are preferred from a concern to match types of play with types of children and disturbances, and to match appropriate toys with children of specific ages. Paul Adams (1974) notes that almost no play gimmick need be taboo if it is used appropriately within the therapeutic context.

The use of toys as a medium of expression in therapy has its limitations, however. Many children who are "wise to the therapist's game" reject toys. Some age groups view certain toys as silly and, if they approach a toy at all, do not play much and produce little fantasy material. Of course, seasoned clinicians have their own ways of dealing with this disinterest or resistance.

Although many 12-year-olds may disdain an office filled with dolls, something about a 12-year-old boy's vulnerability to regression is revealed when he selects a doll from a closet full of assorted toys. Patricia Pothier (1976) noted that children who have a poor ability to fantasize will benefit least from play therapy, although fantasizing can be encouraged in patients through instruction and modeling. Some toys may stimulate fantasy more than others (Sours 1978). A toy's specific value in play therapy seems to depend not solely on its ability to stimulate fantasy, however, as evidenced by the popularity with children of toys which stimulate little fantasy, such as the Nok-Out Bench in Helen Beiser's (1955) study. Toys have other therapeutic value, such as allowing a child to rehearse socially acceptable behavior, externalize and then reintegrate internal conflict, and express emotion. A child who is less prone to fantasize initially may still benefit from these other aspects of play.

Value of the Telephone

This chapter discusses the use of the telephone in therapy with children. The telephone itself is not a toy. Recently it has been used increasingly in therapeutic circumstances for emergency counseling of suicidal individuals, with patients for whom the issue of psychological closeness and distance presents a problem, and where physical distance between the patient and therapist occasionally demands brief therapeutic contacts via telephone conversation (Miller 1973, Rosenbaum 1975). The role of the telephone as a transitional object has also been recognized by some therapists (Blanck and Blanck 1979, Searles 1976).

As a toy for play therapy, the telephone has received little attention. In 1942, M. B. Durfee discussed the use of office equipment in child therapy that focused on children's experiences with a dictaphone and make-believe radio broadcasts which encouraged expression and revealed fantasies. Only tangential reference was made to a patient who had used the telephone to direct information about his father to imaginary relatives he had "called" on the phone. In more recent articles about child play therapy, the telephone still receives only passing reference as a toy among others in the therapist's closet, leaving unexplored its unique use for therapy as a child's "nontoy" toy (Haworth 1964, Piers 1972, Schaefer 1975). In fact, Dell Lebo (1975), using a "verbal index" formula, finds that, although the telephone has been valued theoretically as an expressive toy, it is frequently not rated highly on his index.

The therapeutic value of most toys lies largely in the child's disposition to engage them in natural play, with a secondary effect being the communication of fantasy or information. The telephone, however, is recognized quickly as a *communications* object in itself. The child understands that it is a social instrument. The telephone is also a potentially symbolic play object because it simultaneously combines talking and listening, and responding and asserting, in ways not visible to the party at the other end of the line. In play, these reactions, and their meanings, must be imagined and can be directed by the child. Thus, when children use the telephone in the therapist's presence they intuitively assume the therapist's participation in their end of the conversation, while determining at their own pace just what the therapist "hears," as shown in the following example:

> Les, age 7, picked up the toy phone and "called" his classmates in school to tell them he was visiting "a friend." When asked if any of his classmates knew where he really was, he replied that they imagined he was absent so he could see a doctor, a "shots doctor." Les then turned his back and, with his hand covering his mouth and the receiver, he whispered to his "classmates," "I lied . . . I'm really going to see a doctor but you guys don't have to worry!"

Les was now prepared to deal with his own anxieties about seeing a "doctor." The therapist was also in a better position to help the child understand what he had allowed the therapist to hear. For the child who can imagine conversations at both ends of the telephone, its therapeutic value is immense.

In addition, for many children the use of the telephone symbolizes mastery of adult abilities, including the ability to manipulate the dial, to converse with friends, and to do two things at the same time. Toddlers from the age of 16 months pick up the receiver (or even an object that approximates the shape of a receiver, such as a film cartridge from an Instamatic Camera) and babble into it, an obvious replication of parental behavior. Telephone privileges are a source of considerable excitement for children. They may imitate their parents by clamping the receiver between their ear and shoulder while they busy themselves with some other important task. Using the telephone is perceived as a source of power and control as well as pride. One 9-year-old patient summarized, "I don't like Gramma. If I don't want to talk to her I just don't call her, and if I'm talking to her and I get sad, I *could* just hang it up." A telephone conversation is one of the few social situations in which, if one is unhappy with the proceedings, the interchange can be abruptly terminated. By slamming down the receiver, many children feel they have managed to confine the source of their indignation to the telephone, afterwards often gingerly lifting up the receiver to insure that the other party is, indeed, no longer there.

In therapy, the telephone stimulates fantasy by encouraging a child to conduct a dialogue with an imaginary second party. Whom the child selects to call, what dialogue transpires between them, and what role the child plays as the second party, all reveal much information for the therapist, as the following example shows:

> Sally, an abused 8-year-old, had great difficulty accepting her feelings toward her violent mother. Her descriptions of her mother were of a pleasant, well-intentioned, and nurturing individual. Early in therapy I suggested that she call her mother at home on the toy phone to ask if she could be picked up from school early. Acting in the role of her mother. Sally expressed that having Sally home early would be inconvenient and upset the day. When Sally asked a second time, complaining of a headache, her "mother" promised that Sally would be punished for messing up the daily schedule. Although Sally was unable to confront and accept this image of her mother directly, she replicated a meaningful, typical interchange between them.

The telephone can also be used to fantasize a connection with individual now dead or far away. Children often use the telephone to connect with deceased loved ones, separated parents or even with significant acquaintances from earlier years. When used frequently in this capacity, the role of the telephone as a transitional object must be explored. In other conversations on the telephone, the child's ego may assume the role of the visible party while the child's self-image is projected onto the imagined second party. For example, during an initial interview session, a child called herself on the phone and, assuming the role of an adult, reminded herself not to fear the helpful doctor.

The telephone is also useful in dealing with a child's reluctance toward therapy, especially in beginning sessions. Ten-year-old Billy sat through two intake sessions without speaking when it was suggested that he telephone the therapist and, speaking as his father, try to convince the therapist to see "his son." He was also told that he could then call, as himself, to explain why he would rather not come to therapy. During the enactment of his father, Billy made such an effective case for consultation that he remained on the phone and, still playing his father, revealed much of importance about "his son."

Case Histories

The following four cases illustrate the use of the telephone in play therapy.

Case 1

John's younger brother died of pulmonary complications when John was 8 years old. John had become aggressive since then and seemed to have a wish to be punished for a deeply repressed conviction that he was responsible for his brother's death. John's parents had cared for the brother at home during his last weeks alive. John and they had taken turns monitoring the boy's breathing and tending to his needs. It was an overwhelming task for an 8-year-old. The night John's brother died, John was on watch and had fallen asleep, failing to note a critical shift in his brother's breathing. His brother died as John slept. Had John alerted his parents, probably nothing could have been done to reverse the situation. His sense of blame persisted nonetheless.

In the middle phase of therapy I encouraged John to use the telephone to "call" his brother. I asked them to discuss some good memories they shared as well as some bad ones. After a few sessions, John, enacting the brother, began to wonder whether John was ever jealous of the increased attention he had received or angry about their parents' shortness with John during the many frustrating and weary weeks before his death. Suddenly John threw the phone against the wall and began to cry. He had heard for himself—and very much from himself—what emotional issues were broiling beneath the surface of his aggressiveness and depression.

In subsequent sessions, John wished so call his brother again and apologize for these feelings. The limitation of reality had to be stressed at this point, however, to encourage John's bereavement. This could now occur, unhampered by John's previous hostilities and feelings of guilt. John's inability to use the phone to reach his brother again was a loss similar to the original loss of his brother through death, which John now could mourn more appropriately with support from therapy.

Case 2

Eight-year-old Sally had been in treatment for two years for anxiety neurosis. The termination phase had begun when Sally began to have severe nightmares of being thrown into the sea. She also began wetting the floor of my office. Some of this regression was based on her parents' sudden decision to divorce. Her mother planned to leave the state with Sally, which was going to end treatment earlier than scheduled. Part of Sally's regression was also based on her apparent vulnerability, which had been insufficiently dealt with in therapy. The problem involved Sally's fears of loss of control.

I told Sally to imagine that she was the "central command" of her body and could communicate with her various organs by telephone.

Her duty was to listen to the complaints of these organs and encourage them to carry out their tasks. I was to describe various scenes based on situations in the past where she had lost control or had experienced anxiety symptoms, and she was to monitor the sensations of her body. Partly motivated by the lack of time, which precluded a more nondirective format, I wanted to help Sally desensitize her reactions to stress and control her fear of loss of control.

During the various telephone conversations with her body, Sally revealed much about her sense of body-self and her family's attitude toward physical infirmity (Sally had a limp due to a congenital defect). In many conversations, Sally relegated her parents to her genital organs and was punitive to these members of her otherwise cooperative body system. This material was useful and brought remission of her symptoms. Sally directed her attention to these feelings for the remainder of our time together.

Case 3

Beej was 7 when her parents left her with an alcoholic aunt who, within a year, sent Beej to live with a punitive and possibly mentally incompetent brother and his alcoholic wife. A concerned relative managed to have Beej placed under her care and arranged for treatment to begin.

Beej sat timidly in the waiting room and, when finally in my office, sat with her head buried in her chest. When she noticed the wall full of toys she reached for the telephone and held the receiver to her ear. As I began some preliminary conversation, Beej slammed the receiver down on the phone cradle. Confused about the meaning of this act, I waited a few minutes and attempted to pick up the conversation again. Beej slammed the receiver down on the cradle. I finally understood that she was attempting to shut me up as one hangs up a receiver. I then picked up the receiver of my phone and held it to my ear. We sat like this for the remainder of the session, Beej holding her toy phone to her ear while I held my phone to my ear. We did the same during the next session. In the third session, I picked up my receiver and held it out to Beej. She jumped into my lap, placed the receiver by her ear, and smiled. She sat in my lap holding the phone for the remainder of that session.

I learned later that whenever Beej's parents called her aunt's house to speak with her, Beej's aunt would grab the receiver away from her and slam it down on the cradle. Our therapeutic relationship began with her symbolic act and my fortuitous connection with the rich reality behind that symbol.

Case 4

Nine-year-old Pat was diagnosed as atypical. He heard voices instructing him to hurt people and to kill animals. He had been hospitalized when he attempted to destroy a car he said he was ordered to destroy. Epilepsy and other neurological disorders had been ruled out. Pat came from a violent home, and it seemed clear that his stepfather had attacked Pat sexually about three months prior to his hospitalization, when his symptoms had been first noticed by a school counselor.

As part of therapy, I instructed Pat to take the telephone whenever he heard these voices and speak to them as if they belonged to someone else. Most of the voices seemed to belong to his stepfather. Many of Pat's fantasies as well as his castration anxiety were dealt with in this manner. In later stages of therapy, I assumed the role of the voices so that Pat could begin to conceptualize the difference between the unreality of the voices and the reality of the telephone play.

Conclusion

In play therapy, the telephone is readily assimilated by children wishing to fantasize, externalize affect, or express fears and frustrations. A certain safety exists in speaking to parents, siblings, a therapist, or even oneself behind the one-way screen of the receiver. And because hearing voices on the telephone is expected, a telephone conversation becomes a socially acceptable way for a child to acknowledge inner fears by articulating them in the guise of another party on the line.

The telephone should be used as a therapeutic *aid* and not as a substitute for other intensive therapy. A patient's use of the telephone to avoid conflict or minimize the ego's confrontation with reality is certainly not desirable. A therapist must assess the strengths and weaknesses of a patient to know whether the telephone can be used in such extreme ways as with Pat or John. Communicating through the telephone instead of directly with the therapist for extended periods of time may indicate a client's resistance to therapy. It may also indicate that the therapist has not succeeded in providing a therapeutic atmosphere "good enough" to promote trust and more direct communication. In addition, the therapist should explain that the therapeutic use of the telephone is a privilege of the therapeutic session.

Telephone play should be instituted only with the full understanding of the child's changing levels of awareness, emotional flexibility, and insight. The telephone's capacity to facilitate communication makes it a valuable therapeutic tool, but it is the child's ability and willingness to play that allows the telephone to become a means of expression.

References

Adams, P. L. (1974). *A Primer of Child Psychotherapy.* Boston: Little, Brown & Co.

Beiser, H. (1955). Play equipment for diagnosis and therapy. *American Journal of Orthopsychiatry* 25:761–770.

Blanck, G., and Blanck, R. (1979). *Ego Psychology.* Vol. 2: *Psychoanalytic Developmental Psychology.* New York: Columbia University Press.

Durfee, M. B. (1942). Use of ordinary office equipment in "play therapy." *American Journal of Orthopsychiatry* 12:495–502.

Erikson, E. (1964). Toys and reasons. In *Child Psychotherapy: Practice and Theory,* ed. M. R. Haworth, pp. 3–11. New York: Basic Books.

———— (1972). Play and actuality. In *Play and Development,* ed. M. W. Piers, pp. 127–167. New York: W. W. Norton.

Haworth, M. R., ed. (1964). *Child Psychotherapy: Practice and Theory.* New York: Basic Books.

Lebo, D. (1975). Toys of non-directive play therapy. In *Therapeutic Use of Child's Play,* ed. C. Schaefer, pp. 435–447. New York: Jason Aronson.

Miller, W. (1973). The telephone in outpatient psychotherapy. *American Journal of Psychotherapy* 27:15–26.

Piers, M. W., ed. (1972). *Play and Development.* New York: W. W. Norton.

Rosenbaum, M. (1975). Continuance of psychotherapy by "long-distance" telephone. *International Journal of Psychoanalytic Psychotherapy* 3:484–495.

Schaefer, C., ed. (1975). *Therapeutic Use of Child's Play.* New York: Jason Aronson.

Searles, J. (1976). Transitional phenomena and therapeutic symbiosis. *International Journal of Psychoanalytic Psychotherapy* 5:145–502.

Sours, J. (1978). The application of child analytic principles to forms of child psychotherapy. In *Child Analysis and Therapy,* ed. J. Glenn, pp. 615–646. New York: Jason Aronson.

9

Block Playing

ROBERT J. RESNICK

Human interaction has been described as a communication system characterized by such properties as: time, system and subsystem relationships, wholeness, and feedback (Watzlawick et al. 1967). In examining the structure of communication, Watzlawick and colleagues (1967) have suggested that difficulties occur when meta communicational (messages about the communications) relationship levels are in disagreement but that the resolution of the disagreement occurs on a content level. Thus, disagreements evolve that undercut the relationship between the people involved. Certainly, psychotherapists are familiar with confusions between content and relationship aspects of any particular issue. Sometimes this all-important difference is referred to as talking at a person rather than talking with a person, or hearing the person but not listening to what he is saying. Furthermore, these authors have labeled mature relationships between a husband and wife as parallel since the communications are frequently complementary with many crossovers; in the pathological relationships what is seen is a consistent sabotaging or refusing of the other's attempt to define that relationship with communication. This is done by direct "no" or by multilevel messages in which a covert denial occurs—the classic double bind.

In the parent–child relationship, the child is placed almost universally in an inferior position, having to succumb to the parental wishes either by denial of the communication or by undermining of existing interactions system. With respect to both adult-adult and parent–child interaction several basic terms or theoretical constructs must be understood. As abstracted from Sorrells and Ford (1966) the following theoretical constructs can be indicated: (1) Any behavior which takes place in the presence of another person has communication value and such behavior can be either verbal or nonverbal. Thus, a person cannot not communicate. (2) The message that is transmitted may not necessarily be the message received. (3) Meta communication, which is a communication about a communication, or what is referred to as the music of a communication drawing on the analogy of popular music where there are words and music and one sometimes pays attention to the words without truly comprehending the music. Thus, it seems to be of paramount importance in working on a therapeutic relationship with couples or with a child to improve the communication network between adults and between the child and his parent or parents. Without some improvement in the communication network, the therapeutic task becomes more difficult, time consuming, and costly.

With this brief background, let me move to the technique of block playing. I must pay homage to my then 5½ year old daughter who, one evening when we were playing, brought out her *Playskool* blocks and indicated that we were going to build something. She stated that I was to build a bird house and that she would build a bird house and that she would tell me how to build my bird house to look like hers. Thus, the game was begun and she described to me how I was to put my blocks so that they would resemble hers. I purposely did not put my blocks the way she had indicated and with noticeable frustration in every way she said "Daddy, you are not listening to me." Later that evening I commented on the rather amusing situation to my wife and began to wonder whether this simple child's game could be used with married couples and with parent–child pairs who were having difficulty in communication with one another. At that point I decided to experiment with some young couples and some children that I was working with in therapy at the time. In the less than two years that I have used the technique, I have not used it with every married couple nor with every child that I have seen. I have used it, however, when it appears quite early that there is a breakdown in communication and where people are hearing without listening or, as indicated above, talking *at* rather than *with* each other. In the latter situation, a person talks while the other person is quiet but the second person is not really listening but simply waiting for an opportunity to jump in and defend his position. Thus, there is really no communication since all of the verbiage is going in one ear and out the other and each person is waiting for an opportunity to retort.

The block playing technique is utilized as follows: Two sets of blocks identical in number, color, and shape are given to the people involved.

The instructions are simple: one person is to begin a construction with the blocks, describing to the other person exactly what he is doing. The second person is out of the field of view of the initiator's construction. Commonly, the participants sit back to back or less commonly in adjoining rooms. The "follower" is allowed to ask as many questions as needed and the verbal interaction is solely on the block construction. The construction itself can be as simple or as complicated as the participants see fit. A trial is over when both partners have completed their construction and all questions have been asked and answered. Thus, there is complete interaction in both directions on an equal basis about a very *concrete* task. Following this, the positions are reversed: the follower now becomes the initiator of a construction and the same routine is completed. Usual instructions are to do two constructions with each partner being the initiator every other night. In the one instance where I had the child constructing with *each* parent there were four trials every other night.

This technique concretizes an interaction around a specific content and thus minimizes extraneous or unessential information. In this way, training toward listening with and to rather than *at* another person is actively encouraged. It allows the partners to participate and understand each other's communication without interjecting tangential and potentially toxic information. After the construction is completed there is a new face to face interaction trying to determine how the errors were made and where the errors occurred. The more difficult the communication between the two people is, the wider the discrepancy in their constructions unless they opt for some very simple designs. The technique also provides a vehicle to explore feelings after the construction is completed. However, I usually save the second phase until after the participants are comfortable with the block-playing technique. The second phase is initiated when the participants are instructed to attempt to explore the feelings that they were "reading" from the other person as the construction was going on. The way that they can get at the meta-communication is exclusively through changes in vocal pattern since they are out of each other's field of view. Furthermore, because the situation is focused on the construction the person will have not only feelings to examine, but feelings in relation to a very specific situation. Thus, the participants can learn to pick up meta-communications on a very simple level as ground work for picking up more complicated feeling tones in the nuances of later developing communication.

There are other advantages of this technique. It does get the involvement of the patients early in the therapeutic process. Related to this also is the notion of homework in therapy. By providing the patients with homework, it keeps their interest in the therapy motivation higher, and structures some continuity in the therapeutic process. Customarily, at the beginning of each session, we talk of the block designs: who led, the nature of and severity of the errors, the feelings engendered by the reception of changes in vocal qualities (phase 2) and the nature of the face-to-face interaction following completion of the technique. It is interesting to note that as the toxic communication becomes more benign, the confidence of the people goes up and their designs become not only more complicated, but the errors lessen. The nature of the design (e.g., simple or complex) may also provide the therapist with information about the perception of one partner by the other.

To illustrate the block-playing technique, three examples will be mentioned:

> First was an adolescent boy of 13 who had a particularly toxic relationship with the mother, who reciprocated the toxicity. Both could readily acknowledge that quite early in the course of an argument the cause of the argument was lost and it was simply a matter of waiting their turn to shout at the other person. I instituted the block-playing technique; they used it once and discontinued. When asked whether the technique was being used, a plethora of excuses was evoked. Such things as club meetings, too tired, homework as well as good old "I forgot" were utilized. I then dropped the weekly inquiry about the technique. As I utilized more conventional means of adolescent therapy, the relationship to his mother improved. At this time, I brought the mother and father in and discussed with them (with the patient's permission) the progress made thus far. The mother was greatly relieved at hearing some of this information and spontaneously the block-playing technique was resurrected. Within a week's time the mother and son were having very complicated but identical designs.

The second illustration is that of a married couple with no children who were having grave problems in not understanding the nature of the meta-communications. The husband and wife both reported a reduction in tension or, as they put it, the usual "walking on eggs in the house" after utilizing the technique for a week. In fact, they were using the technique daily and found it to be of great value in working through problems in communication utilizing this very concrete mode of interaction. Thus, the technique had trained them to communicate directly with each other

without being drawn into their previous hidden-message mode of interaction.

Third was a 12-year-old child who was having difficulty relating to
both parents. The block construction was used with both parents every
other night as indicated above. At termination they felt that this technique was such a meaningful part of the therapeutic process that they had
bought their own set of *Playskool* blocks for their son and are continuing
to use this technique whenever they feel there has been some disruption
in the communication process.

As a measure of success of the technique, I have used simple kinds of
feedback, that is, number of errors, length of time to construction,
complexity of construction, and so forth. In order to test the efficacy of
this technique in communication enhancement. I asked couples, as well
as parent and children who are having difficulties, to use the block
technique with my standard set of instructions. Invariably there was a
shorter time to errorless constructions without any of the toxicity indicated in the interactive process. Thus, this technique is a way of actively
encouraging changes in the communication pattern via the exploration
of feelings, that is the meta-communication, once the technique is firmly
established. The technique may be of value in the reduction of the total
number of therapeutic sessions as well as the maintenance motivation
between sessions. Its greatest virtue is that it provides a mode of interaction on a concrete level where feelings can be explored within a relatively non-toxic parameter—obviously while building blocks it's difficult
to make some sarcastic remark about the mental health of your mother-
in-law!

References

Sorrells, J., and Ford, F. (1966). Toward an integrated theory of families and family
    therapy. *Psychotherapy: Theory, Research & Practice* 6:150–159.
Watzlawick, P., Beavin, J., and Jackson, D. (1967). *Pragmatics of Human Communication.*
    New York: Norton.

PART II
Play Techniques Using Natural Media

10

Sandplay

JOHN ALLAN
PAT BERRY

Sand often acts as a magnet for children, and before they realize it their hands are sifting, making tunnels, and shaping mountains, runways, and river beds. When miniature toys are added, a whole world appears, dramas unfold, and absorption is total. In this chapter we describe the use of sand play for counseling children.

Background

According to Stewart (1982), the first description of sand play as a counseling technique came from the British pediatrician, Margaret Lowenfeld (1939). In the 1930s, she established the London Institute of Child Psychology. She recalled reading H. G. Wells's (1911) book *Floor Games,* in which he described the great animation when he and his two boys played on the floor with miniature soldiers.

In the Institute, Lowenfeld added to the playroom two zinc trays half filled with sand and provided water and implements for shaping. The toys were placed in a box, and the children who came to the Institute combined the toys with the sandplay and started to call this box of toys "the world." In turn, Lowenfeld (1979) called this method of play, "The World Technique."

The method was brought to the United States by Buhler (1951), who used sandplay mainly for diagnosis and research. It is the Swiss Jungian analyst, Dora Kalff (1966, 1981), however, who has had the greatest impact on developing the approach, formulating theoretical principles, and training many practitioners throughout the world.

Expanding on the works of Neumann (1954, 1973), Kalff viewed the development of a healthy ego as a critically important task for children. The function of the ego is to balance and mediate between inner drives and the outer world. To Kalff, the ego is strengthened by a deep, internal feeling of mother–child unity that develops slowly from birth and culminates during the second and third years of life. Disturbed children are those who have experienced breaks in attachment bonding that damage the inner feeling of wholeness and impair ego functioning. In sandplay, the child has the opportunity to resolve the traumas by externalizing the fantasies and developing a sense of mastery and control over inner impulses.

Method

The sand tray itself is a container, approximately $20 \times 30 \times 3$ inches. Usually two waterproof trays are available: one to contain dry sand and the other damp sand. The inside is painted blue to simulate water when the sand is pushed to the side. The dimensions are important and specific, so that the sand world can be taken in at a glance without unnecessary head movement. Hundreds of miniature toys and objects from which the child may choose are made available. Categories for the selection of toys and objects include (a) people: domestic, military, fantasy, mythological; (b) buildings: houses, schools, churches, castles; (c) animals: tame, wild, zoo, prehistoric, marine; (d) vehicles: land, air, water, space, war machine; (e) vegetation: trees, shrubs, plants, vegetables; (f) structures: bridges, fences, gates, doorways, corrals; (g) natural objects: shells, driftwood, stones, bones, eggs; and (h) symbolic objects: wishing wells, treasure chests, jewelry.

Some counselors place the toys in categories on shelves so that they are readily visible. Others present them randomly on a large table. We recommend that families of items be available, such as a sow and a litter, three dinosaurs, four snakes, and a small doll family.

Sandplay is the process, sand tray the medium, and sand world the finished product. The process begins when the counselor invites the child to play with the sand and to choose from the assortment of miniatures. Each object has its own physical structure and symbolic meaning, and each tends to trigger a fantasy reaction. Kalff (1981) stated that "the symbols speak for inner, energy laden pictures of the innate potentials of the human being" (p. 29), which, when expressed, facilitate psychological development.

The counselor plays a key role in providing the safe and protected space where the inner drama and healing potential of the psyche can unfold. Such a space is the sand tray and the therapeutic relationship. Most practitioners emphasize the value of unconditional, positive regard and minimal verbalizations by the counselor. Interpretation is seldom needed because the psychological issues are resolved or understood on an unconscious, symbolic level. The counselor is there as a witness to the process of play. The process of play makes the inner problem visible and allows therapeutic movement and growth. Toward the end of a session a child may announce "goodbye," "I'm finished," or just sit silently in front of the sand world. Often, there is a recognizable point at which the process of play stops and a finished work is evident.

Buhler (1951) developed an observation form on which one may record prevalent themes in the play, and Reed (1975) devised a rating scale for children. Some counselors draw a quick sketch of the sand picture, whereas most take a slide photograph of each sand world. At the termination of treatment (often after 8 to 10 sessions in the school), the counselor shows the child all the slides as a means of review and discussion.

Overview of Common Stages in Sand Play

As the sand drama and play unfold, children tend to portray chaos, struggle (organized fighting), and resolution in recurring cycles.

Chaos

In this stage, often the first stage, the child may literally dump ten to three hundred toys and objects into the sand tray. There is no order, only a vast upheaval and intermingling of sand and toys. The toys do not seem to be chosen deliberately. There may be an absence of animal, plant, or human life. The land may be barren and dry, and often crops or vegetation is in ruins. This stage reflects and objectifies the emotional turmoil and chaos in the child's life. In other words, the child's ego may be overwhelmed by distressing emotions. Depictions of this stage may occur once or continue for two or three counseling sessions.

Struggle

In this stage many battles occur as monsters fight monsters, robot man wipes out armies, and knights tirelessly joust each other. Anything that moves is shot, destroyed, or blown up. Often, in the beginning, both sides are annihilated; there is no winner, and the dead are left in a heap in the corner. Over the weeks, the battles become more intense and more organized, and the struggles are more balanced. The adversaries are not killed but imprisoned, and a hero emerges who wins in the battle against the "dark forces" (i.e., destructive impulses).

Resolution

In this phase, life seems to be getting back to normal. Order is being restored, and there is a balance between nature, people, and the rhythm of daily life. Animals are in their correct habitat, and fences protect the sheep and cattle. Roadways wind evenly through town and country, and the crops and trees bear fruit. The counselor senses a resolution of a problem and the feeling that the child is accepting a place in the outer world. Often the child will say, "I don't need to come anymore," and this statement is often confirmed by the teacher. Symbolically, the feeling of completion and wholeness is demonstrated by such images as squares, rectangles, and circles (Kalff 1981, Kellogg 1970). There is an ordering of the sand world and an integration of libidinal forces manifested earlier.

Teacher's Reactions to Sand Play

When the child returns to the classroom after sandplay, teachers often comment on the child's relaxed mood and his or her ability to become involved in schoolwork. The child seems calmer, happier, and exhibits a sense of humor. After eight to ten sessions, there is often dramatic improvement, and the child begins to respond to normal controls and limitations imposed by the teacher.

Noyes (1981) found that when sandplay was used as part of her remedial reading program for sixth graders, it deepened rapport and intimacy, improved self-esteem, helped resolve inner conflicts, and increased reading scores in all students from a range of 2.0 to 5.5 years.

Case Study

James (a pseudonym), a second grader, was referred for counseling because he exhibited inappropriate behavior in the classroom and on the playground. Two years earlier, he was moved several hundred miles to live with his father (whom he did not know), his stepmother, and her two older daughters. When introduced to sandplay, he immediately became involved with the materials.

Session 1

Many animals and vehicles (cars, trucks, jet planes) were precariously and chaotically piled at one end of the sandplay, held down by two snakes. At the bottom of the pile was Pegasus, the winged horse, and at the top, a jet. It seemed that the jet, with all its power, was unable to move out from under this serpent's domination and control.

Session 2

Many of the same objects were used, but this time there was order and regulation. The planes and the police helicopter were ready for takeoff. The cars and trucks were lined up as if waiting for a signal to go. One ambulance was in readiness in the corner. All of the animals, however, were prone. It was as if they could not move even though they were no longer in the grip of the snakes. Two exceptions were a crocodile and a tiger walking toward each other across a lake as if in preparation for attack and a fight.

Sessions 3, 4, and 5

These sand trays showed more organization. Vehicles were stationed in appropriate bays. There was a house, a boy, and two women. A tree grew in one corner and Pegasus reappeared. Just before he left Session 5, James placed two men in the sand tray: an older man with the two women and a younger man by himself in the corner.

Sessions 6 and 7

During these sessions two sand worlds appeared whose themes seemed to be extensions of the other sessions but more enriched. Animals were standing, and growth was symbolized by trees and foliage; a red wizard, the magical helper, was riding Pegasus.

Sessions 8 and 9

The theme and toys were similar, but to his world James added several black wizard helpers. As he was leaving to go back to the classroom, he returned to the sand tray and silently added Pegasus. Then he stood the younger man on his feet. He turned and left the counseling room.

During this period in counseling James painted two pictures. The first showed a fox hiding from a huge mammoth creature. The fox had several places to hide. The second depicted two mammoth creatures in the water with a small fish swimming between them. He added a castle and a Canadian flag with a king standing watch.

Session 10

This was his last sand world. In it James showed a circle of his family members including the older man. The family truck and a house were depicted as was a jet plane, all part of the circle. After a period of concentrated attention, Pegasus was placed in the center of the family circle. James looked up and smiled as he quietly said, "He's magic you know, and no one can see him but the boy."

Discussion

Initially during counseling, James was quiet and tentative. He tended to ignore the counselor and immersed himself totally in his sand worlds and paintings. Slowly, he opened up and began to talk more about his sand worlds and his dreams. In the sand trays the counselor was able to see the movement from chaos to struggle to resolution. The early phase of chaos reflected the inner turmoil in James, as many of his emotions were confused and intertwined. He was unable to use the energy of the jet (a symbol of adaptive movement in the outer world) and the energy of Pegasus (a symbol of inner strength) to help him in his life. He was feeling controlled and trapped by negative external forces (as symbolized by the snakes), and his ego was overwhelmed by psychological pain (Allan 1978).

In the subsequent sessions the counselor began to see the slow process of differentiation, regulation, and separation of various emotions, symbolized by planes, trucks, and an ambulance. The animals were not active (i.e., prone) except for two aggressive forces (crocodile and tiger). Slowly, family members appeared as helpers and symbols of vegetative and instinctual life. Order and identity were restored (the king and the Canadian flag), and the family seemed more intact. It is significant that Pegasus played a major role in the sessions. It is common for many children to be attracted to one key symbol that will appear, disappear, and reappear throughout their treatment (Allan 1986). Pegasus, of course, was invisible. He reflected the healthy essence of the boy's spirit, which became alive again in him.

Treatment ended at the close of the school year. Follow-up sessions indicated that James's impulsive, aggressive behavior had diminished, his social skills had improved, and he was channeling his energy into art and soccer.

Conclusion

Sand play as a technique for counseling elementary children may be implemented by counselors who have had basic training in play therapy.

Kalff (1981) warned against the use of interpretation. The crux of sand-play therapy is not that it must be interpreted but that it must be witnessed respectfully. The counselor's attitude for this process is one of "active being" rather than one of direction and guidance. The process of play and dramatization seems to release blocked psychic energy and to activate the self-healing potential that Jung (1964) believed is embedded in the human psyche. Sandplay counseling is challenging and has no age barriers. It has been used with children as young as 2 years old and with adults of all ages. The unleashing of repressed energy transforms that energy so that it may work productively for personality development and for future learning.

References

Allan, J. (1978). Serial drawing: a therapeutic technique with young children. *Canadian Counsellor* 12:223–228.

Allan, J. (1986). The body in child psychotherapy. In *The Body in Jungian Analysis*, ed. M. Stein and N. Schwartz-Salant, pp. 145–167. Wilmette, IL: Chiron.

Buhler, C. (1951). The world test: a projective technique. *Journal of Child Psychiatry* 2:4–13.

Jung, C. (1964). *Man and his Symbols*. New York: Doubleday.

Kalff, D. M. (1966). *Sandspiel*. Zurich: Rascher Verlag.

_____ 1981). *Sandplay: A Psychotherapeutic Approach to the Psyche*. Boston: Sigo.

Kellogg, R. (1970). *Analyzing Children's Art*. Palo Alto, CA: Mayfield.

Lowenfeld, M. (1939). The world pictures of children. *British Journal of Medical Psychology* 18:65–101.

_____ (1979). *The World Technique*. London: George Allen & Unwin.

Neumann, E. (1954). *The Origins and History of Consciousness*. Vols. 1 and 2. Princeton, NJ: Bollingen.

_____ (1973). *The Child: Structure and Dynamics of the Nascent Personality*. New York: Harper Colophon.

Noyes, M. (1981). Sandplay imagery: an aid to teaching reading. *Academic Therapy* 17:231–237.

Reed, J. P. (1975). *Sand Magic Experience in Miniature: A Nonverbal Therapy for Children*. Albuquerque: JPR.

Stewart, L. H. (1982). Sandplay and Jungian analysis. In *Jungian Analysis*, ed. M. Stein, pp. 204–218. La Salle, IL: Open Court.

Wells, H. G. (1911). *Floor Games*. New York: Arno.

11

Water Play*

RUTH E. HARTLEY, LAWRENCE K. FRANK, AND ROBERT M. GOLDENSON

Anyone who has watched a 3-year-old zestfully wash and rinse and squeeze a pair of doll socks cannot doubt the irresistible attraction that water holds for the very young. The child's utter absorption in this rhythmic activity and the almost hypnotic effect it has upon him inevitably calls to mind the fascination of a waterfall or of waves rising and falling on a beach.

In view of this fascination, one would expect that water would be given a conspicuous place in programs designed for preschool and kindergarten children. It certainly is easily obtainable and little expense is involved. It is one of the few basic substances still easily available for exploration by urban children. It lends itself to a variety of activities and offers a wide range of manipulation and learning. But it has not merely learning values to recommend it; it has something even more valuable—the absorbed delight and joyous enthusiasm of the children as they play with it. Yet, in spite of the fact that contemporary psychology tends to accept the child himself as the best indicator of his needs and regards need fulfillment as a necessary precursor to healthful advances in development, strangely enough, the child's apparent urge for free and unin-

---

*This chapter was originally written specifically for teachers of very young children—nursery school and kindergarten—and reports observations and experiences in the use of water play as part of a research project of the Caroline Zachary Institute. It is included in this volume since it is the only extensive treatment of this play medium in the literature. It is felt the same implications for the use of water obtain for the somewhat older, but emotionally immature and disturbed child, as for the younger "normal" child described in these pages. Most of the illustrative cases have been deleted, as well as portions more specifically addressed to the teachers of young children.

terrupted experimentation and exploration with water seems to have been almost completely overlooked.

It might be appropriate at this point to consider the contributions of water play to child development from a more theoretical point of view. Most children in the preschool age range have not yet completed the adjustment tasks set by society in relation to the control of body processes—oral, anal, and urethral. Although their experience is still largely in terms of sensation, their urge to explore is constantly being curbed. Food is to be eaten, not played with, and feces and urine, which have a very intimate connection with their selfhood, are never to be handled at all. In the child's view, body products are as legitimate as any other substance, and his desire to learn about them is particularly urgent since they have been part of himself. To deny him this right is, in a sense, to alienate him from part of his being. Now, we know from recognized studies in genetic psychology that children are able to accept substitutes for activities that are denied them and often seek them in proportion to the degree of deprivation. We know, too, that they frequently equate water with urine. In view of all these related facts, it therefore seems logical to assume that free access to water will give children an opportunity to satisfy in substitute fashion legitimate needs which our child-rearing practices usually frustrate.

The Feeling of Mastery

In addition to the wealth of sensory pleasures and learning experiences offered by water, it is a basic material through which a child can experience early the satisfactions of mastery and achievement. For some youngsters, particularly those with few adjustment problems, the primary gratification found in water play seems to be connected with the control of a fluid medium.

For uncertain children who are generally constricted in movement and show little or no initiative in attempting new activities, blowing soap bubbles seems to offer tremendous opportunities for ego building. Children not only are avid for the activity and participate for long periods at a time, but also talk about it with unmistakable satisfaction.

Satisfactions for the Immature

In many ways water appeared to be the royal road to the hearts of children who were behind others in social development, attention span, and initiative. They seemed most avid for all kinds of play with water, concentrated much longer on it than on any other activity, and seemed to derive the keenest pleasure from handling it as they wished. For these youngsters—whatever their actual age—it seemed to minister to two general types of needs: oral and tactile pleasure and the expression of aggressive impulses. It was therefore especially important to include such accessories as bottles and nipples, small cups, soft cloths, and sponges. Their play was usually extremely simple, repetitive, and organized around one theme, but the expressions of delight, the jealousy with which they guarded the implements, and the tenacity with which they returned to the activity in spite of interruptions and distractions testified to its importance for them.

Outlet for Aggression

In addition to the pleasure it affords, water play offers inviting channels through which aggressive impulses can be released. But we generally need running comments of the children themselves to prove that they are covertly expressing sentiments they dare not express more openly—sentiments such as resentment, defiance, and hostility.

[An] instance of the close connection between water and very primitive hostile impulses is found in the behavior of Bud. A study of his play also illustrates the necessity of making numerous observations before the full intent or meaning can be discovered. For, in his case, we first noticed only indiscriminate delight in playing with water, but as we continued our observations we began to understand that water meant much more to him. For example, in his first session with miniature life toys he splashed some water on the floor and explained that the toy horse he was playing with had urinated. And another time, he used water to obliterate a male figure which he had molded of clay during a series of hostile fantasies.

Relaxation and Absorption

In contrast to some of the statements cited above, other teachers emphasized the soothing and absorbing qualities of water for children ordinarily rather scattered and explosive in their play. For example, one teacher of very young children in a guidance nursery said

Water is a relaxing kind of thing; it is good in that very few aggressive feelings are expressed there. A very disturbed child, Beth, would be happy at water and retreat to it and play for a long time. We have used water play to relax a child when he was disturbed. When the kids were hectic and wild we would take a group to the water, especially on rainy days. We could accommodate about seven children at one time. Outside we used water for painting and for scrubbing with soap. The children had a lot of tea parties, pouring the water; they used water in the sandbox too. This would make a noticeable difference in them.

It would be a mistake, therefore, to believe that ministering to oral and aggressive needs is the only advantage of water play. It seems outstandingly fruitful in these directions for very young or very immature children. But for older children and for other kinds of children it seems to offer additional benefits. Many aggressive children are definitely soothed, relaxed, and quieted by a chance to play freely with water while other children, who are ordinarily extremely inhibited, become stimulated, gay, and free, even inviting social contacts that they cannot ordinarily undertake.

Liberating Effects

Teachers who recognize the release and stimulation derived from water play are often particularly impressed with its catalytic effect on youngsters who are ordinarily solitary and lost. Not only do they mingle with other children during the activity, but afterward they freely approach materials which they had been hesitant to use. An uninterrupted session with water will often prove the "open sesame" to activities with clay, finger paints, or the easel.

The Versatility of Water

Viewed in perspective, the observations of teachers and special observers present a challenge on theoretical grounds. Why should this simple substance have such varied effects? No other material, not even clay or finger paint, has its protean quality to the same degree. For one thing, the repetitious and somewhat monotonous nature of water play, together with the soft and yielding quality of the material, may account for its relaxing effect on tense and anxious children. The fact that it demands no special skills and involves no achievement goals may explain why it neither threatens nor thwarts the anxious child who cannot take the pressure of social contacts or the adult-directed use of other materials. Again, its mild yet pleasurable sensory qualities afford withdrawn, constricted youngsters stimulation without excitement. Likewise, the chance to pour and splash and mess offers these children, as well as more active and outgoing ones, not only a means of expressing aggression but also a way of escaping the pressures of growing up and of regaining the privileges of infancy. Moreover, clinical reports on inhibited children often reveal that they have responded to parental prohibitions by a generalized lack of interest and venturesomeness. They retreat into safe and "good" behavior—but free play with water gives them a chance to explore and experiment with a medium that has been denied to them. Time and again we have seen water play lift the burden of anxiety and release hidden resources of interest and vitality.

But what of the possibility of arousing guilt reactions which might block any benefits that water play could hold for the child? We can only report that not one of the hundred and more children we observed seemed to suffer sufficient anxiety to interfere with enjoyment. In only two cases was some tension reported. In one, the child simply refused to play with water at first, but after a period of observation came to accept it fully. In the other, a 3-year-old was reported to need assurance after pouring water over miniature life furniture. Close contact with the teacher and assurance that it was all right to play with water at a special time and with special toys were enough to relieve this child's mind.

The neutral quality of water is another reason for its enormous flexibility and varied effects. Because it offers so little resistance and makes so few demands on the children, yet lends itself to so many satisfactions, the range of its appeal is unlimited. As we have pointed out, the very young child finds in it a substance that he can manipulate and master more easily than any other—provided adults do not interfere. He can transform it into almost anything and use it to experiment with his own powers and with the qualities of other materials.

We have not discussed the contribution of water play to a sense of participation in the adult world. Cleaning up offers an opportunity for identification with grownups. Unfortunately, however, some teachers regard water play as largely a girl's activity and limit it almost completely to cleaning dishes, bathing dolls, or washing doll's clothes. But in centers where water is freely used as a substitute for paint—water painting—as well as for washing surfaces such as tables and walls, for blowing masses of bubbles, and pouring from vessel to vessel, boys are just as eager to participate and frequently remain at the activity longer than girls do. It may very well be that in the cleaning-up function boys can find an acceptable channel for identification with a mother figure which they need at the preschool level, but cannot find in other activities because of cultural taboos against male interest in "women's work."

Conclusion

To sum up, water play has many values and can be used for many purposes in the preschool and kindergarten program. To the development of sensation and feeling it offers more varied experience and a keener pleasure than any other material except finger paint; to intellectual development it contributes its great flexibility and vast opportunities for experimentation and exploration. It stimulates the inhibited child and soothes the explosive. Scattered, disorganized youngsters are able to concentrate on it for long periods of time. Those who are uncertain of themselves gain a sense of achievement and find in it a channel for expressing emotions not condoned in their primitive forms. Many children who have had trouble in the group situation begin their adjustment through water play. Others who are tense, fearful, withdrawn, and inhibited indicate a general loosening up and growth in spontaneity by their acceptance of water as a medium and by their increased freedom in using it.

A few words of caution seem appropriate here. Because of the striking and varied advantages of water play, there has been a tendency among educators to expect it to be a universal panacea. This we must guard against. We have no evidence that it is effective in every kind of developmental problem or personality difficulty. Our evidence simply indicates that it is particularly valuable where there is a question of overactivity or constriction of interest or movement. We have reason to suggest, too, that the child who "gets stuck" with water play and who uses it repetitively in the same patterns or around the same theme needs special help in finding other avenues of expression and special encouragement to grow beyond the joys of infancy.

12

The Use of Food in Therapy

MARY R. HAWORTH AND MARY JANE KELLER

The use of food in the playroom has not been widely discussed in reports of play therapy. Most well-equipped playrooms probably provide baby bottles for regressive play, but this discussion refers to cookies (such as vanilla wafers) or hard candies which are made available to the child. Occasionally, real milk has been provided in the baby bottles for autistic children and for others known to have suffered severe infantile deprivations. Ice cream or Cokes are especially liked by preadolescents. Children respond in a variety of ways to these oral supplies. The child's eagerness for treats or his refusal of them are pertinent aspects for therapeutic handling, while his spontaneous offer to share the food with his therapist adds yet another dimension.

The present authors have elsewhere reviewed (Haworth and Keller 1962) the literature on the symbolic meanings attached to food and eating, as well as the significance of various types of reactions to food in the diagnostic setting and in psychotherapy.

The early association of pleasant experiences surrounding food and feeding with feelings of love, comfort, and security has been frequently pointed out in the psychoanalytic literature. Therapists such as Sechehaye (1951, 1956), Federn (1952), Rosen (1953), and Schwing (1954) have reported the introduction of feeding situations as a vital part of therapy with seriously disturbed adult patients in an attempt to re-create the initial mother–child relationship and to work through early affectional deprivations.

Probably the earliest report of the use of food in therapy with children is to be found in Slavson's (1943) descriptions of therapy sessions with groups of boys. He points out rather definite stages in the boys' attitudes to the snack times which were provided toward the close of each session. First there was a stage of shyness and tentative holding back, then overreactions of horseplay and messiness, until finally the refreshment period became a time for relaxation and mutual social interchange.

Reports of therapy with young autistic children, such as Waal (1955) and Alpert (1959), describe the child's reactions when food has been offered. These may include gorging on the food or hoarding of crumbs and pieces, as well as leading to further exploration of his own, and the therapist's, mouth and teeth. Kaufman and colleagues (1957) briefly discuss the values inherent in the use of food with the psychotic child as a means of building up the ability to accept gratification and of reassuring the child that his oral needs are not dangerous.

Only quite recently has the meaning of the patient's offer of food to the therapist been treated at any length. In a paper by Anthony (1961) and its discussion by Kramer (1961), two opposing theories are proposed to explain the meaning of this act. In discussing his analysis of an 18-year-old girl, Anthony describes her bringing him a cookie which she had baked, and at the end of each hour she would take it home, only to bring it back the next day. "Both in real life and in her dreams, she was haunted by the anxiety that what she offered would prove unacceptable. If I ate what she produced, it would be proof that I was accepting her since I would be assimilating her products. Something from her would have gotten right inside me" (Anthony 1961, p. 213). Kramer (1961) presents an alternate hypothesis: "I wonder, though, whether the act of feeding the analyst is not also an attempt to . . . assert a degree of independence from him" (p. 249). Kramer proceeds to describe the usual infant's attempts to stuff food into his mother's mouth and interprets such behavior "as one of the earliest efforts at establishing the child's identity separate from his mother. There is a display of purposeful activity where only passivity was present before." He suggests that Anthony's patient was demonstrating both the wish to merge with him and the wish to become free and grow up.

The material to be presented here represents the authors' experiences in work with neurotic children. The general types of reactions these children exhibit toward food will be discussed, as well as a more detailed description of food behavior from one child's therapy.

In providing food for the child the therapist is, in effect, presenting herself as the all-giving, good, and nurturant parent. But the child may experience such a situation as very threatening, since it may dramatize his conflict between wanting to receive such nurturance and his feeling that this food is somehow forbidden or potentially dangerous. It may be too difficult an act to spontaneously reach out to take a bite of food in the presence of an adult. If the therapist points out the availability of the food or specifically offers it to the child, he may withdraw even more. The therapist's exact role, beyond making certain that the cookies are at hand for each session, cannot be specified in advance, but must be adapted to the child's idiosyncratic reactions to the situation.

While he may not refuse a bite outright, the child may take only one, and this when the therapist's back is turned. Even then, he may not eat it, but slip it into his pocket. Guilt and shame reactions, as well as fearfulness, may have become associated with the child's earlier experiences with food, and these will be reflected in his present pattern of denial and inhibition. Negative feelings related to infantile oral deprivations may now be transferred from the mother to the therapist and become manifest in this tangible eating situation.

As children come to feel more at ease in the playroom, they may help themselves more openly to the contents of the cookie jar, but they are apt to want to wrap the cookies in a paper towel to take with them when they leave. As therapy progresses in all areas, changes will also be noticed in such secretive food reactions. The child will gradually take more than one piece, eat these in front of the therapist, and count out fewer to take home. When the constricted child spontaneously offers cookies to his therapist at the same time that he is eating freely and with enjoyment, definite gains in other aspects of therapy as well can probably be observed.

Suspicious, paranoid children may have fantasies that the food is bad, or dirty, or poisonous.[1] They may refuse food for long periods of time. When they do finally give in, they have been observed to hold a cookie between their teeth for several seconds before chewing it. One boy, who was sensitive to being watched, would close his eyes as he reached for the cookie jar.

In contrast to the inhibited child, others, who still bear sensitive scars of earlier deprivations, are apt to gorge themselves with cookies or candies, at first seeming to never get enough. They will notice at once if the jar is not in its accustomed place and be in near panic until it is produced. As they gradually come to feel secure and satisfied, if not actually satiated, the number of cookies will be reduced and the sense of urgency toned down to reasonable proportions. Again, after many

---

[1]Rosen (1953) relates poison fantasies to infantile reactions to the "perverse mother" who was not attuned to her child and failed to meet his oral needs.

weeks, such a child may suddenly wish to share his treasure with his therapist.

Once the initial reactions to the food have been worked through, regressive feeding behaviors are often observed. The child may pretend to be a baby and ask the therapist to feed him, piece by piece. Others will take a handful of cookies to a play shelf, crawl up in a fetal position, possibly covering the opening with a blanket or towel, and indulge in cozy solitude. Food has also been noted to serve a comforting role as the child progresses to more normal functioning. One 10-year-old boy engaged in many target shooting contests with his therapist and always took a cookie whenever he lost a bout. Children who may not ordinarily take cookies have been observed to do so the last session before a vacation period.

Aggressive reactions toward food also occur, sometimes as an initial behavior, but always as an expression of hostility. Rather than eating the cookies, the child may crush them to bits or throw them across the room. This may represent an aggressive act directed toward the therapist and her "gift," or reluctance to admit to strong oral hungers, or a form of self-punishment and denial. One boy offered a cookie to his therapist after first concealing a thumbtack in the bottom of it. Other children have shot at the cookie jar with water pistols, with or without first making sure the lid was tightly in place. A quite hostile and jealous youngster emptied the cookie jar each week so there would be none left for "the other children who come here." Diminution of such aggressive acts with time, along with an increase in pleasurable eating, represent indications of therapeutic gains.

One further behavior frequently noted pertains to parental reactions. Once they are aware that their children are being given food, some mothers have developed a routine of stopping on the way to the therapy session, to buy the child a Coke or ice cream cone, thus beating the therapist at his own game! A healthier reaction was noted in one case when, after six months of therapy and when real gains were becoming evident in all areas, the child announced that his mother had started buying him a treat on their way home from their concurrent sessions.

Some procedural aspects should be pointed out with respect to the use of food in the therapy hour. It is important to determine whether the child has any allergies that would prevent his being able to eat certain foods. It does not seem sufficient to merely have the food available. To be therapeutic one should verbalize the permissiveness of the situation and stress over and over again, "How nice it is to be able to have all the cookies you want" or "It feels good to be able to have them all," and so forth. In this connection, the number of cookies in the jar becomes quite important. Some therapists feel they can demonstrate their all-givingness best by filling the jar but, ironically, this makes it practically impossible for the child to eat them all and so to experience the joy that comes with feeling they can *all* be his. On the other hand, too few cookies may be regarded as niggardliness on the part of the therapist in spite of his protestations of magnanimity.

It should go without saying that as the various meanings of food to the child and his reactions to the situation become evident, the therapist should reflect and/or interpret as he would in any other play situation.

The therapist wisely lets the child set the pace as to when he offers cookies to the therapist and how many he wishes to share. As discussed earlier, Kramer (1961) points out the possible dual aspects of such offerings—either the desire to be incorporated by the therapist or a demonstration of separateness and independence. The latter explanation has seemed more relevant in the authors' experience. When children reach this giving stage it seems to represent a real milestone; it is as if they have achieved a new maturity in now being able to give, where formerly they have been preoccupied with receiving. The therapist is then viewed in a new perspective, as an individual in her own right, rather than just a familiar fixture in the playroom.

Excerpts from the therapy of a 7-year-old boy have been selected to demonstrate many of the symbolic and supportive uses to which cookies were put during a year and one-half of therapy.

During the first session, Billy did not appear to notice the cookies until time to leave. He then asked if he could "have a few" and took two, saying, "Two is a few." Halfway through the second session he ate one cookie. Later in this hour, he sucked water out of two bottles at once and said, "These are the mother's." In the next four sessions he continued taking only one or two cookies, while his play themes during this time were concerned with symbolic birth fantasies and much interest in sucking activities.

In the seventh session he displayed more anxiety than usual and played out various representations of his guilt and fears concerned with looking and seeing. He accompanied these activities with constant eating of cookies and also offered one to the therapist for the first time.

In the ninth session he drew several pictures of "statues of eagles." At one point he got up to get a cookie, but, due to an oversight, none were available that day. He said he really didn't mind since he hadn't gotten used to them, and so he didn't miss them. Later in this same hour he reported the following dream: He had shot a mother eagle and brought back the babies—they were almost starved to death; he had fed the babies and sold the mother for a lot of money. When the therapist suggested that the babies were starving because the mother had not fed them or taken good care of them, he denied this vigorously and blamed it on himself (in the dream) for shooting the mother bird. (While he can immobilize the depriving mother eagle in his drawings and shoot her in his dream-fantasy, on the conscious level he must stoically deny his oral needs and take the blame for the infants being deprived.)

Sessions ten to fourteen were occupied with activities symbolically representing comparison of size, strength, and virility in phallic rivalry with his father. It is interesting to note that he did not eat any cookies in these sessions.

The next twelve sessions were marked by much oral emphasis as he struggled with his fears of eating and his desires to be fed. First he set up situations in which he would beg for toys and objects which he knew the therapist could not let him have, thus putting her in the role of the depriving mother. In the following session, he mixed plaster-of-Paris with water to form a thin milky substance which he poured into the baby bottles to "fool the baby." Then he fashioned three oral receptacles out of clay—a canteen bottle, a cup, and a bowl. He saw the cookie jar and announced he was "going to eat cookies today." He held his first one in his teeth a long time before chewing it, while he drew a target and shot at darts. Once he started eating, he made repeated trips, finally asking the therapist to bring the jar over to him and hold it for him. His desire to be given *all* he wanted, especially of food, was repeatedly pointed out. He made quite a point of leaving two cookies in the jar and said he'd get sick if he ate them. The therapist remarked that he seemed to be afraid that something bad might happen if he took all he wanted of anything. He immediately became unusually spontaneous and quite daring in his play, as if a great load had been removed.

The following session Billy took the cookie jar to his play area and ate many of them. He offered one to the therapist, but refused to accept any that she offered to him, preferring to pick out his own. He commented he was saving the *last* cookie for her and again she reflected that he didn't ever seem to want the last ones, that maybe he felt it's bad to take all he wants, or that he might get sick, or something bad might happen to him. Toward the end of this session he had been mixing red paint with sand; then he suddenly darted to the shelf for two small bottles. He filled them with red and green paint and specified that these were "poison" for the therapist. (The paranoid attitude to food is clearly evident with the fear of getting sick and so not taking *all* of the food; then he expresses the wish to poison the agent of his food deprivations—the mother-therapist—by first giving her the last, bad cookies and then by mixing up a concoction for her which he labels directly as "poison.")

The next session he inspected the cookie jar at once and said, "Oh, you got a lot because you knew I was coming." He ate many as he played and once the therapist put one up to his mouth which he opened so wide that he engulfed the whole cookie and managed to suck momentarily on her fingers. (Only after having "poisoned" the therapist can he let himself actually be fed by her.) He avoided further opportunities to be fed, kept the jar close and helped himself often, and again made a point of giving the last cookie to the therapist. He denied her reflection of his fears about eating or taking all of anything.

The following five or six sessions were marked by much regressive play with sand and finger paints, accompanied by baby talk and gross eating of cookies. He would stuff several in his mouth at a time, completely emptying the jar and often getting still more from the supply box. At the close of one of these sessions he took two cookies with him "for me and mama." Another time he set up a "tea party" of cookies and water, giving the therapist more cookies than himself because he wanted to see her get fat. He crushed some of his cookies, later asking if he could also crush pieces of chalk and expressing concern about wasting the chalk or the water when he let it run for a long time. It also became obvious, during this period, that whenever he was told his hour would soon be over, he would go at once for more cookies.

An eventful session (the twenty-sixth) occurred the day before he was to go on a long summer vacation. He was engaged in cleaning out the sink with soap flakes and brought the cookie jar to the sink so the therapist could put cookies in his mouth as he worked. She deliberately fed him in steady succession, and he seemed to settle into a comfortable, relaxed regression—wallowing in cookies, soap, and water. When the therapist once did not observe that his mouth was empty, he said, "Cookie, please. No, *not* please." The therapist commented that he seemed to feel she should know when he was hungry without his having to beg, to which he agreed. She then discussed his great need to be given things, that children have a right to feel their mothers will feed them good things without their having to ask, it's fun to be given all you want, and so forth.

He ate cookies throughout the first session following the vacation, but from then on he largely ignored the cookie jar or ate only a single cookie at the end of the hour. The last session before the Christmas holiday he again showed interest in the cookies, eating throughout the hour, asking the therapist to feed him, and offering one to her.

During the next four months his general play themes were becoming less symbolic and more creative and constructive in nature. Cookies held little interest for him. Only when termination plans were being discussed did he return to the cookie jar at one point when he was verbalizing some of his concerns and questions about the future.

Three weeks before his final session he brought a bag of hard candies to the playroom and offered some to the therapist. She pointed out that before this time he was *getting* things in the hour while now he was able to *give* and that this was a real change, to which he agreed. In his next to last session he once more stuffed his mouth with cookies, but did not seem to notice them in his final hour.

In summary, Billy's use of food can be divided into several stages. At first he was very constricted, denied his desires for food, or allowed himself only one or two cookies in an hour. Only after he acted out his fears of the bad food and retaliated against the bad mother could he then permit the therapist to feed him. This rapidly led to much regression in play and gorging of cookies as he played out pleasurable infantile feeding situations. As gains were noted in all areas of his play, his need for cookies also diminished, and he used them only when he needed extra support, for example, at the close of an hour or before a long vacation. Finally, he brought in food to give the therapist which signified a newly achieved stage of maturity for him.

References

Alpert, A. (1959). Reversibility of pathological fixations associated with maternal deprivation in infancy *Psychoanalytic Study of the Child* 14:169–185. New York: International Universities Press.

Anthony, E. S. (1961). A study of "screen sensations." *Psychoanalytic Study of the Child* 16:211–245. New York: International Universities Press.

Federn, P. (1952). *Ego Psychology and the Psychoses.* New York: Basic Books.

Haworth, M. R., and Keller, M. J. (1962). The use of food in the diagnosis and therapy of emotionally disturbed children. *Journal of the American Academy of Child Psychiatry* 1:548–563.

Kaufman, I., Rosenblum, E., Heims, L., and Willer, L. (1957). Childhood schizophrenia: treatment of children and parents. *American Journal of Orthopsychiatry* 27:683–690.

Kramer, P. (1961). Discussion of Dr. Anthony's paper—a study of "screen sensations." *Psychoanalytic Study of the Child* 16:246–250. New York: International Universities Press.

Rosen, J. (1953). *Direct Analysis*. New York: Grune & Stratton.

Schwing, G. (1954). *A Way to the Soul of the Mentally Ill*. New York: International University Press.

Sechehaye, M. A. (1951). *Autobiography of a Schizophrenic Girl*. New York: Grune & Stratton.

_____ *A New Psychotherapy in Schizophrenia*. New York: Grune & Stratton.

Slavson, S. R. (1943). *An Introduction to Group Therapy*. New York: Commonwealth Fund.

Waal, N. (1955). A special technique of psychotherapy with an autistic child. In *Emotional Problems of Early Childhood*, ed. G. Caplan, pp. 431–449. New York: Basic Books.

13

Mud and Clay

ADOLF G. WOLTMANN

The child's handling of form and color through the use of pencils, crayons, or water colors has been the subject of extensive studies. Comparatively little attention has been paid to the factors involved in the processes through which the child learns to master three-dimensional materials and to employ them as means of projecting his drives, feelings, and desires. An attempt is being made in this chapter to roughly trace the maturation factors which lead the child from the undifferentiated approach to creative structuring of pliable three-dimensional materials and to their use as a means of projection.

The term *plastic* will be used throughout this chapter. This word should not be confused with the more modern meaning of this term which is given to a variety of chemical products which are now used for the manufacturing of diverse utensils. The term *plastic,* as used in this chapter, is employed as a collective term for mud, clay, and plasticine. It denotes pliable, three-dimensional materials which can be structured and which offer to the child different creative outlets than the so-called graphic or two-dimensional media.

Nearly every infant, at one time or another, discovers the plasticity of his own feces. Mashed vegetables and similar baby food offer endless varieties of play patterns which, in a large measure, are determined by tactile stimulation. As the child grows older he learns to play with sand, water, and mud. Sand lends itself to a variety of play patterns. Through a combination of elevation and indentation the child can build tunnels, hills, rivers, and numerous landscape and geological formations. Sand is stable and gives support to the child's body and to the things which he places in it. Any object that is placed in the sand remains there. Water, on the other hand, is a fluid medium which does not allow for the creation of permanent structures. It is unstable and does not give body support. Objects placed in the water either swim, float, or sink.

> In playing with both media the child quickly realizes that sand makes things dirty, but that water cleans them. This results in a play pattern which can roughly be called "washing." Children seem to enjoy cleaning things as well as dirtying them. Once or several times during the day he experiences the transition from dirty to clean on his own body. Water and sand as play media enable him to experiment with things around him as "wet" and "dry," thus reviving earlier infantile experiences. By mixing water with sand a new plastic medium—mud—is created. By varying the proportion between water and sand, all kinds of consistencies from dirty water to a plastic mass can be made and played with. By throwing sand or mud or by squirting water, the child has in these three media excellent weapons of aggression and defense. The child also sees in them potential threats to his own welfare. There is the danger of catching cold, drowning, or choking. Sand, water, and mud adapt themselves particularly well to group activities. [Bender and Woltmann 1941–1942, p. 31]

These raw media are important developmental aids, because through them the child learns a great deal about the physical properties of his environment. He becomes aware of basic physical laws. Things are experienced as solid and liquid, as warm and cold, as dry and wet, as stable and unstable. Play with mud offers an excellent substitute for an early inhibited play with feces. At the same time, socializing factors appear when several children play together with sand, water, or mud.

The so-called normal child will learn to handle clay or plastic materials between the ages of 4 to 5 years. Sometimes other children revert back to the above-mentioned primitive play media. This happens if the child in question either has a very immature ego, if he suffers from a developmental retardation, or if the child is emotionally blocked and unable to compete with children of his own age group. The same applies to children with inadequate language development or with poor language facilities. Before any intensive therapeutic work can be started with such children, one should let them slide back, so to speak, to a more primitive developmental level of playing with sand or mud.

As the child grows older, sand, water, and mud play patterns slowly diminish in importance and are taken over by clay and plasticine. Plasticine is preferred because it does not harden and can be used over and over again. By the time the child comes in contact with plastic material, he usually has had some experiences with graphic media. A comparison between graphic and plastic media reveals that both have advantages and disadvantages. Graphic creative work is carried out with the use of one hand whereas plastic creative work calls for the coordination of both hands. In graphic creative work, forms are created through the use of lines and of color. Once a picture has been drawn or painted its contents remain stationary. The finished picture cannot be changed unless one erases, paints over, or destroys the original painting and makes another one. By using clay or plasticine, a constant change takes place because the medium is responsive to the slightest touch or impression. The consequent changes do not destroy the medium as happens if one erases or tears up paper. Graphic art is a two-dimensional medium and an indication of perspective is nothing but an optical illusion. Plastic material is three-dimensional and as such comes much closer to the representation of real objects. If a human figure is drawn from the front view, one can never see the sides or the back of this figure. A human clay figure automatically is three-dimensional and offers exploration as well as experimentation with all sides.

Graphic creative art allows for a defiance of physical laws, especially of the law of gravity. If one draws falling objects such as bombs dropping from an airplane or a person diving into the water, such drawn objects always remain suspended in mid-air. Plastic materials, on the other hand, are subject to physical laws. A combination of line and color offers more opportunities for realistic representation, but even at its best each portrayed action is but a frozen segment comparable to the individual photograph in a motion picture. Clay and plasticine usually are unicolored materials but the pliability somehow compensates for the lack of color. One should mention here that both graphic and plastic creative work very often are accompanied by acoustics. If children draw an airplane or make one out of clay, they like to imitate the noise of this object. This acoustic forms an integral part of all play patterns of children because the noise supplies a very necessary and realistic aspect in the child's attempt to master his environment.

A brief restatement of the factors cited above shows that plastic material has certain advantages over graphic material. Instead of handling one medium (pencil, crayon, or brush) with one hand and using it on the second medium (paper), the child handles the plastic material directly with both hands. This leads to early bilateral coordination of arms, hands, and fingers.

Both graphic and plastic materials are eminently suited for projective processes because both media are unstructured. They constitute the tools. The child, in creating something with both media, is free to select the content.

> The child learns how to master plastic material through maturation cycles, which are initiated by the sheer love of motor activity directed at the material offered. The early stages of this cycle, during which creative intentions are absent, may be called the kneading period or stage of nonspecific treatment which corresponds to the scribbling period in drawing. It is an investigation of the external world by rhythmic movements out of which patterns are built. An accidentally gained form or shape may be given a name and may become the carrier of a meaning. A more integrated rhythmic rolling seems to be characteristic for the next higher level of maturation during which attempts in object representation appear. The first real form mastered by a small child is usually a rolled cylinder which is comparable to the loop, whirl, and circle which form the primitive units of visual motor *gestalten* in graphic work. Through handling and turning, the cylinder can easily be changed into an arc, a ring, or a spiral. Out of these primitive geometrical forms more complex entities can be created. Rolled balls to which cylinders are attached, are usually the first attempt to create a "man." The plastic creative work of the child is no longer sheer motor exercise, but the representation of real objects to which meaning and emotional values are attached. This, in turn, stimulates the child's fantasy life and leads to the expression of problems which the child may have.
>
> This is one of the reasons why plastic creative work is of such great value in the observation and treatment of behavior problems in children: because it enables the child to clarify more freely and bring to conscious, tangible levels his own phantasies, which are thus accessible to therapeutic procedures.
>
> Aside from the quicker maturation cycles, plasticine offers other advantages. It lends itself extremely well to the repetitive-aggressive-destructive-constructive modes of behavior which seem to characterize the normal development of children and which are so evident in their play patterns and verbalizations. [Woltmann 1943, p. 299]

One may therefore consider the plastic creative work of the child as an expression of his own motility, as his aggressive investigation into the world of reality, as his drive to produce patterns on the receptive material with which he can express his emotional and social problems and his tendency to solve many of his problems through these experiences. These latter parts take place as soon as the child has reached the stage of object representation. Object representation may occur in the following stages (Bender and Woltmann 1937, p. 285):

1. Form as produced by motor impulses.
2. Form reproduced as seen or in imitation of other children.
3. Form which arises from the body image or postural model of the body and its manifold sensory and conceptional experience.
4. Form as an expression of phantasy, emotional, and social problems.

Before more attention is given to the stage of object representation, an account of the preceding stage of nonspecific handling is included because it shows that even before the child is developmentally ready for the creation of objects, unstructured clay or plasticine offers many valuable outlets for the small child. The following observations were made of nursery children from 2 to 5 years of age and also of older children who were either mentally retarded or emotionally blocked, so that they were unable to make the proper motor, intellectual, emotional, or social adjustments of the child above the nursery level.

Their approach to plastic material is that of an experimental investigation. They examine the plasticine by looking at it, smelling it, poking and hitting it, by putting it into their mouths, trying to chew and swallow it. They might drop it on the floor, throw it away, or watch the other children. One or two children will begin to hit the plastic material. Soon the others will follow. First each child will hit the clay in some kind of "individual" rhythm. Before long, the children will coordinate their "individual" rhythms into one steady group beat. While this goes on, new discoveries are made. Because of the repeated hitting, the plasticine lumps will take on a flat shape. One child will suddenly stop and exclaim, "Look what I made! I made a cake!" These activities are repeated over and over again. Once the children have released their undifferentiated motor drives, they soon become interested in the plastic material itself. They take it apart and put it together again. Other children might push holes into the plasticine or even use their fingernails or teeth to make indentations. Various forms and shapes are thus made. A flat piece of plasticine will be called a "cake." A polymorphous lump of clay with a little piece protruding from it is identified as a mouse. The children are happy about their discoveries, show them around, and enjoy having their creations admired by the group. On one occasion, a 6-year-old girl attached a piece of clay to one end of the armature stem.[1] On top of this, she put another piece of plasticine in the form of a rolled cylinder. She called her creation a "baby." She showed it to a 3-year-old boy and said, "You can't hit my baby." No sooner had she said this than the boy took the armature stem and began to hit the baby. Instead of being angry or upset, the girl laughed and screamed with joy whenever the boy touched or hit the clay baby. After it was completely destroyed, she made another one, and this play activity was repeated over and over again.

The emotional implications in this instance are especially interesting because this little girl was on the observation ward together with her 18-month-old brother. The two children were rejected by their mother and showed clear signs of sibling rivalry for the scant bit of maternal affection that the mother had to share between them.

At this stage we also notice the possessive nature of the child. It seems that the children are never satisfied with the amount of plasticine given to them and try to get as much as possible from the other children. They do not work in social groups yet although working alongside of each other and observing the activities of each other is not only important insofar as their own activities are concerned but this also points toward socializing factors which, at the next higher level, lead to the formation of social groups. [Bender and Woltmann 1937, p. 286 f.]

Since the preschool child usually handles both graphic and plastic media, one might expect overlappings in their creative endeavors. It is not at all uncommon that a young child will create a solid human figure out of clay. Instead of adding to it a solid hat, the child might form the outline of a hat by rolling clay into a thin, snake-like cylinder and bending this form into the proper shape. This sort of hat, in contrast to the three-dimensional body, has a definite two-dimensional appearance. Other children might attach the clay outline of a torso to a three-dimensional head.

The stage of preoccupation with investigation into the body image and postural model of the body is very well known in graphic art and has been used as a maturation test by Goodenough. The development of the

---

[1]An armature consists of a square-shaped board of 6 × 6 with a hole in the middle. Into this hole is inserted a round dowel.

same processes in plastic art has not been standardized. However, the so-called tadpole stage *(Kopffüssler)* in graphic arts has its equivalent in plastic creative work. Many young children leave out the body and attach the clay arms and legs directly to the head.

It was pointed out above that feces are among the earliest plastic materials with which the child comes in contact. Plastic material, due to its softness and pliability bears, for many children, a striking resemblance to fecal matter. Whereas the play with feces is usually strictly inhibited and curbed, clay and plasticine become a socially accepted symbolic substitute for feces. It is not surprising, therefore, that preoccupation with the anal region and elimination is common in the child's handling of plastic material. The child does not always adhere to the anal content but combines it with allied problems such as the proper body posture maintained during the process of elimination and also with larger social issues. Children sometimes are puzzled over the fact that the intake of food is a social occasion in which the whole family participates. The elimination of food, however, is a purely individual and private activity from which others are excluded. In an earlier publication Dr. Bender and this author (1937) refer to several plastic creations which deal with toilets. One 7-year-old boy built an individual toilet for every member of the family. Another boy, slightly younger, created a "community toilet" by pushing five holes into a piece of clay. He placed five round sticks of clay on each hole and called them "father, mother, two sisters, and the baby." The top ends of these so-called human figures were slightly twisted because, using his own words, "they turn their heads away while they sit down there." We have on record other plastic creations of this sort in which anal and sexual content are symbolically expressed. One 7-year-old boy created a bathroom scene in which two toilet bowls looked like doughnuts. He rolled another piece of clay into a round cylinder, bent down one end and used his creation as a gun. For a few minutes he ran around in the playroom, shooting at everybody present. Then he examined his gun very carefully and said, "This looks like something you use in the toilet when you pull the thing. I am going to make a toilet now. I am going to make a big toilet, a fat toilet." He straightened out the gun and placed the elongated clay piece between the two doughnut-shaped toilets. He added two round clay balls to the upright structure and referred to his whole creation as "This is a frankfurter with two meatballs and two doughnuts on each side." He was highly amused by his creation and showed it around to the other children in the room. The other children, too, laughed. When he finally presented his creation to this author, he had a serious expression on his face and maintained with an artificial air of sincerity that he only had been joking and that his real intentions had been to build a toilet.

Psychoanalysis has taught us that the anal contents and references in folklore, slang, and dreams very often carry a decided note of contempt. The following brief case history is included here to demonstrate that cathartic release of contemptuous feelings can be obtained through a very primitive, unspecified handling of plastic material alone. Richard, a 9-year-old boy, was referred for psychotherapy because his mother found it impossible to handle him. The family owned a home in a small community. Richard refused to conform. He had broken several windows, destroyed property, and on one occasion had even tried to set the house on fire. Occasionally he truanted from school and was extremely aggressive toward his younger brother. This boy was seen three times a week in hourly sessions for a period of two years. Treatment attempts were extremely difficult in the beginning because Richard was mean, negative, and aggressive. Several times he sneaked up behind this author and hit and kicked him. Puppets were introduced which from then on received the full fury of his aggressive contempt. After a year and one-half of stormy sessions, during which Richard enacted many family scenes, he suddenly became interested in dollhouse furniture and in animals. Richard identified himself with the snake. He surrounded the snake with other animals who were away from home and who would come at nighttime and try to break in and destroy the house while his father, mother, and younger brother were asleep. One day he suddenly discovered a large play toilet which originally had served, thanks to the inventiveness of fun-loving manufacturers, as a dispenser of cigarettes. Richard immediately turned this play object into a flying feces factory. He attached two clay hoses to the toilet and made believe that one squirted out urine and that the other shot out feces. After building a bedroom, living room, kitchen, and bathroom, he would hold the toilet in his hand and make believe that the whole house was thoroughly drenched with urine and feces. Not satisfied with this, he allowed the snake to sneak into the house at nighttime and to deposit lumps of clay throughout the whole apartment. Richard had a fiendish glee on his face when this "fecal matter" was placed in the stove and in the coffeepot. He danced around and shouted, "Tomorrow morning, when the mother starts the stove going, this will stink up the whole house and they will drink shit instead of coffee for breakfast." His preoccupation with fecal matters increased from one session to the next. He was no longer satisfied with placing feces into the apartment, but began to bombard his house with huge lumps of clay. He rejoiced when during this process the whole apartment was reduced to shambles. Since it did not occur to him that his parents and brother might fight back, this writer took the initiative by attaching a clay penis to the father figure and by making believe that the father tried to urinate against the flying feces factory as a measure of defense. Richard fixed that. During the night the snake came into the house, castrated the father and touched the genital region of the mother figure. Then Richard said, "They won't be able to make piss at me any more. From now on they always will have to run to the toilet, but only water will come out. The piss will stay inside of them and before long they will get sick and will have to go to the doctor. Now I can throw all the piss and shit at them and they can't fight back."

This intense fecal play lasted for approximately three months. Whereas formerly the boy had been aggressive toward the therapist, he now devoted all of his time and effort to annihilating his family by choking them with and drowning them in urine and feces. Richard was so preoccupied with this play that it was impossible to suggest other play patterns or to engage him into a discussion about the meaning of this play. I therefore took this boy one day to the zoo. While we watched the chimpanzees, one of these primates suddenly began to poke a finger into his anus and to extract fecal matter by force. In true monkey fashion he cleaned his hand by inserting it into the mouth. Richard had watched all of this with great fascination. Then he turned around and said, "Let's go. This is disgusting. Whoever heard of a monkey sticking his finger in his behind and then into his mouth." I explained to him that fecal play is very common among animals and young babies and that he probably, as an infant, had acted like the monkey. Richard flew into a rage. He denied ever having had an interest in fecal matters. He stormed into the hotel lobby where his mother was waiting for him and shouted, "Mother, did I play with shit when I was a baby?" After the thoroughly embarrassed mother and this writer had brought Richard to the privacy of the therapist's office, the mother explained to her son that he had played with his own feces from the age of 6 months till he was nearly 2 years old. This unexpected revelation came as a shock and a surprise to the youngster. He was quiet and pensive. When he returned for the next session, he again built an apartment for his parents and younger brother but refused to play with the toilet and clay. Instead he sent over the elephant to the house to ask whether the snake and the other animals could come for a visit. As soon as permission was granted, all of the animals moved into the house and were cordially received by the family. During the following play sessions all of the animals went to school during the day and came back to the house in the evening with very good marks. The mother reported spontaneously that a complete change of behavior had taken place in her son after the incident at the zoo. Shortly after this Richard was discharged from treatment because he no longer was mean and aggressive. Although Richard had never once modeled objects out of clay, he had used plastic material in its primitive, unstructured form for the release of his pent-up aggression and for the working through of numerous problems on a developmental level which was far below his chronological age.

Problems connected with the size, shape, and functions of the genital regions can likewise be investigated and experimented with through plastic media. Interestingly enough, genital preoccupation, as evidenced through plastic creative work, seems to be much more prevalent among boys than girls. Boys very often endow their clay figures with penises of various sizes and shapes. We have on record the creation of an 11-year-old boy who attached six clay testicles around the clay penis. Sometimes the clay penis is left out but the nose of the clay man might become the object of experimentation. It also happens that a human clay figure is endowed with a penis and an anus. Experimentation with such concepts might lead to an enlargement of both areas so that, for instance, the anus may reach all the way up to the nape of the neck.

The release of sexual fantasies in experimentation with clay was observed by the author in group activities of five boys between the ages of 7 to 10. Ordinarily, sexual knowledge is inhibited, but the uninhibited expressions of one member of the group quickly remove the thin veneer of custom and education from the rest of the group. It is as if the group activity sanctions the collective thoughts of all those who comprise such a gathering. It was of interest to note that all of these activities were carried out with a total absence of fear, guilt, shame, or modesty. At the same time interesting mechanisms of projection were observed. Several of the clay objects were destroyed because they did something bad (sexual activities). In other words it was not the ideations of these boys that was at fault, but the blame was shifted and projected onto the clay objects which these boys themselves had created. The permissive attitude of the therapist, who allowed the boys to act out their repressed and inhibited problems, greatly helped toward bringing this material to a tangible level, so that later on it could be handled therapeutically.

Masturbatory activities which might give rise to castration fears are occasionally encountered. A 7-year-old boy made a human figure out of clay which was devoid of arms but had a penis. He told this writer that his clay boy had been playing with his "dicky" and that God had punished him by cutting off his arms. "The boy knows that it is wrong to play with his dicky, but he cannot stop it. He tries to use his feet, but God will punish him and also cut off his feet. Then the little boy will have no arms and no legs, and he cannot walk no more, and his mother will have to feed him and he cannot play with his dicky no more."

Only once, during several years of daily contacts with groups of children, suffering from a variety of behavior problems, did this writer encounter a plastic creation in which fellatio was the theme. This boy was over 12 years of age. He produced a man, kneeling behind a machine gun. His real intentions were obvious to a group of boys who had been watching him work with clay. After much giggling and snickering the boy finally admitted that the so-called machine gun was in reality a huge penis which the kneeling figure tried to insert into his mouth.

Anyone who observes children and their handling of plastic materials will be struck by the fact that a snake-like figure occurs very frequently in the plastic creative work of children.

> This constant appearance of the snake in the clay work can partly be explained as follows: As mentioned before, the rolled cylinder constitutes the first basic, elementary form the child masters once he has reached the stage of object representation. By rolling a piece of clay with his hands, an oblong, snake-like object is the inevitable result. This explanation covers only the formal aspect but not the emotional contents which point toward a diversified use of one symbol. [Bender and Woltmann 1937, p. 295]

Most of the children who produce snakes in their clay work have never seen a real living snake. In some instances, the snake is a phallic symbol. In other cases, the snake might represent aggressive parents or siblings. Very often the snake is the protector or a punishing agent who kills "bad" people. We also have seen plastic creations in which the snake appears as a tame friend of people. An individual study should be made in each case to determine what the snake means to the child and what it supposedly represents.

Among the many plastic creations of children which include snakes, the following one is singled out because the mechanisms of projection are especially clear. What this 12-year-old girl worked out in her plastic creation constituted a great deal of her own personal experiences. Gwendolin made many tall and small snakes out of clay which she put together into some sort of a community. She identified her objects as father snake, stepmother snake, dead mother snake, a snake minister, a snake sitting on the toilet, snake children, and as a lake with a fish in it.

She called her creation a "garden of snakes" and told the following story about her clay work:

> Adam and Eve have sinned in the garden because of the snake. God put all the snakes in this garden because the snakes had started the first sin in the world. The snakes have to stay in the garden for a whole year. They were hidden away from the rest of the world. In this garden there was only one fish. The snake that did the most work should get the fish. So these two lazy snakes started to fight for it. One snake killed the other snake and ate up the fish. After this, God comes and says, "A woman should tread on every man's head because the man snake killed the lady snake." The wife of the snake is dead. He killed her. You see, they were lazy. They didn't want to do the work. There was only one fish in there and the wife said she should have it because she is the lady. He said he should have it because he is a male. So they started fighting and he bit her near the heart and she died.

Gwendolin was asked if the snake would be punished for killing the wife. She answered, "Not yet. He doesn't know that his new wife has a temper. She will beat him up. See these little snakes here? She is their stepmother."

How does the stepmother treat the little children? "Pretty good as long as she is only engaged to the man. After she is married to the man for a couple of days, she gets very nasty. She makes the kids sweep the floor. . . . The stepmother wants presents from the children so she is good to them for one day because it is her birthday. The children give her a present, a big ball. She thinks it is a chocolate ball, but it is made out of rock. She puts it into her mouth and breaks all her teeth. She goes around teethless. She can't eat. All she can take is soup and water."

Will she punish the children for this? "No, because they tell her that the preacher has sent the candy. So she goes and hits the preacher over the head. The father can't do nothing. She hits him over the head with a rolling pin."

Gwendolin had a stepmother with whom she could not get along at all. Many of her behavior adjustment failures are related to a very unsatisfactory home situation. Her story contains many of the unpleasant home episodes and also a simple but very effective plan of revenge in which the hated stepmother is deprived of her oral aggression, of her strength and her vitality. Instead of bossing the children around, she has to live on soup and water. The symbolism involved does not require further comment. It is of interest to note how the biblical content in the beginning of her story is twisted around. The biblical animosity between man and snake is changed to hostility between male and female.

It would be erroneous to assume that the plastic creative work of children deals primarily with oral, anal, and genital content. They are experimented with if the child encounters disturbing problems in these areas. For the greater part children use plastic material as a medium into which they project their own ideologies and curiosities and use it for working out their own specific problems. It should be mentioned here that a child should be allowed to create freely. Any attempt toward formal instruction and teaching children to create objects such as cups, ashtrays, or vases automatically inhibits spontaneous expression. If a group of children is left alone in a permissive atmosphere, an amazing variety of plastic creations will be the result. It is possible that one child might borrow an idea from another child. This is perfectly permissible because the borrowing child will change the idea according to his degree of motor development and maturation, the intensity of his own problems, and his degree of socialization.

One should never be satisfied with looking at the finished creation, but should try to learn from the child what his creative intentions were and what his creation means to him. The child should be encouraged to speak freely about his finished clay work. The above-mentioned snake story gave real meaning and an understanding of Gwendolin's problems to the otherwise well made but static "garden of snakes." The plastic creative work of a child does not bring forth all of his problems and should therefore not be used as a single criterion. Its chief value lies in the fact that the child brings to a tangible level some of his problems which can be seen, discussed, experimented with, and changed. To create a permissive attitude and to allow children to express themselves in plastic creative work is an activity which teachers, settlement house workers, recreation workers, and nurses can and should carry out. The evaluation and interpretation of such creations should be left to the specially trained therapist.

A brief description of other plastic creations made by children is given in an attempt to show the range and variety of problems which children bring to a realistic level. An 8-year-old boy showed a great deal of preoccupation with the figure of what he called "a good man." First he referred to a piece of clay as a house and that a good man lived in the house selling vegetables. Then he changed the story and said that the house was full of candy and that all of the candy belonged to the man inside the house. Finally he made a clay face of a man which he covered completely with little bits of clay. He said, "The man is good because his whole face is covered with candy." This boy came from a broken home which the father had deserted. His preoccupation with the good man obviously was an attempt to create an ideal image of the father figure and the wish to have the father come back. It also turned out that this boy, who could not accept the harsh reality of the irresponsible father, had to convince himself over and over again that there was such a thing as a good father.

Fred came to the hospital at the age of 7. His father deserted when he learned that his wife was pregnant again. Shortly after the desertion Fred began to stay out late and, on several occasions, was picked up by the police during the wee-hours of the morning and returned home. Finally the mother's condition made it impossible for her to care for this boy and he was therefore recommended to the hospital for a period of observation. At first, this boy was very shy and taciturn. He participated little in the group activities and stayed more or less on the fringe of things. Little by little he became interested in working with clay and began to make crude household utensils. Among his creations were a basket full of eggs and a rolling pin which his mother used when baking bread. Fred received intensive individual psychotherapy during which the attention was focused on the fact that before long there would be another baby in the family. His mother visited him regularly at the hospital and, at our suggestion, discussed with him the changes that would take place in the family and the adjustments which would necessitate living in a family with two children and without a father. Fred understood, because before long he began to make mother figures out of clay. Soon he added little babies to the mother figure. Most of the time the clay mother would be holding the clay baby in her arms. He was very glad when he finally learned that he had a baby sister and eagerly looked forward to going home in order to resume a new life with his mother and sibling. He adjusted very well to the new situation.

A number of the clay creations which have come to this writer's attention clearly deal with feelings of loneliness and being deserted. A 9-year-old boy created a clay scene in which a clay boy stands under a lamp post. Nearby is a fence on which a cat is walking. The boy, according to his story, ran away from an orphanage because he didn't like it there.

The cops go after the boy. They will get him and bring him back to the orphanage. He now will like it there because he had no right to run away. He should have stayed there. This all happens at night time.

What is the cat doing there?

Oh, nothing, the cat just happened to walk by.

This boy had a history of truancy and of running away from home. His clay scene depicts a boy who is out on the street in the middle of the night. He is all alone, has no bed to sleep in, no money with which to buy food. Instead of meeting with excitement and adventure, he finds himself devoid of human contacts and is glad when the police return him to his environment. It is one thing when a child speaks about being lonely. It is quite another thing when he gives creative expression to his feelings, because the desolateness of a few pieces of clay put together gives spatial dimension to the feeling of being all alone.

Here and there in this chapter reference has been made to the fact that clay and plasticine are very good outlets for aggression on several developmental levels. The following observations are included because they reveal children's attempts to experiment with and to repeat various forms of aggression.

Richard and Walter, two 7-year-old boys, made airplanes out of clay and played with them. Both planes had a machine gun and were shooting at each other. After some flying around and shooting, both planes collided in mid-air. These collisions were repeated a few times during which the boys held the clay models in their hands. Then they decided to let them crash and dropped the clay figures on the floor after each collision. After this had been carried out a few times, the airplanes lost their shape and became lumps of clay. Instead of letting them drop again, the clay was picked up and thrown down. Richard would leave his piece of clay on the floor and Walter would try to hit it with his piece of clay and vice versa. The boys would say, "He's hitting my airplane" or "He's killing my airplane." After these repeated acts, both boys hurled their pieces through space in projectile-like fashion trying to hit other objects. When class was over, Walter begged us to let him stay saying, "Let me take another shot at that," pointing to a chair.

These play activities, which lasted approximately twenty-five minutes, showed some of the characteristics inherent in child's play. I would call it repeated experimentation in aggression. Each aggressive act is repeated over and over again. As the child grows older, his problems of aggression become infused with general social problems. It is, therefore, not surprising that quite a number of the plastic creations of older children have to do with social scenes in which bad people murder good people and then are apprehended by the proper authorities and brought to justice.

Aggression may not always be directed toward the outside world but may also take on forms of defense, as is illustrated in the clay work of a 13-year-old boy who had below average intelligence and who was physically handicapped. He created a monster out of clay and had the following to say about his plastic creation:

> I was thinking the other day what I'll do when I was big. I decided to get rich. It is easier to get gold than it is to get money. But all the gold mines are discovered already and guarded, so when I get big I want to go to Africa. There is some dynamite that hasn't been discovered. If I go to Africa I need protection. It costs money to have a guard, so I make my own guard. I get tusks from a lot of elephants and make one great big tusk. Then I get all the feet of the gorillas and make two big feet out of them. Then I put the eyes of an eagle in the front and the eyes of a hawk in the back. Then I get the horns of all the rhinoceroses and make great big horns out of those things. Then I give it the brain of a dead human being. Then I cut the head, the tusks and the feet of an elephant so that just its belly is left. Then I put all the things together in the belly and fill it with the blood of a vicious animal. Then I put a tube down his heart and pump it and then it will become alive. Before I do that I put him into a steel cage so he can't hurt anybody. Then I train him that he likes me and do what I say. Then I take him to Africa. If the savages or animals start out with me, he protects me. I give him the skin of a crocodile, so that bullets wouldn't hurt him. I give him the voice of a lion. With his mouth he can swallow a couple of million guys in one gobble. With each horn he can stick through twelve thousand men at once. If a herd of elephants attacks me he can swallow seven or eight elephants at a time. His tail can wrap around seven thousand men at one time, choke them to death and throw them away. He stays up all night and if a crook comes he will kill him. I will get all the diamonds. In the jungles he can kill plenty of animals but it costs plenty of money to feed him in the city. I know what I do. I give him the scent of a bloodhound so he can follow after the crooks and kick up the house with one foot and kill all the crooks.

Frankenstein seems to be an ineffective amateur next to this clay creation. The interesting part of this clay work lies in the fact that this boy surrounds himself with an all-powerful fantastic monster which keeps away from him injury and ridicule. This boy suffered from a speech defect and was partially paralyzed. A long period of hospitalization had interfered with his educational development. He could compete neither intellectually nor physically with children of his own age group. His speech impediment often made him the target of other children's fun. The creation of the clay monster must therefore be taken as an attempt to retaliate and to express his hidden aggression.

It is impossible to comment on every type of plastic creative work that children may produce. The few examples cited in this chapter may suffice to point out that plastic materials play just as important a role in the development of the child as do graphic media.

> When a child works with plastic material, a definite intention to create specific objects is not always present. The activities based upon motor patterns may lead to forms which suggest definite objects which might be elaborated with secondary intent. When a plastic object is created it is not merely considered as an image with more or less similarity to the object, but it is also endowed with function. This function might be a passive one and the object might be merely played with. It might also take over the role of aggressiveness; it may talk and act. In this way, the plastic figure becomes an object of importance in the child's life. The child is given a chance to "create" his conception of the world in a real, visible and tangible form. Consequently, all these activities constitute a great emotional release for the child. [Bender and Woltmann 1937, p. 299]

The combination of a child's creative work and his own story are as revealing as Rorschach responses and stories told to the pictures of the Thematic Apperception Test. Plastic creative work is a projective technique in the true sense of the word because, according to Lawrence K. Frank, the child, when given plastic material, does not create what the therapist arbitrarily has decided the child should make. The child is confronted with an unstructured, polymorphous, pliable, three-dimensional material, which he must structure and endow with this own meanings, desires and idiosyncrasies.[2]

---

[2]The author is greatly indebted to Dr. Lauretta Bender, Senior Psychiatrist, Psychiatric Division of Bellevue Hospital, New York, for her help and encouragement in many of the original studies and for giving valuable information which greatly enhanced this selection.

PART III
Drawing and Art Techniques in Play Therapy

14

Finger Painting

JACOB A. ARLOW AND ASJA KADIS

Originally introduced as a form of play and a medium for artistic expression, finger painting is now a recognized psychotherapeutic technique. Shaw (1938), who invented the medium, was quick to see how it enabled her pupils to overcome their inhibitions and permitted fuller expression of their fantasy life. Painting out hostile fantasies served as a means of catharsis for conflicts.

In addition to the therapeutic possibilities as a play technique, which it shares with the graphic arts (Bender and Woltmann 1941–1942), finger painting has several peculiar advantages. It is a socially sanctioned form of playing with mud. Both Spring (1935) and Mosse (1940) emphasized the utilization of the anal regression. Finger painting requires little technical skill and permits the use of larger muscle groups. Fleming (1940), working with adult neurotics, related the character of the painting movements to personality types. Other authors have attempted to interpret finger painting through a universal symbolism of form and color, even suggesting that specific colors are related to definite clinical entities (Obendorf 1940). Shaw and Lyle (1937), who use the medium to encourage fantasy expression in children, warned against the danger of arbitrary interpretation of finger paintings.

In the work which forms the basis for the present chapter we attempted to integrate finger painting with the total psychotherapeutic situation, using the medium as a form of projective play, as a study of motility, and as a source of fantasies and free associations. No attempt was made to analyze the paintings by themselves; at all times they were viewed within the context of the therapeutic situation.

We described the process of finger painting to our patients, but in order to avoid the suggestion of any technique, it was not rehearsed in practice. No suggestion was made concerning colors or themes. Unlike other authors (Mosse 1940), we did not leave the room while the patient painted. We adopted instead an attitude of passive objectivity, observing the patient in the same spirit as an analyst observes the patient, taking note of the patient's behavior as well as the content of his productions. As much can be learned from the approach to the new situation of painting as from the drawing and the fantasy. Finger painting gives the painter liberty to create as well as to destroy his creation, without actually being destructive. From the same material he is able to obliterate and create again and again, and is spared the humiliation of asking for fresh material.

If the patient is not observed during his experimentation with the medium, important material is missed by the observer which the patient may conceal with a stroke of the palm. Conversely, the metamorphosis of forms often reveals the condensations and distortions which are used to disguise the expression of conflicts and wishes. For example, when a patient with a few strokes of his fingers converts a rabbit into a small child, one may anticipate that the rabbit and child may unconsciously have been equated. We thus observe at first hand a graphic presentation of the dream work.

Although the medium properly used may give rise to intriguing designs and artistic patterns, we have not found it necessary to praise or encourage the patient's efforts. After a relatively short period of time, he comes to appreciate finger painting as a medium of self-expression and uses it accordingly. In this respect finger painting commends itself to children because no great skill or experience is required, and is a distinct advantage over other forms of drawing or painting. The painter is not discouraged by experiencing failure or inadequacy.

While the patient paints we observe how he applies himself to the task, the rate and rhythm of his work, the colors he employs, types of lines, and so forth. After the child feels that the picture has been completed, he is asked to tell the story of the painting. Then we inquire whether he is reminded of anything by the painting. How the material is used depends primarily upon the level to which the therapeutic process has advanced. The following case reports will demonstrate how the material is integrated with treatment.

Case 1: Harry S., a 10-year-old boy, was brought to the clinic by his mother as a behavior problem. Presenting the clinical picture of a mild Froelich's syndrome, with an undescended testicle on the left side, he had been receiving endocrine therapy but with little result. His testicle remained undescended and his weight continued to increase. His mother complained that Harry was completely unmanageable. He was involved in endless quarrels with his mother, usually nagging her over some exorbitant demand which she had not fulfilled. His misbehavior would begin shortly after his mother had denied a request. Requests ranged from a watch, a football, a young dog, to a younger brother. During these periods of frustration the boy's appetite became insatiable. He would descend upon the refrigerator and gorge himself with all it contained. The fluctuation of his weight curve on the clinic chart was one of the surest indicators of his behavior during the week. School behavior was similarly disturbed so that performance on tests ranged from excellent to extremely poor. Intelligence was slightly above average.

The mother's attitude toward the boy was characterized by extreme ambivalence, the result of conflicting rejection and guilt. If not for the patient, she would have left her husband for whom she felt temperamentally unsuited. She sometimes indulged the boy's every wish and on other occasions denied the most modest request. For example, for a while she had considered placing the boy in an institution, yet a few months later she applied at a foster home agency for a child in order to satisfy Harry's intense wish for a baby brother, which she was unable to satisfy because of a hysterectomy.

Harry's behavior in painting was characteristic of his general attitude. He could not get enough of anything nor could he get it quickly enough. He used too much water and too much paint; he mixed the colors indiscriminately in massive quantities, resulting in an unpleasant brown or gray effect. He spread the paint well beyond the limits of the paper onto the linoleum used to protect the table. As often as not his picture extended right onto the linoleum. His movements were rapid, restless, and definitive, giving the lines of his drawing a bold character. Despite this turmoil, the content of the drawing was always something very simple—something this frustrated little boy desired: a football, a pipe, and so on.

The following two instances illustrate how unexpressed wishes or even unconscious wishes can find expression in painting.

During the period when Harry's feelings of inadequacy about his small genitalia and undescended testicle were being discussed, he kept making drawings of a tremendous football which he wanted his parents to get for him to replace an old small football which he had lost. In the playroom he modeled a human figure out of clay and then made a large penis which he placed in the appropriate position. Smiling, he removed the penis, placed it in the figure's mouth explaining: "It's a cigar." Immediately after, he drew a large male face with a tremendous cigar in the mouth, a very clear example of symbolization and displacement from below to above. (One of his problems was smoking.)

Among the many things that Harry demanded of his mother was that she present him with a younger brother. He also wanted a puppy but she refused because it would entail too much work. Harry painted a picture of a boy seated in a chair, arms outstretched to receive his dog. The dog, however, was not pictured on the floor but in the air at the level of the boy's arms, revealing the obvious intention to hold it as one holds a child. More interesting, however, is the fact that a year earlier Harry drew practically the same picture as a pencil sketch for another examiner. There were two differences: in the earlier sketch the dog was on the floor, but his head was unmistakably that of a child. Thus Harry's wish for a baby brother transformed into the desire to get a puppy found expression in identical drawings on two separate occasions more than a year apart. This illustrates what we have found to be true in our experiences: that the pictorial productions and fantasies which the patient creates about them are characteristic for him and undergo relatively minor modification with the passing of time.

Case 2: Paul O., a 14-year-old boy, was brought to the clinic by his mother. When asked what was wrong, he burst into tears and complained that "things are phoney, I don't feel real. I don't feel like myself." He was unable to leave the house unaccompanied. When an attack overcame him at school he would either run home or return to his "home class" where in the presence of his male teacher his anxiety would abate. The feeling of complete unreality and the feeling of body change which he experienced during the attacks were the most disturbing symptoms.

Paul appeared short and young for his age, which was a definite family trait. He had two older sisters and a younger brother. Many symptoms pertained to the younger brother, of whose whereabouts Paul had to be assured constantly. He felt no antagonism toward any members of his family and was unaware of any interpersonal conflict.

It was Paul who took the initiative in incorporating finger painting into the therapeutic process. While trying rather unsuccessfully to explain how he felt during an attack, he suddenly turned and reached for the painting which he had made a few minutes earlier. In pale yellow he had drawn two indistinct figures at opposite ends of a road. He pointed to the more distinct one, and said: "I'm this person. But during an attack I feel that I may be this one (pointing to the opposite figure). Or I'm here and sometimes I feel that I'm there. During an attack I don't know who I am or where I am." Using the painting, he thus gave us not only a graphic description of his sensations during an attack, but also an invaluable clue to its psychological significance, for we later learned that identification with another person was a most important dynamic factor in his illness.

Paul's manner of painting was characteristic. In a series of over fifty paintings he deviated only two or three times from his customary approach. After mixing his colors, he spread the paint over the paper in smooth, even strokes, then stopped and stared at the paper in a sort of trance. Following this he would draw in a very deliberate manner, changing, erasing, and adding, then stop suddenly and say: "It's finished." He explained that he always knew when a picture was completed because a certain feeling of uneasiness within him disappeared.

Following the original drawing, Paul painted a series of twelve to fourteen pictures, all of which were related by two closely connected themes: either a young child was lost or killed, or the smaller or younger of two objects or persons was destroyed. He was unaware that his paintings and fantasies told an identical story in an almost compulsive manner, until it was brought to his attention when he related several dreams, of which the following two are typical.

Paul dreamed that he was helping his brother up a mountainside when the brother lost his grasp and plunged down the mountain. He woke from his dream in one of his attacks. He dreamed that he was offering condolences to a neighbor who had lost the younger of her two sons. In explanation of this dream Paul stated: "She really has three sons but my mother has two, myself and my younger brother."

At this point, with the aid of his own drawings, we were able to demonstrate how an unconscious thought may act in a dynamic fashion and force itself into his creations and his behavior. He showed genuine amazement when we demonstrated to him the persistent recurrence of these themes in his paintings. He insisted that he never knew beforehand what he was going to draw. We questioned him on many occasions in order to ascertain that this was so and in order to eliminate the possibility that the theme of the painting had been suggested by us.

The next turning point in treatment occurred when the patient became aware that he was not only thinking of his younger brother's death, but was wishing for it to take place as a result of his own efforts. Once again this was made clear by the paintings. Paul drew a picture of the body of a young boy and a ball lying at the foot of a tree. In explanation he said that the boy had climbed into the tree to retrieve his ball. Having gotten it, he lost his footing, and fell to the ground injuring himself seriously. Paul was ready to leave discussion of the painting when he was asked whether the picture reminded him of any specific events in his life. After a few moments two childhood incidents occurred to him which he had forgotten. Both events occurred in the country where his illness began. In the first situation the younger brother had climbed into a tree to retrieve his dog. Paul, standing on the ground, urged his brother to throw the dog to him. When the little boy refused, the patient threatened. The intimidated youngster finally yielded to Paul's demands. Paul, however, permitted the dog to fall to the ground. He was immediately overcome by guilt and remorse, feeling that the dog had been killed. In the second incident, Paul threw his younger brother out of the tree under the pretext that he was not coming in for lunch promptly enough. Fortunately the boy was not injured, but Paul responded as on the previous occasion, with guilt and remorse.

These revelations were followed by a series of paintings in which Paul kept rescuing his younger brother from danger. Then he produced a painting in which the tree reappeared. This time a small chipmunk was in the branches while below stood a young boy poised to kill the animal with a stone. To this Paul associated the many times when he had killed frogs, squirrels and rabbits, and felt guilt later. He finally renounced this destructive pastime and felt only extreme gentleness and solicitude for animals. Having already equated the little animals with his brother, his unconscious wish to kill his younger brother was now apparent to him from his own drawings. We were further able to point out that the sequence of drawings in which the theme changed from overt hostility to stories of rescue, recapitulated Paul's attitude toward animals and toward his younger brother: first destruction, then extreme solicitude.

In a drawing which he made sometime later, the patient revealed that, out of guilt, he had identified himself with the object of his destructive wishes. In this painting two boys are walking on a road in which an excavation is so covered over with leaves that travelers are unaware of the danger. Paul explained the picture: "My brother and myself on a road in the forest, the pit is like an animal trap. One of the boys falls in." (Which one?) Paul remained silent for a moment, then smiling very sheepishly, meekly said: "I fall in." He explained that he had meant to say the brother fell in, but had changed his story when he became aware that the pit reminded him of a grave. (Prior to the painting we had been discussing Paul's first acquaintance with death—the funeral of his grandfather.) He continued by saying that the structure at the bottom of the pit, which he had noticed during his explanation of the picture but about which he had made no comment, reminded him of a coffin.

The painting thus demonstrated to Paul how, on becoming aware of his death wish toward his brother, he substituted himself for his victim. This sequence of events, now made conscious, was used to explain the genesis of his attacks in which Paul felt that he was dead or dying. As in the painting, so in the attack; Paul felt impending death only after he had first thought of or fantasied the death of some other person.

We have presented the above case in some detail because the observable content of the drawings reflected very closely the content of the fantasies which the patient created about his paintings. This correlation of drawing and fantasy is not always the rule. Younger children, particularly those under 5 years of age, are more likely to use finger painting to gratify their need for emotional outlet in the form of overt motor activity. As a medium of expression this relates finger painting closer to dancing than to the graphic arts. We might say that our patients "danced with their fingers" on the paper, expressing in their movements the mood at the time of painting.

Some of our patients assaulted the paper, smearing the paint about in swift, aggressive strokes, often tearing the sheet. One girl, on the other hand, after evading discussion of her bed wetting, painted like a dilettante, flicking the paint about with the nail of her little finger in a thoroughly supercilious manner. She thus made known to us beforehand that her resistance to discussing bed wetting would not be overcome through painting.

Sylvia, a 14-year-old girl, ordinarily painted with deliberation and planning, and her drawings were usually organically related to her productions. After a quarrel with a friend, however, she expressed her mood in a purely motor form. She poured a generous amount of brown paint on the paper and kept rubbing with both hands, making ceaseless, vigorous, circular movements. Nothing appeared on the paper but two boldly drawn, overlapping circles, concerning which she stated: "This drawing is a forest. There are brown leaves all around. My friend is a forest. There are brown leaves all around. My friend is dead and I am burying her and burying her. I am so mad with her, I could kill her." This regression to a more immature way of using the medium, unusual for a girl this age, may be related to the fact that Sylvia was inhibited in verbal expression by a stammer.

The cathartic value of this particular painting technique is quite apparent. A combination of the use of motor activity and drawing content for cathartic purposes is clearly seen in the case of an 8-year-old boy who, shortly after being admitted to a children's institution, kept painting and destroying a "bad man" over and over again. He related the "bad man" to the enemies of his country, but also to his father who had been instrumental in having him institutionalized.

The correlation between the observable content of the painting and the patient's fantasy story about it, we have found to be an almost infallible index of the degree of ego development; in children, it is a measure of the progress of treatment. The restless, aggressive child finds it difficult to inhibit his motor activity long enough to plan and execute meaningful forms in his finger painting; he has already abandoned formal language when he begins to express his conflict in the form of misbehavior and symptoms. Following psychotherapeutic treatment more formal means of speech and behavior are adopted. There is also a greater degree of self-criticism which results in increased appreciation of the environment. The child relates himself more objectively to his surroundings and begins to use patterns of speech, behavior, and drawing which are more meaningful to the observer. This process has been observed in several severely disturbed children.

Case 3: When Allan, age 4½, came to the clinic, he raced through the halls at top speed, shrieking loudly and slamming doors. In the playroom he ordered the other children about and climbed on top of the toy chest. At home he had thrown food out of the window, smashed dishes, and started several fires. Because of his marked restlessness a diagnosis of post-encephalitic behavior disturbance was entertained for awhile.

On the first day of finger painting Allan made no picture at all; he got so excited he fell into the pail of water that was used to moisten the paper. Later, when he did paint, his creations were meaningless jumbles of lines with no discernible form, pattern, or organization. His verbal productions in relation to these drawings were at first equally incoherent and unintelligible. After months of treatment he was able to tell stories about the paintings that made sense, but the paintings themselves remained without form or meaning. These stories, which usually centered about a sinister and threatening figure called "the Shadow," led to the youngster's fear of his cruel and abusive father. As Allan was able to discuss his problem, in part, his mood became more tranquil. This turn in the treatment was reflected in a short time when he was able to draw an easily recognizable pair of green curtains. A well-executed boat on a blue sea followed soon after. This improvement in his ability to express himself in drawing was paralleled by concurrent improvement in his symptoms.

Case 4: Bernice, a 7-year-old girl, was first observed when she was at the height of a sexual affair in which she masturbated a 16-year-old boy.

Her symptoms consisted of disobedience, begging and stealing, exposing herself, and masturbating in public. Her excitement never abated. When asked to relate some incident or tell a story, she produced an incoherent mixture of fact and fantasy.

Her early finger paintings were equally incoherent and the fantasies concerning them equally senseless. As in the previous case, the story the little patient told about the pictures became intelligible long before the painting showed any discernible patterns or forms. Bernice would point to some part of the maze of twisted lines and say: "This is a bad man with a big knife, who is chasing the little girl to her house." Man, knife, girl, or house could be recognized nowhere in the drawing. The theme of impending assault persisted, however, and the patient was not able to express any other fantasy in relation to her paintings. Finally, through her drawings, we became aware of her sexual behavior.

As treatment was continued and the problem discussed, her anxiety and excitement began to abate. The progress of treatment was clearly recorded by the finger paintings. Soon a man, a knife, a girl, and a house could be recognized in the drawings. The threatening man characteristically appeared in the same part of the painting each time. Bernice showed her readiness to renounce her interest in the object of her sexual play when she spontaneously blotted out that part of her painting which the threatening man usually occupied. Liberated from this all-encompassing interest, the compulsion to tell the same story about each painting disappeared. The choice of subjects for her paintings was now much wider and varied over the range of a child's normal interests. She was able to paint with greater ease, using fewer movements, better planning, and several distinct colors, instead of an over-all mixture of many colors.

In the dynamics of therapy, finger painting may be used by the patient for purposes of resistance as well as overcoming resistance. We have cited several typical examples of children who were aloof and indifferent to their creations, as if to indicate that they felt only distantly related to their paintings. This attitude may be expressed both in the manner of painting and in the content of the picture. Other children, or the same children at other times, may paint with obvious emotion. In such instances, even before the content of the drawing or the fantasy is made known, the intensity of the patient's movements and his application to the task foretell the revelation of significant data. Often it was possible to circumvent a patient's resistance during an interview by shifting from conversation to painting.

In Case 2, while discussing the death of his grandfather, for example, Paul became aware that he could think of nothing further to say. At this point it was suggested that he paint. Though unable to talk, he was able to paint, and produced the picture with the hidden pit in the road. The painting plainly revealed the cause of his resistance. During the discussion of his grandfather's burial, Paul was struggling with a fantasy of burying his brother. The painting thus acted like a dream made to order for the purpose of overcoming the resistance.

When resistance is strong, the patient may become completely inhibited; that is, he may be unable to paint at all, and may experience uneasiness and anxiety. This situation may persist for varying lengths of time but is usually dissipated because the patient finds a discharge for his anxiety in the motor activity of the apparently meaningless smearing movements. These early movements of spreading the paint, so aimless and neutral, seem very safe to the patient and help to assuage his anxiety.

The conflict between the resistance and the emerging unconscious wish is often dramatically acted out by the patient while he is trying to paint. This was obvious in the case of Paul. After having spread the paint over the sheet, he was unable to proceed. Several times he moved his fingers toward the paper, but withdrew them. He then drew an animal, but instantly marked it out. Again he stood before the sheet unable to proceed, appearing very tense. He finally drew the animal and completed the picture by drawing a young boy pursuing the animal with a stick. When he had completed the painting he said: "I have a very funny feeling." Later he explained that he had tried very hard not to draw the animal, but try as he might, nothing else would come to his mind and he felt compelled to return to the theme of the fleeing animal. On only one occasion was this patient completely unable to paint. This occurred after his wish to do away with the younger brother was clearly revealed. Naturally, the question arose: What possible motive could he have for such an impulse?

Paul failed to keep his next appointment. At the following session, after preparing his sheet he was unable to paint. He turned to the examiner after a painful pause and said: "I can't paint today. . . . I don't want to paint . . . You tell me what to do. . . ." Since this was a departure from his usual practice he was asked to explain. He explained that while traveling in the subway to the interview, he had thought of the dream he was going to tell. In his dream, he and his younger brother are escaping from some danger. They come to a picket fence. He gets by successfully, but the brother does not. Then for the first time he thought in advance of a possible subject for his painting. It occurred to him that a picket fence and a small boy would be a good theme. Suddenly there flashed into his mind the thought: "No, don't! That would be giving too much away." The patient thus confessed that he did not trust himself to paint for fear of revealing too much repressed material. As it developed, the picket fence dream and painting were a repetition of an almost identical event which served as the precipitating incident of the neurosis.

At some period in treatment almost every patient produces a characteristic painting which we have come to recognize as a "resistance painting." Such a drawing consists of a simple design repeated over and over again so as to cover the sheet completely. The wish to "cover up" is acted out. The children themselves learn the implication of these paintings very quickly. One little patient after completing such a painting, looked at it, laughed and said: "I guess I'm not going to do much talking today." This was true.

Very frequently abstract forms are painted by the patient with such persistence that one suspects important material with emotional coloring is hidden behind a screen of abstract designs. In such instances, if the patient is left undisturbed, he may ultimately gather enough courage to commit himself in a painting. A 9-year-old boy persisted in drawing abstract forms about which he could produce no fantasy. The intensity of his movements, however, suggested that something very disturbing was hidden behind the abstractions. At last he painted a picture of a dancing girl but threw the painting out of the window before he thought anyone had seen it. In explanation he stated that he had been thinking of something which no good boy should ever do. Later interviews revealed a conflict over masturbating to the fantasy of dancing girls.

The manner in which the finger painting and the fantasy express resistance to therapy is very similar to that of the dream. As a matter of fact, the parallelism between dreams, painting, and fantasy is most striking in relation to the problem of resistance. One patient, for example, was quite surprised when one of his paintings pointed to his sexual experiences. The interpretation of the painting was confirmed by a dream which the patient had had the previous night which he had intended to withhold. The themes of the dream and the painting were identical, but a slight change of locale in the painting led directly to the interpretation of the traumatic situation. This unexpected revelation apparently came upon an insufficiently prepared patient. He did not keep four of the next eight appointments. He was much disturbed, trying to decide whether to continue treatment. During this period of indecision he made the following paintings.

1. A boy arrives at a fork in the road; cannot decide which way to turn.
2. An armed guard is protecting a precious storage tank against sabotage by enemy spies. The tank he associated with gas tanks near the Mental Hygiene Clinic.
3. Two boys are on a road which winds endlessly toward the horizon.

This painting was made twice. He identified the two figures as himself and his illness. The road to recovery seemed long and endless.

The ending of this period of resistance was foretold in another painting in which a boy comes upon a huge stone which blocks his path. At first he is undecided whether to walk around the stone or to tackle it directly and roll it away. The decision in the fantasy to roll the stone away indicates the patient's readiness to talk about his sexual problem. The painting part of the session was terminated and in the ensuing interview the patient finally resumed discussion of his sexual conflict.

We might say briefly that almost every dynamic mechanism of defense observed during psychoanalysis has some counterpart in the patient's relation to his finger painting.

The choice and use of colors proved of singular importance. The particular color selected was an almost unfailing index of the mood of the patient and the theme of the painting. One girl used light blue for a painting, the "Ship of Success" coming into port; green for a study of music and the musical instrument which she hoped would bring her recognition; brown for the burial of a faithless friend; black for a drawing of bars which reminded her that living in an institution was like being a prisoner.

Paul (Case 2) once made two companion paintings on the same day. The first, a young boy at the bottom of a pit, unable to escape and doomed to die, was painted in black. The second was that of an older boy at the top of the pit having successfully evaded death, which was painted in light blue. The color selections were made quite unconsciously; even before he knew what he was going to draw he searched through the jars saying: "Where are the darker colors?" This infallibly predicted the type of painting. Death was invariably executed in black; themes of hostility or aggression were executed in brown or black.

As a rule this was true of all our patients. A young refugee boy, who had been through the London blitz and had developed a severe neurosis upon separation from his parents, could paint nothing but fighter planes crashing to the earth in black, brown, and red. His theme and selection of colors never varied. Conversely, bright colors were chosen for happy scenes.

An interesting use of color was made by Muriel, age 11, who was a bed wetter. She identified herself with the color yellow. She was a middle child who resented the attentions showered on her younger brother, the only boy. The one occasion which he had not spoiled for her was the only birthday party her parents had given her, for which they had bought her a bright yellow dress. Her paintings repeated the theme of three siblings quarreling with each other; and whether these were pictured as animals, flowers, or humans, she was invariably identified with the yellow one.

Very few children chose red as the sole color for a painting. A notable exception was a 6-year-old boy, who was on a fire-setting spree. A few enuretic girls also drew burning houses repeatedly in red.

Younger children, age 4 to 10, preferred to use several colors, usually the primary ones, which they frequently employed in striking combinations. Their reactions indicated immediate color appreciation, showing a very primitive pleasure of color. As a rule they did not mix colors to produce any of the intermediate shades. Older children preferred to use a single color, usually an intermediate shade, apparently centering their interest on the form and content of their paintings. Inhibited, frightened, and insecure children were partial to the darker colors and, in the younger groups, used only one color as a rule. Such children may be unable to adapt themselves to finger painting as such; instead they may dip an individual finger into the paint jar and use the finger as a pencil or crayon, thereby indicating reluctance to avail themselves of the less formalized means of expression which finger painting permits. Those children who fail to cover the sheet completely with paint may be suspected of being inhibited or frightened. Conversely, the inability of a child to limit himself to the paper is important diagnostically. Such a child may be suspected of being too aggressive or insufficiently inhibited. He can no more limit himself in painting than he can in other life situations.

The habits and technique employed during finger painting reflect very accurately the personality and habits of the painter. Together with the fantasy material which is elicited with relative ease in relation to these paintings, we are afforded quick and valuable insight into the organization of and the conflicts within the personality. The parallelism observed between the dream life and the fantasies concerning finger paintings is consistent and striking. It demonstrates clearly the significant role played by unconscious forces in the elaboration of daydreams and in the process of artistic creation. We hope through finger painting to make a further study of this problem.

Shaw (1938) has suggested that the neurotic child, by repeatedly painting his fears onto paper, may discharge his anxiety and free himself from his symptoms. We have not found this to be the case. Although finger painting may be used as a locus for displacement of anxiety, it does not relieve the anxiety per se. The way in which the anxiety-producing fantasy reappears and is elaborated in finger painting is most impressive. The fantasy persists in an almost compulsive manner restricting the patient's productivity and interests until the underlying conflict is resolved either by life or by psychotherapy. Our case material has demonstrated that it was the resolution of the underlying conflict which caused both the persistent fantasy and the related symptom to disappear. Getting the child to express his fantasies during finger painting is therapeutically futile unless his productions can be related to the traumatic life situation from which they've originated. In other words, the experiences derived from finger painting must be integrated with the developing ego.

In personal conversations we have heard the opinion expressed that finger painting may prove to be further destructive to a disintegrating ego which has already begun to abandon reality, by encouraging fantasy formation and facilitating the appearance of more symbolic rather than more concrete forms of expression. The feeling is that on a psychological plane finger painting fosters chaos. The premise upon which such a fear is based is incorrect. Like other forms of behavior and expression, finger painting is but a manifestation of the capacities and organizational strength of the ego. A disturbed personality will produce chaotic finger paintings. As the individual responds to therapy, the paintings become more explicit. The cases of Bernice and Allan illustrate the course of events. When these two very severely disturbed children were finally able to cope with their fears, they were also able to paint explicitly, using concrete symbols in well-defined patterns. Often only through finger painting were we able to discover the disintegrating element in the personality.

In our experience the consistent use of finger painting has proved very valuable in treating children with behavior problems and neuroses. Within the framework of a controlled situation it permits observation of personality and motor patterns. It facilitates the emergence of fantasies and personality trends. The finger painting acts both as a record of the psychotherapeutic experience and as an objective measure of the progress of treatment. Above all, it affords an excellent means of confronting the individual with trends in his own creations. Since these productions are recorded in paint in his own unmistakable style, the young patient finds it very difficult to repudiate them. He "sees" what he has been doing.

References

Bender, L., and Woltmann, A. G. (1941–1942). Play and psychotherapy. *Nervous Child* 1, 1.

Fleming, J. (1940). Observations in the use of finger painting in the treatment of adult patients with personality disorders. *Character and Personality.*

Lyle and Shaw. (1937). Encouraging children to express their phantasies. *Bulletin of the Menninger Clinic* 1, 3.

Mosse, C. P. (1940). Painting analysis in the treatment of neurosis. *Psychoanalytic Review.*

Obendorf, C. P. Quoted by Mosse.

Shaw, R. F. (1938). *Finger Painting.* Boston: Little, Brown.

Spring, W. J. (1935). Words and masses. *Psychoanalytic Quarterly.*

15

The Squiggle-Drawing Game

LAWRENCE CLAMAN

The resistance of latency-age children to direct discussion of their problems and feelings has stimulated child psychotherapists to seek additional ways to communicate. Traditional nondirective play therapy is limited in its ability to focus verbally on the child's problems. Though projective and semi-projective techniques have been used in diagnostic evaluations of children, these techniques have not been utilized therapeutically in a systematic fashion.

Winnicott (1971) introduced his squiggle technique to communicate by metaphor with his child patients. He utilized a squiggle-drawing game as the core of his short-term consultations. The goal of the technique was to establish communication with the child's inner thoughts and feelings through an interchange that "unhitches something at the place where the patient's development is hitched up." Winnicott's largely intuitive approach was based on his cognitive-emotional assessment of the child's developmental level, and was a short-term intervention (1 to 3 interviews). He felt more long-term use of the technique would be ineffective because "the problems of the transference and resistance begin to appear."

Gardner (1971, 1975) and Kritzberg (1975) developed more systematic techniques of therapeutic communication by metaphor for children in psychotherapy.

Gardner (1971) stated: "Few children are interested in gaining conscious awareness of their unconscious processes let alone utilizing such insights therapeutically." He felt that children enjoy telling and listening to stories, and that this approach could be used for "the imparting and transmission of values and insights. . . ." He developed a mutual-storytelling technique to implement this approach, which he later elaborated technically by utilizing additional play materials and by developing the Talking, Feeling and Doing Game (a board game).

Kritzberg (1975), who worked collaboratively with Gardner, built on Gardner's concept more systematically in his structured-therapeutic game method of child analytic psychotherapy. He developed two games, TASKIT (an adaptation of the popular Scrabble game) and TISKIT (a game almost identical to Gardner's Board of Objects Game which utilizes objects to elicit thematic material) and designed a structured means of communication with the child through metaphor.

It is the purpose of this chapter to present the application of the approach of Gardner and Kritzberg to utilizing Winnicott's squiggle technique as a therapeutic modality in child psychotherapy. The following aspects of the squiggle-drawing game will be discussed: (1) technique of the game, (2) therapist's role, (3) child's drawings and stories, and (4) therapist's drawings and stories. A review of the relevant literature will be included.

Squiggle-Drawing Game

The mechanics of the game are introduced after ascertaining that the child is interested and willing to draw. The child is asked if he would like to play a "fun drawing game—the squiggle-drawing game."

The game is explained as follows: "Each of us will have a piece of paper and a pencil. I will draw a squiggle and you will make any kind of drawing you like out of it, then you'll make up a story about your drawing, and I will ask a few questions about it (your drawing and story). Then you will draw a squiggle which I will make a drawing out of, tell a story about it, and you can ask me questions about it." Thus the game involves making a drawing out of a squiggle, telling a story, asking and being asked questions and taking turns. A squiggle is any variation of a straight, curved, wavy or zigzag line. Skill in drawing is unimportant, and there is mutual interaction and sharing of thematic material. After the explanation, or while giving it, the therapist and child sit down side by side at a table or desk. The therapist provides the child and himself with paper and pencil for drawing. He also provides himself with a piece of paper for taking notes. The therapist initiates the game by drawing the first squiggle on which the child is supposed to build. It is desirable for the child to develop the first story so that the therapist is better able to decide what theme to use on his turn. If the child does not understand the directions, the order may be reversed and the child draws the first squiggle. Once initiated, the game is continued as long as it is therapeutically productive and interactively enjoyable. The following examples illustrate the child's response in playing the game:

Case 1

Aaron, an 11-year-old boy, was in psychotherapy because of compulsive rituals which he used to ward off angry feelings. He was a shy, quiet boy of above-average intelligence who did well in school but had poor peer relations. He appeared to be a good candidate for a drawing game since one of his rituals was drawing detailed maps. The squiggle-drawing game was introduced in the third interview. In the fourth interview, his third drawing (Figure 15–1) was of a "prehistoric animal who survived in a warm valley and finally found a friend of his own kind outside the valley and wasn't sad anymore

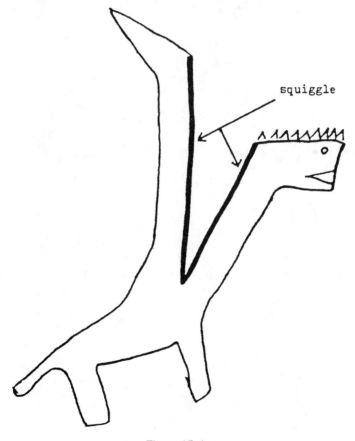

Figure 15–1.

because he had a friend." This clearly dealt with his peer relationship problem.

Case 2

Beth, an 11½-year-old girl, had been seen in psychotherapy every other week for almost two years because of behavior difficulties, poor school performance despite average intelligence, feelings of insecurity and inadequacy, poor self-image, and poor peer relations. She made good use of projective game techniques including the squiggle-drawing game. Two months before terminating treatment, she was physically in early adolescence without having started her menses. She played the squiggle drawing game and her second drawing (Figure 15–2) was of "Cleopatra riding on her camel

squiggle

Figure 15–2.

and having snakes on her head . . . kings and queens of Egypt have snakes on their head . . . Cleopatra is going to exercise and ride all over the desert." The drawing and thematic material suggested a significant improvement in her self-image through identification with Cleopatra.

Therapist's Role

The role of the therapist in the game is to carry out an empathic, collaborative, interactive psychotherapy focused on the child's problems and stage of development. The therapist is guided by the content and structure of the child's drawings and stories to help the child express his thoughts, feelings, and concerns in displaced, thematic form. The therapist shares through his own drawings and stories his understanding of the child's problems and suggests possible solutions. The therapist is not only challenged by this technique, but is helped in the process because the participant child enjoys his own drawing and story-telling as well as the therapist's. The game is truly collaborative and is part of an ego-oriented psychotherapy.

The Child's Drawing and Stories

The child's drawings, although symbolic, are primarily a means of getting the child to tell about himself in displaced fashion. The stories are as essential to specific, clear understanding of the child's drawings as associations are essential to understanding dreams. The child may be asked to rotate the squiggle in making a drawing to stimulate associations and is told to make up a story about imaginary persons, things, events, and experiences, not about himself, people he knows, or his own experiences. The child is encouraged to start his stories with the phrase "Once upon a time, far, far away, a long time ago. . . ." The child is helped to understand that his story should fit an action model of experience. As Kritzberg (1975) has stated, such a story "means that something happens to someone, or some animal, or something; that someone or some thing does something, and that most stories have a beginning, a middle and an end." The child is also asked if his story has any special message so that he can summarize its meaning.

The following example illustrates the varied thematic material in the squiggle-drawing-game stories told by one child in a single interview:

Beth, the 11½-year-old girl, played the squiggle-drawing game and produced the following four stories and drawings (Figures 15–3, –4, –5, and –6).

Figure 15–3.

Self-Portrait (with a rose in her hair): She is holding flowers and giving them or selling them to people for a dime.

Proud Horn (deer) in India: He is looking over the hill. If anybody comes or hurts the other deer, he would go and prong them with his horn. He also fought the other deer for the female. She (girl) wishes she had a real horse so she could ride him everyday.

Snail Eating a Tomato: He goes out at night and eats people's tomatoes which they have grown. He is real mean and has real sharp teeth.

Big Kitten: He is a tramp and he sings "I like cat food." He walks through the house and wants to get out and all the cats go by and meow at him because they like him. "He is our cat."

The pictures and stories suggest the girl's core conflicts. She has conflict in her identity in being feminine or masculine. The self-portrait and story suggest she feels she has little to offer as a girl. The proud-horn drawing and story suggest strong identification with aggressive masculinity, though she would also like males to fight for her favors. Her wish to ride a horse every day appears to be tied in with her masculine strivings (she rides occasionally in real life). Her pride and identification in being a cat-tramp who is liked by everybody further asserts her masculine strivings, but also represents a wish for herself in real life (long-term experience of being rejected by peers). The story in connec-

Figure 15–4.

tion with the snail drawing suggests she feels she has to be mean and steal to meet her needs.

The Therapist's Drawings and Stories

The therapist's primary role is to help the child express his own thoughts, feelings, and concerns in displaced thematic form. The therapist needs to share through his own drawings and stories his understanding of what problems the child is struggling with and suggest possible solutions. In carrying out this task, the therapist must be guided by the content and structure of the child's drawings and stories.

When the therapist makes a drawing from the child's squiggle, he must be free to interact with the squiggle as a percept. Hopefully, a number of possible drawing choices will come to mind, and he will choose a useful metaphor to generate a meaningful story for the child. More often than not, the therapist will not know the story he is going to tell until he has completed the drawing. It is not a disadvantage for the therapist to draw poorly. This makes it easy for the child to feel he can

Figure 15–5.

Figure 15–6.

draw as well if not better than the therapist, and can be encouraging to the child.

Kritzberg (1975) suggests that the therapist create an action story with characters (animate or inanimate), a plot and some sort of outcome. The story should have a lesson or main idea which encourages the belief that the child can master his problems as well as suggesting a way to do so. This can be summarized when dynamically indicated.

Kritzberg (1975) proposes three categories of therapist stories that are useful: The "mirror story," the suggestive-directive story, and the indirect-interpretive story. The therapist should always be prepared to use a mirror story if he is unable to decide on a dynamically helpful story from his squiggle. In this story, the therapist repeats a story of the child from earlier in the same interview with minor changes in the characters, the situation and the action. For example, in a child's story involving a chase, the lion can be changed to a bear, a forest to a mountain, and the outcome specifics altered slightly while conveying the same message. This supports the child's self-expression.

The suggestive-directive story presents themes about life that encourage the child to feel he can master his problems. These themes can be categorized within a libidinal-psychosocial developmental framework. They can be related to specific tasks of development for the latency-age child. And they can be expressed in colloquial phrases that have specific meaning for the child. The following categories are based on Kritzberg (1975):

1. *Trust theme.* "You need to try to trust people." "Give people a chance before you decide they're against you." "Don't be afraid of people."

2. *Being-assertive theme.* "You can stand up for yourself." "Don't let other kids push you around." "It's okay to be aggressive and fight for yourself."

3. *Persistence theme.* "Keep going." "Push on." "Don't be discouraged by obstacles." "If you stick with things, you'll succeed."

4. *Peer-relationship theme.* "It pays to have friends." "It's fun to have other kids to play with." "Don't be afraid of kids picking on you."

5. *Value-of-talking theme.* "Talking is helpful." "Let people know how you feel." "It's good to have someone listen to you."

6. *Value-of-exploring theme.* "It's worthwhile looking into things." "Explore further; there are interesting things to find out." "There are always new things to find out about."

In telling stories on the value-of-talking and the value-of-exploring themes, there are many metaphoric representations of therapy. Kritzberg (1975) suggests the following: a jungle safari, underseas exploration, archaeological expedition, investigation of outer space, or finding a cure for a disease; a conversation or talk with a teacher, old friend, minister, wise man, guru, doctor, or counselor; a productive or work activity such as altering or repairing houses or cars; an artistic or creative activity such as writing, painting, sculpting, or designing.

The following story summaries show how to use different theme categories (more than one category may be utilized in a sample story)— these pictures and stories were used by the therapist in two different interviews with Aaron, the 11-year-old boy:

1. *Being-assertive theme.* Picture: surfer riding a giant wave. Story: the surfer rides the wave successfully because of his skill and courage despite being scared and almost engulfed.

2. *Value-of-exploring theme.* Picture: three men in a canoe paddling along a winding river lined with trees. Story: three explorers in Africa who are looking for a lost African tribe that has a secret early language which tells about the beginnings of man.

3. *Being-assertive and persistence themes.* Picture: high, old-fashioned car. Story: demolition derby where car looks different and is strong, has a skillful driver, demolishes fifteen other cars and becomes the champion even though badly damaged.

4. *Peer-relationship theme.* Picture: two protozoa in the process of fusing with each other. Story: two protozoa who are frightened of each other, feel each other out, make contact, fuse and become one larger stronger protozoan.

The therapist hopes that the child has understood the story and will respond to it by using some part (element of theme) in his next story.

The indirect-interpretive story focuses on a current problem of the child. It may also include transference and resistance issues encountered in therapy. A story dealing with a current problem can involve a latency-age child who is afraid of the water and of learning to swim. His mother is trying to get him to take swimming lessons. The child has avoided discussing the problem in therapy. The therapist can tell about a young beaver who is so afraid of the water that he cannot learn to swim even though all beavers swim. His mother is unable to coax him into the water. Then a friendly, playful older boy beaver comes along, starts playing games with the young beaver, gets him to play in the shallow water so that he has fun, and helps him overcome his fear enough so that he learns to swim and is no longer afraid of the water.

Discussion

To understand children's drawings and stories, the therapist must consider psychodynamic issues, the kinds of symbols used, how feelings are experienced and understood, and the level of cognitive functioning.

Children's drawings and stories usually include a representation of themselves as a part-symbol of a good or bad aspect or attribute. For example, a policeman can represent a child's "good" controlling part (superego) and a robber his "bad" impulsive part (id). Pitcher and Pre-linger (1963) studied the stories made up by a nonclinical population of preschool age children to determine the most common themes and defenses. The most common themes involved abandonment and separation, fear of getting pregnant, sibling rivalry, fear of sex, oedipal themes in boys, and the wish of girls to be a boy. The most frequently used defenses were denial, undoing, and repression. Rationalization, reaction formation, identification with the aggressor and intellectualization were less often used.

Kritzberg (1975) has discussed the categories of symbols children use in their stories in detail. Three main categories are: (1) symbols of objects (actors, characters or participants in events); (2) symbols of action, events and happenings; and (3) symbols of impulses, affects, moods, and feelings.

Object-symbols include person-symbols and animal-symbols of both sexes, and inanimate object symbols (natural and man-made). Parents can be represented by a real or imaginary person who is good or bad such as a teacher, principal, doctor, lawyer, general, king, queen, devil, witch, or fairy. The possibilities for person, animal and inanimate symbols are limitless and can encourage the imagination of both the child and therapist. The choice of symbols is dynamically meaningful. Kritzberg (1975) emphasizes the value of symbols in providing the child with psychological distance from his interpersonal problems while allowing thematic expression of them. Animal-symbols have special appeal for children and are to be encouraged because they provide distancing.

Impulses, affects, moods, and feelings can be expressed directly or through symbols. People, animals, and even inanimate objects are described as feeling scared, angry, happy, sad, friendly, jealous, or loving. The symbols often represent energetic, powerful, explosive natural or man-made forces. They usually represent threatening impulses, feelings, and ideas. Kritzberg (1975) provides an imaginative list of possibilities: "fire, hurricanes, storms, tornadoes, the sea, floods, raging rivers, earthquakes, blizzards, atomic explosions, bacteriological and chemical warfare agents, diseases, etc."

It is important to inquire about any story to clarify its meaning and the feeling involved. For example, the child is asked in a patient, encouraging manner to fill in the details about what kind of person or animal is involved, and what he felt at key points in the story.

To inquire appropriately about feelings, it is important to know how latency-age children experience and understand emotions. Taylor (1974) studied a nonclinical population of 256 grade-school pupils to determine the processes by which emotions are named and described. The pupils were asked how they experienced or might describe physiologically toned words such as hungry, thirsty, and sleepy, and psychologically toned words such as sad, happy, angry, scared, and nervous. A significant developmental discrepancy was noted. Children of all ages were able to define what they wanted to do when they felt hungry, thirsty, and sleepy.

However only among the older children could a majority say what they wanted to do when they felt sad, happy, angry, scared, and nervous. Not surprisingly, the older children relied more on internal cues instead of external cues to describe their emotional experience. Similarly, the older children more often provided a given emotion with an internal locus or body zone. For example, thirsty was associated with mouth and throat, hungry with stomach, angry with head and brain, and nervous with extremities. The older children also avoided sad feelings and used coping tactics for angry feelings.

To understand a child's stories and carry out an inquiry, it is also important to understand the latency-age child's cognitive functioning. Elkind (1973) has discussed latency behavior attributable to the child achieving Piaget's developmental cognitive stage of concrete operations. He details three important attainments of the latency-age child in interpersonal communication and relations: "First, the child at this stage can take another person's point of view and engage in true communication, with give and take about a particular subject. Second, the child at this level is capable of comparing what he hears and sees with what he knows and is, therefore, able to make judgments regarding truth and falsehood and regarding reality and appearance. Third, the latency-age child is now able not only to reason from premise to conclusion but also from general to particular instance so that he can now operate according to rules." Elkind emphasizes how the child's ability to understand another's point of view leads to his assimilation into the peer culture. This "provides the child with modes of peer interaction, such as jokes, jeers, taunts, superstition, quasi beliefs, ritual and so on." This can only be learned from peers. This assimilation causes an estrangement from some fantasies such as Santa Claus, fairies, giants, and the like. "The latency-age child may still enjoy such fictions but he makes it known that he is well aware that they are not real and are merely make believe." Elkind also discusses latency behavior attributable to egocentrism. This involves the child's tendency to reject or alter facts so that they fit his own hypotheses. This is operating according to "assumptive realities." The latency-age child assumes that adults are not very bright and can be easily outwitted when they are discovered to be wrong on occasion and not omniscient. This cognitive conceit supports the child's egocentrism and presupposes a world which children can master because they can make facts do their own bidding. This is why children like stories of mystery, adventure, and magic.

The potential value of communicating with children through stories is supported by Bettelheim's (1976) detailed review of the meaning and importance of fairy tales to children. Fairy tales appeal to children according to their stage of emotional development. These tales picture an imaginary world in black and white terms in which good wins out over evil. They encourage the hope that the child can emerge victorious in his struggle against the unavoidable dangers and difficulties of life.

References

Bettelheim, B. (1976). *The Uses of Enchantment.* New York: Alfred A. Knopf.

Elkind, D. (1973). Cognitive structure in latency behavior. In *Individual Differences in Children.* New York: Wiley.

Gardner, R. A. (1971). *Therapeutic Communication with Children: The Mutual Storytelling Technique.* New York: Jason Aronson.

_____ (1975). *Psychotherapeutic Approaches to the Resistant Child.* New York: Jason Aronson.

Kritzberg, N. I. (1975). *The Structured Therapeutic Game Method of Psychoanalytic Psychotherapy.* Hicksville, NY: Exposition.

Pitcher, E. G., and Prelinger, E. (1963). *Children Tell Stories: An Analysis of Fantasy.* New York: International Universities Press.

Taylor, E. K. (1974). The developmental study of the language of emotions. *Journal of the American Academy of Child Psychiatry* 13:667.

Winnicott, D. W. (1971). *Therapeutic Consultations in Child Psychiatry.* New York: Basic Books.

16

The Emotional Barometer

SUZANNE ELLIOTT

The first few minutes of the counseling session are important in setting the tone and preparing the client for counseling. In working with elementary age children, counselors' valuable time can be lost through exchanging pleasantries before getting to relevant issues. To solve this problem I have developed a graphic aid called the *emotional barometer* to help engage elementary age children in the counseling process in a nonthreatening manner.

Background

Initially, as a counselor trying to focus on how students feel or what might be an issue with them, I frequently resorted to a system used when I was a teacher. While moving around the class in the morning to check homework assignments, I would ask my students to rate how they felt that day on a 10-point scale ranging from *awful* (0) to *excellent or super* (10). Thus, I was quickly able to assess the mood of my students and consequently know who might need some special attention that day. This same method has worked in counseling sessions as an ice breaker and a graphic record of students' feelings over time.

The 10-point scale was developed into a graphic emotional barometer after I read LaFountain's (1983) description of a graphic checklist used to promote communication and change with self-referring students. While trying out the barometer in an elementary school counseling setting, I have added additional parts from the creative ideas of students.

The emotional barometer refers to a visual scale with happy faces. It is a valuable graphic aid to help children understand the concept of a rating scale ranging from 1 to 10. When introducing the barometer (see Figure 16–1) I am able to determine each client's emotion and feeling vocabulary as the faces and the area in between are discussed. Thus, the "0" end of the scale becomes "life is the PITS," whereas the "10" represents "life is GREAT."

With additional use the barometer has evolved into a more sophisticated form. A score of − 5 has been added to the bottom of the scale to indicate that life is the "SUPER PITS." As one of my students contemplated the smiling face one day, he commented that, "He's so happy that he's bursting!" Therefore, space has been added to the top of the scale to indicate that life is "better than great."

Method

At the start of each session, I ask clients to draw a line on the barometer to indicate how things are going for them. Clients will often choose to draw a tie, a star, or a corresponding facial expression if they are between the − 5 and 0 scores or between 0 and 10. A few children like to shade in the barometer like a thermometer. Sometimes students use different colors to shade in the space, relating colors to feelings (e.g., warm colors for relaxed and contented feelings).

To be more directive, I ask clients to indicate how things are going

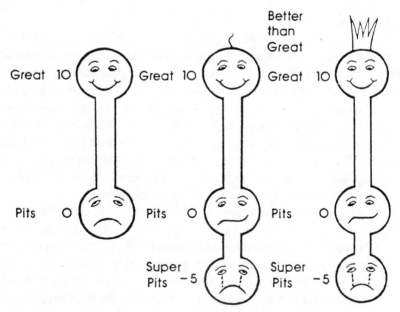

Figure 16–1.   Evolution of the Emotional Barometer

for them in a specific area, such as home, schoolwork, or friendships. At times I ask for an indication from more than one area of their lives. After a few sessions, I find that clients, when asked how things are going for them, often indicate these key areas on their own.

After I have the indication of how things are on the barometer, I often write the negative and positive things that are happening to the students on opposite ends of a "balance" (see Figure 16–2). This visual "teeter totter" or scale allows the counselor and students to see:

1. Personal strengths and weaknesses of students
2. The degree of ego strength
3. The number of positive or negative aspects existing in their lives and which is predominant
4. Awareness of others' perceptions (teachers and parents) of the existing problems
5. Areas of immediate concern.

I have found that after these issues are out in the open they seem more real and the child can relate to something concrete. When the counselor focuses on one of the issues, the student can refer to the barometer to relate what it is like when that particular issue arises. Because the issue has become more concrete and seems less threatening to the client, the counselor can gain access more easily to the client's feelings and move to more inner work.

If I have a nonverbal student and the barometer indicates that things are not going well, the opportunity arises to do some reflective work regarding the client's feelings and to relate present issues with past problems. When the barometer indicates things are going well, students are usually willing to talk about positive things that are happening in their lives. Discussion of these positive things provides opportunities to review growth as well as to reevaluate counseling goals with the children.

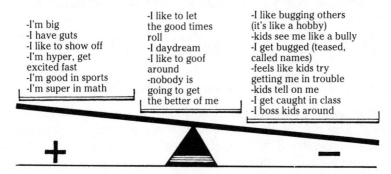

Figure 16–2.   The Balance (Example of an Intake Session)

Results

Using the barometer usually stimulates students to raise the issues that are pertinent to them, thus allowing the counselor to work in a less threatening manner. Getting the issues out in the open creates a catharsis for the client and provides a path for action and change. An example of a session using the barometer follows.

> *Counselor:* Hi, Cathy. How are you? How has the week been? I wonder if you would mark on the barometer how things have been for you since we met on Monday?
>
> *Cathy:* Hmmm, I guess it's been about a 4. (Cathy places a line across the barometer at 4.)
>
> *Counselor:* Gosh, Cathy, I'm sorry to hear that things haven't gone very well for you. Would you tell me a little bit about what hasn't gone smoothly for you?
>
> *Cathy:* Well, when I go home after school, I have to look after my little brother because my mom's at work and he never does what I tell him. Then when my mom comes home she gets mad at us and everyone gets in a bad mood. I hate the yelling and fighting. It reminds me of when we lived with my dad.

Using this example, one can see how quickly children move into talking about real issues that concern them. After many sessions of using the barometer to determine how specific things are going in their lives, children will typically lead the counselor directly into these important issues.

> *Counselor:* Good morning, Geoff. It's good to see you today. I wonder how things have been going for you since we met on Tuesday? Could you mark the barometer to show me what life's been like for you?
>
> *Geoff:* Well, it's kind of mixed. At school I'm about a 9 because I'm getting all my work done. But the kids have been teasing me again about playing with younger kids, so that's about a 3. At home things are about a − 5 because mom's gone on a holiday and my dad's looking after us. (Geoff marks these areas on the barometer as he talks.) I hate it when my mom goes away because. . . .

When I initially ask children how they are, they will often say "fine" or "okay." This is a nebulous, distancing response, yet when clients mark their barometer at a 6 or 7, it gives more insight into what they are thinking and feeling. At that point, the counselor can say, "Jody, I heard you mention that things are fine, yet I notice your barometer reads about a 6. I wonder if there's something happening that's hard for you to talk about right now?" The counselor will usually notice a recognition reflex or the child will mutter an "uhhm." The counselor, through some reflective work on feelings, can then ascertain the level of pain or discomfort.

If clients are not forthcoming with information about what is happening in their lives, I have found it helpful to ask: "What kinds of things might have to change for you to feel like a 10?" or "Could you tell me a little bit about what is happening to you just now that is getting in the way of things being a 9 or 10?"

Imagery can also be used with clients to illustrate what might be damming up or blocking the barometer from reaching a 10. The client and counselor can brainstorm a list of things that might be creating the dam. In addition to providing a record of client concerns, the list enables the clients to see graphically what the issues are as they draw a dam and fill it with the problems. Imagery also provides an opportunity for counselors to use art or play media with their clients by having the children draw a picture of these "blocks" or their feelings concerning the issues. If the drawing process augments verbal interaction with the child, the counselor may want to pursue a directed art counseling approach (Allan and Clark 1984) or a technique called serial drawing (Allan 1978) as an effective treatment technique. All of the techniques mentioned above provide further graphic avenues for exploring the client's unconscious world.

Discussion

One of the more beneficial aspects of using the emotional barometer is that it seems to take the focus away from the stressful aspect of coming in and talking with the counselor about issues that are painful. The focus shifts from the child to the less direct approach of communicating through the images on paper. After using the barometer, several of my students have chosen to draw and reproduce their own copies (see Figure 16–3) for their personal record to be used outside of the counseling sessions.

Whether using their own barometers or the ones I provide, students enjoy looking back at previous barometers to see how they are progressing. From this record they can begin to see the positive side of the balance and not just focus on the negative issues. Additionally, the recorded barometers become a great self-esteem builder as students' concerns move toward the positive side of the balance. It is exciting to watch the response of students as they see the changes they have been able to effect through counseling. After a list of blocks is written on the scale, students can determine the issues within their control. Work can then begin on those

Figure 16–3. Barometers Drawn by Students

changeable issues as counseling moves into a problem-solving and action mode with a visual balance of counseling goals.

Conclusion

The emotional barometer can be an extremely useful counseling technique for many reasons. The barometer is a nonthreatening way for students to identify pertinent issues while enabling the counselor to zero in on relevant data. Second, the barometer provides a record of the students' highs and lows and enables the counselor to see any patterns that may evolve. Third, progress toward goals can be readily evaluated. Through reflecting on the issues and reviewing the recorded barometers, the counselor can identify areas in which more in-depth work is necessary, tie up loose ends, and summarize changes. In summary, the emotional barometer can be used as a simple graphic tool by the counselor for the initial counseling session or as an in-depth record of counseling progress. The barometer technique provides a visual impression for students to monitor their own growth and progress toward positive self-esteem.

References

Allan, J. (1978). Serial drawing: a therapeutic approach with young children. *Canadian Counsellor* 12:223–228.

Allan, J., and Clark, M. (1984). Directed art counseling. *Elementary School Guidance & Counseling* 18:116–124.

LaFountain, R. (1983). Referrals and consultation. *Elementary School Guidance & Counseling* 17:226–231.

PART IV
Storytelling, Role-Playing, and Imagery Techniques

17

Mutual Storytelling

RICHARD A. GARDNER

The Mutual Storytelling Technique (Gardner 1968, 1969, 1970a,b, 1971), devised by the author as a method of communicating with the child patient at his own level, is useful in the treatment of a variety of psychogenic disorders of childhood. In this chapter, the basic technique will be reviewed and its utilization in child psychotherapy will be discussed.

Many techniques in child therapy are centered around the elicitation of stories. Each attempts to use such stories therapeutically. Some try to give, or help the child derive, insights into his stories. Others consider insight of little significance therapeutically. It is the author's opinion that some children can profit from insight and for others it is of little value. There is, however, a group of children who will tell stories, but who have little ability or inclination to derive conscious insights into their meaning. The author's technique enables the therapist to communicate meaningful insights to such children. It is based on the principle that although the child has communicated with stories, the therapist traditionally has been attempting to communicate at a different level, namely, analytic, educational, and so forth. If the therapist were to communicate to the child stories of his own which were meaningful and pertinent to the child's problems, he would be speaking the child's own language and would have a greater chance of being heard.

In this technique, the therapist, on hearing a story, surmises its psychodynamic meaning, selects one or two important themes, and then creates a story of his own, using the same characters in a similar setting. However, the therapist's story differs from that of the child in that he introduces healthier resolutions and maturer adaptations.

This approach employs one of the most ancient and powerful methods of communication. The fable, the legend, and the myth have proved universally appealing and potent vehicles for transmitting insights, values, and standards of behavior. The child is spared the anxiety he might experience with more direct attempts to impart or elicit conscious insights. One could say that the interpretations bypass the conscious, appeal to and are received by the unconscious. Direct verbalization, confrontation, and interpretation—so reminiscent of parents and teachers—are avoided. Psychoanalytic interpretations, often too alien for the child's comprehension, need not be employed.

The most common modalities around which stories are related are drawings, dolls, puppets, and other toys. The tape recorder has certain advantages over these more traditional devices. With it, there is total absence of stimuli which might restrict the story or channel it into specific directions. Eliciting a story with it is like obtaining a dream on demand. Since it is the author's instrument of choice, it will be used to demonstrate the details of his therapeutic technique. With minor modifications, the basic method can be utilized with dolls, drawings, blocks, and other toys.

I introduce the child to the game by first pointing to a stack of tapes, each of which has a child's name clearly written on the end of the box. I tell the patient that each child who comes to my office has his own tape for a tape-recording game that we play. I ask him if he would like to have a tape of his own. The child generally wants to follow usual practice, and having his own tape enhances his feeling of belonging. If he assents, I take out a new tape and let him write his name on the box.

I then ask the child if he would like to be guest of honor on a make-believe television program on which stories are told. If he agrees— and few decline the honor—the recorder is turned on and I begin:

> Good morning boys and girls. I'd like to welcome you once again to Dr. Gardner's "Make-Up-A-Story Television Program." As you all know, we invite children to our program to see how good they are at making up stories. Naturally, the more adventure or excitement a story has, the more interesting it is to the people who are watching at their television sets. Now, it's against the rules to tell stories about things you've read or have seen in the movies or on television, or about things that really happened to you or anyone you know.

> Like all stories, your story should have a beginning, a middle, and an end. After you've made up a story, you'll tell us the moral of the story. We all know that every good story has a moral.

Then after you've told your story, Dr. Gardner will make up a story too. He'll try to tell one that's interesting and unusual, and then he'll tell the moral of his story.

And now, without further delay, let me introduce to you a boy (girl) who is with us today for the first time. Can you tell us your name, young man?

I then ask the child a series of brief questions that can be answered by single words or brief phrases such as his age, address, school, grade, and teacher. These simple questions diminish the child's anxiety and tend to make him less tense about the more unstructured themes involved in making up a story. Further diminution of anxiety is accomplished by letting him hear his own voice at this point by playback, something which most children enjoy. He is then told: "Now that we've heard a few things about you, we're all interested in hearing the story *you* have for us today."

At this point most children plunge right into their story, although some may feel the need for time to think. I may offer this pause; if it is asked for by the child, it is readily granted.

While the child is engaged in telling his story, I jot down notes, which are not only of help in analyzing the child's story, but serve also as a basis for my own. At the end of the child's story and his statement of its moral, I may ask questions about specific items in the story. The purpose here is to obtain additional details, which are often of help in understanding the story. Typical questions might be: "Was the fish in your story a man or a lady?" "Why was the fox so mad at the goat?" "Why did the bear do that?" If the child hesitates to tell the moral of his story or indicates that there is none, I usually reply: "What, a story without a moral? Every good story has *some* lesson or moral!" The moral that this comment usually does succeed in eliciting from the child is often significantly revealing of the fundamental psychodynamics of the story.

For younger children, the word *lesson* or *title* may be substituted for *moral*. Or the child might be asked: "What can we learn from your story?"

Then I usually say: "That was a very good (unusual, exciting, etc.) story." Or to the child who was hesitant: "And you thought you weren't very good at telling stories!"

I then turn off the tape recorder and prepare my story. Although the child's story is generally simpler to understand than the adult's dream, the analysis of both follows similar principles. At this point, I will present a few of the fundamentals of story analysis.

I first attempt to determine which figure or figures in the child's story represent the child himself, and which stand for significant people in his environment. It is important to appreciate that two or more figures may represent various facets of the *same* person's personality. There may, for example, be a "good dog" and a "bad cat" in the same story, which are best understood as conflicting forces within the same child. A horde of figures, all similar, may symbolize powerful elements in a single person. A hostile father, for example, may be represented by a stampede of bulls. Swarms of small creatures such as insects, worms, or mice, often symbolize unacceptable repressed complexes. Malevolent figures can represent the child's own repressed hostility projected outward, or they may be a symbolic statement about the hostility of a significant figure. Sometimes both of these mechanisms operate simultaneously. A threatening lion in one child's story stood for his hostile father, and he was made more frightening by the child's own hostility, repressed and projected onto the lion. This example illustrates one of the reasons why many children see their parents as being more malevolent than they are.

Besides clarifying the symbolic significance of each figure, it is also important to get a general overall feel for the atmosphere and setting of the story. Is the ambience pleasant, neutral, or horrifying? Stories that take place in the frozen tundra or on isolated space stations suggest something very different from those that occur in the child's own home. The child's emotional reactions when telling the story are also of significance in understanding its meaning. An 11-year-old child who tells me, in an emotionless tone, about the death-fall of a mountain climber reveals not only his hostility but also his repression of his feelings. The atypical must be separated from the stereotyped, age-appropriate elements in the story. The former may be very revealing, whereas the latter rarely are. Battles between cowboys and Indians rarely give meaningful data, but when the chief sacrifices his son to Indian gods in a prayer for victory over the white man, something has been learned about the child's relationship with his father.

Lastly, the story may lend itself to a number of different psychodynamic interpretations. In selecting the theme that will be most pertinent for the child *at that particular time,* I am greatly assisted by the child's own moral or title.

After asking myself, "What would be a healthier resolution or a more mature adaptation than the one used by the child?," I create a story of my own. My story involves the same characters, setting, and initial situation as the child's story, but it has a more appropriate or salutary resolution of the most important conflicts. In creating my story, I attempt to provide the child with more *alternatives*. The communication that the child need not be enslaved by his neurotic behavior patterns is vital. Therapy must open new avenues not considered in the child's scheme of things. It must help the child become aware of the multiplicity of options that are available to replace the narrow self-defeating ones he has chosen. My moral or morals are an attempt to emphasize further the healthier adaptations I have included in my story. If, while I am telling my story, the child exhibits deep interest, or if he reveals marked anxiety, which may manifest itself by jitteriness or hyperactivity, then I know that my story is hitting home. Such clear-cut indications of how relevant one's story is are not, of course, always forthcoming.

I now present two verbatim therapist–patient story sequences that demonstrate specifically how one uses the technique.

Example 1

Bill, a 7-year-old boy was referred for therapy because of poor school performance and impaired peer relationships. Although very bright, he was not applying himself adequately to his school work. He had no friends because of refusal to share, domineering attitude, and bullying. He told this story during his fourth month in treatment.

Patient: Once upon a time in the ocean there was a boat and a sea diver went down from the boat. Always when the man went down, the man in the boat always went to town and then came back for the sea diver. And then one day he [the sea diver] ran out of air and the boat wasn't there. The man had taken the boat to town. And he had to wait a long time for the boat to come. And then the boat came and he hopped back on and then they went home, and he always made the boat stay there from now on. The end.

Therapist: I see. And the lesson of that story?

Patient: I can't think of the lesson.

Therapist: Hmm. Okay. Thank you very much. Now it's time for me to tell my story.

I considered the sea diver to represent the patient and the man in the boat his parents, especially his mother. They are the ones who supply him with vital sustenance, that is, oxygen. And the oxygen supply line symbolizes the umbilical cord. The story reveals Bill's concept of his parents as unreliable regarding their continually supplying him with vital nutriment. The boat in the story goes to town, leaving the diver alone without his oxygen supply. Bill cannot trust his parents. At any time he may be abandoned. The patient's parents were, indeed, extremely inhibited in their ability to express affection and were only intermittently capable of doing so. The story well reflects their impairment. However, the story reveals a healthy attempt by Bill to rectify the situation. He does not passively suffer the deprivation, but actively seeks to ensure his parents' continuing presence: "and he always made the boat stay there from now on." This represents advancement for this boy who, earlier in his therapy, did not even fantasize (let alone act on) asserting himself in the attempt to gain more involvement from his parents. Earlier stories of mine encouraged him in this regard and this story reveals that my messages were being heard. There is also an unrealistic wish fulfilled here as well, in that the story ends with his being successful in obtaining his goal of a constant permanent tie with them. They were in fact incapable of providing him with the depth of involvement he craved. With this understanding of the patient's story, I related mine:

Therapist: Once upon a time there was a boat in the ocean and there was a sea diver on it and the boat took the sea diver out into the ocean and the sea diver went down underneath the ocean. And while he was down there the boat left, and the sea diver was running out of air. He had some air but it was getting less and less and he had to wait a long time. Then finally the boat came back and he was kind of scared that he would have been completely out of air; that he would have been left without any air.

Well, after that he spoke to the boat and he said to the man in the boat, "Well, that was a terrible thing you did, leaving me there without air. I'm scared of going out with you again. If you're going to do a thing like that you can't expect me to go out with you."

Well, the man in the boat heard what the sea diver said and he began to be a little bit more concerned and would stay there most of the time, but not always. And then the sea diver realized that it would probably be a good idea for him to make other arrangements. He couldn't be sure that the boat would be there all the time; just some of the time. So he brought down a spare oxygen supply with him so that in case the boat left for a long time he would have his own oxygen supply. In addition, he made friends with another sea diver who had a boat taking him and at times he would go down together with that boy who was sea diving, and then he was less scared because he was with someone else who had oxygen. Also there was another boat there—the boat of the other boy sea diver. Also he had his own spare oxygen supply.

And the lesson of that story is what? What do you think is the lesson?

Patient: That if you're going to go down underneath the sea and you run out of oxygen, make the boat stay there?

Therapist: Well, he tried that, but the boat didn't always stay there so then what did he do?

Patient: He found another sea diver.

Therapist: Right, that was one thing he did and what was the other thing he did?

Patient: Brought more oxygen.

Therapist: Right. He had an extra supply of oxygen. The lesson is: if a person doesn't give you the things that you want—if you can't depend upon a person to do the things you want—then try to get them from other people and also do it on your own. This boy got oxygen from others and had others stay around when his boat wouldn't, and he also did it on his own by getting his own extra supply of oxygen. And that's the lesson of my story. The end.

In my story Bill is encouraged to utilize a number of alternative adaptations to his parents' impairments in providing him with adequate affection. First he is encouraged to communicate directly his frustration: "that was a terrible thing you did, leaving me without air." He advises them that such rejections will only result in his fearing and withdrawing from them: "I'm scared of going out with you again. If you're going to do a thing like that you can't expect me to go out with you." Hopefully such assertion will result in his parents providing him with more attention. However, as mentioned, they were significantly limited in this regard and so Bill had to be provided with reasonable alternatives. He is advised to seek his own sources of gratification (his own oxygen supply) and to involve himself with others who might provide him with affection (he made friends with another sea diver). More reliable adults as well might give him some compensatory affection (Also there was another boat there). Getting the patient to figure out the morals of my story is a good way of determining whether my messages are sinking in. Bill's responses in our interchange revealed that my messages were indeed being heard.

Example 2

John, a 6½-year-old boy was referred because of a severe stuttering problem. He was a "model child," markedly inhibited in asserting himself and expressing emotions, especially anger. He told this story during his second month of treatment (John's stuttering is not transcribed, but it was pervasive):

Patient: Once there was a kangaroo and this kangaroo could jump very high and he could jump over a two thousand and fifty hundred and eighty million height mountains. So one day he just tried something and he tried to jump over a mouse, but he *couldn't.* And he tried to jump over mountains and he *could.*

Therapist: Wait a minute. He *could* jump over mountains but he *couldn't* jump over a mouse?

Patient: Yeah.

Therapist: I see. That's funny. Go ahead.

Patient: Know why?

Therapist: Why?

Patient: Because he was afraid of mice.

Therapist: I see. He was afraid of mice. Then what?

Patient: Then he never jumped over a mouse again. So then one day he said, "I'm going to jump over that mouse!" So he did. And he was never afraid of mice again. The end.

Therapist: The lesson of that story?

Patient: If you think you're afraid and when you try you're not afraid.

Therapist: I see. Excellent story. Thank you very much. I have a question to ask you about your story. What was it exactly that he was afraid of with that mouse? Why was he scared of the mouse?

Patient: Because mice always bothered him.

Therapist: How did they bother him? What did they do?

Patient: Well, like they kept going in his baskets.

Therapist: They kept going in his baskets? Oh, you mean in his pouch—his belly?

Patient: Yeah.

Therapist: I see. They kept going in his pouch. I see. Is that it? Were you thinking of that before when you were telling the story?

Patient: Yes.

Therapist: That the mouse would jump into the pouch. What would the mouse do in the pouch?

Patient: He would tickle him.

Therapist: He would tickle him. And why was he afraid of that?

Patient: Because it made him fall.

Therapist: I see. It made him fall. I see. Okay. Very good. Thank you very much. Now it's time for me to tell my story.

Demonstrated here is the importance of the post-story inquiry in fully appreciating the meaning of the child's story. Although John admitted that he was thinking that the kangaroo feared that the mouse might jump into his pouch, he did not verbalize this information—so vital to the understanding of the story. The mouse symbolizes the patient (small and impotent) and the kangaroo his mother (the pouch, of course, represents her womb). I considered the mountain to stand for John's father (large and imposing). His mother is perfectly capable of jumping over the father, that is, getting close and intimate; but feared such involvement with John. The mouse, we are told, would tickle the kangaroo and make him fall down. Even playful involvement, as symbolized by tickling, was too much for her to bear. The fantasy reflects John's feeling that his mother considered taking care of him a burden—too heavy to bear—a weight which could cause her to "fall." In reality, John's mother enjoyed her social involvements, both with her husband and others, far more than child rearing. The anger John felt because of this rejection was repressed and its feared expression was playing a significant role in his stuttering problem.

The story reveals an improvement in the mother's relationship with John. She overcomes some of her fears of allowing him to get close to her, of allowing him to derive dependency gratification from her. This is well revealed in the lesson: "If you think you're afraid and when you try you're not afraid." The story reflects, at a symbolic level, changes that were occurring clinically. As the result of my work with John and his mother, both were getting closer to one another. The mother was becoming more comfortable with gratifying those dependency needs of John's that were appropriate to his age as well as other requests of his for closeness. With this understanding of the patient's story, I related mine:

Therapist: Once upon a time there was a kangaroo and this kangaroo could jump over mountains. She was a very big and strong kangaroo, but this kangaroo had a very funny idea about mice. This kangaroo thought that if a mouse were to go inside her pouch, which she had on her belly, that something terrible would happen. She was scared that the mouse might tickle her and that would be uncomfortable or she thought the mouse would be too heavy inside of her and would drag her down. So when she saw a mouse once she said, "You stay away from me, mouse. I don't want to have anything to do with you." The mouse said, "Why not?" And she said, "I just don't want to have anything to do with you." And the mouse said, "Tell me what's wrong?" And she said, "Well, I think you're going to be too much of a burden. You're going to be too heavy and you'll pull me down." The mouse said, "You'll see. I won't pull you down. I'm not that heavy. I won't stay in you all the time, I'll just stay in you part of the time and part of the time I'll be out and be on my own. But I won't hang onto you all the time."

And the kangaroo was afraid that the mouse would stay there all the time and weigh her down all the time. So she said, "Okay. Let me try you out." So she tried it out and she saw that the mouse was right—that sometimes he did get a little bit heavy, but other times he'd go out and play by himself. When the kangaroo felt that the mouse was a little too heavy she'd say, "All right, you go out and play now." And when he wasn't too heavy she would let him stay inside there. And she realized that he was right, that he didn't have to weight her down and be too heavy. Also she found that sometimes it was fun being with him and he would tickle her inside her pouch. And other times she said that she didn't like that tickling too much and then she would tell him. And the two of them found out that they could get along quite well together if each would tell the other when they wanted to stop having fun together and each would tell the other when they wanted to have fun together.

Do you know what the lesson of that story is? See if you can figure it out? What did the kangaroo learn?

Patient: She learned that the mouse wasn't heavy, sometimes.

Therapist: Right. What else did she learn?

Patient: That when he was heavy he could go out and play.

Therapist: Right. And what did the mouse learn?

Patient: Hhmm.

Therapist: The mouse learned to tell the kangaroo that he wasn't that heavy and that when he started to get heavy he would go out and he also told the kangaroo that he wouldn't tickle her always—that if he tickled her and she wasn't in the mood to be tickled that he would stop it. And if she was in the mood to be tickled he would do it. So that he learned to try to find out how she felt and she learned to try to find out how he felt. That's what each of them learned. Okay?

Patient: Okay. Good-bye.

Therapist: Tell me something before you say good-bye to everybody. Did you like that story?

Patient: Yeah.

Therapist: What part did you like the most?

Patient: Where the mouse tickled her in her pouch.

In my story I tried to further entrench the clinical improvement revealed in John's. I tried to impart the notion that his mother's tolerance for "carrying the load" of his dependency was limited, but that she still did have definite capacity in this regard. He would do best for himself to be sensitive to her feelings, to gratify his needs when his mother was inclined to satisfy them, and not to coerce her when she was disinclined. He was encouraged to communicate his desires and to learn of and be sensitive to her degree of receptivity to him at any given time. He was advised also that he can engender in her a similar attitude of consideration for his feelings. It is through mutual communication, respect for one another's desires, and appreciation of each other's limitations that interpersonal problems may be resolved. These examples demonstrate certain aspects of the Mutual Storytelling Technique. I consider the method a valuable therapeutic modality. It is not a treatment per se, but one technique in the therapist's armamentarium. It has applicability to certain children only, namely those who will tell stories but who cannot directly analyze them. It should be used in conjunction with other aspects of treatment to a greater or lesser degree depending on the individual patient. Those interested in the application of this technique to a wide variety of childhood psychiatric disorders should refer to my full-length text. (Gardner 1971).

References

Gardner, R. A. (1968). The mutual storytelling technique: use in alleviating childhood Oedipal problems. *Contemporary Psychoanalysis* 4:161–177.

_____ (1969). Mutual storytelling as a technique in child psychotherapy and psychoanalysis. *Science and Psychoanalysis* 14:124–135.

_____ (1970). The mutual storytelling technique: use in the treatment of a child with posttraumatic neurosis. *American Journal of Psychotherapy* 24:419–439.

_____ (1971). *Therapeutic Communication with Children: The Mutual Storytelling Technique.* New York: Science House.

Hogrefe, C. J., ed. (1970). Die Technik des wechselseitigen Geschichtenerzählens bei der Behandlung eines Kindes mit psychogenem Husten. *Fortschritte Psychoanalyse* 4:159–173.

18

Creative Characters

ROBERT BROOKS

In the past 15 to 20 years mental health practitioners from different theoretical backgrounds have developed a variety of innovative structured strategies for use in the diagnosis and treatment of children (Halpern and Kissel 1976, Nickerson 1973, Prout 1977). Examples of innovations in clinical child intervention techniques include Gardner's (1975) use of storytelling and board games, Gittelman's (1965) behavior rehearsal, Lazarus and Abramovitz's (1962) "emotive imagery," Marcus's (1966) use of costumes in play therapy, Meichenbaum and Goodman's (1971) self-instructional training techniques for impulsive children, Minuchin and colleagues' (1967) program to strengthen listening and cognitive skills in delinquent children, Proskauer's (1969, 1971) time-limited therapy, Santostefano's (1971, 1975) diagnostic and therapy approaches in the areas of both affect and cognition, Schachter's (1974) kinetic group psychotherapy, and Winnicott's (1971) squiggle technique.

The number of structured interventions that have been introduced suggests that many child therapists have found, as the author has, that if one or two critical issues are selected for therapy and these issues then serve as beacons of light in determining (a) the particular tasks, games, books or toys that are presented by the therapist, and (b) the therapist's response to a child's material, the therapy endeavor has greater direction and is facilitated. Needless to say, a therapist must always guard against being too intrusive when providing certain structured tasks lest the treatment be disrupted. Much sensitivity, thought, and flexibility is demanded of the therapist in selecting and managing the key issues and in knowing when to address new issues when so dictated by the treatment material.

One medium for providing structure in child therapy involves the therapeutic use of stories and books. There is a growing literature in this particular area. For example, a number of articles have been published on the general subject of bibliotherapy (Berg-Cross and Berg-Cross 1976, McKinney 1975, Morgan 1976, Nickerson 1975). Gardner (1971) has developed the Mutual Storytelling Technique as a very useful therapy strategy. Robertson and Barford (1970) described the use of story-making for chronically ill children as a means of helping children in the hospital to express, deal with, and master their anxieties through characters in a story. In addition, Carmen Goldings (1968), Herbert Goldings (1974), and Goldings and Goldings (1972) have discussed the use of literature as a medium for the child therapist. Also, there has been a proliferation of children's books dealing with a variety of emotional issues (e.g., Fassler, 1972a,b, Gardner 1972).

The Creative Characters Technique

One therapeutic technique which I have found very useful, especially with latency-aged children, is predicated on creating stories. In this particular technique, which I call Creative Characters, the therapist selects the major emotional issues confronting the child and then develops characters (quite often animals) and involves these characters in situations reflecting the core issues in therapy. These characters and the experiences they face are typically elaborated upon by the child and therapist over a number of months and the stories provide very rich material for treatment. The following points highlight the critical features of the Creative Characters technique:

1. This technique is one possible strategy that the therapist can employ. It is not assumed to be the major nor the only technique available to the therapist. I have introduced the Creative Characters technique in therapy as a way of eliciting and highlighting certain themes for children who might be seen as more passive or reserved as well as a way of articulating and more clearly defining those themes for children who would even be considered more productive in treatment. In general, I have found that the technique can be presented at almost any phase or point of treatment and is applicable to children who present a wide range of emotional problems and defensive maneuvers. Creative Characters should not be viewed as a last resort strategy to be used only when nothing else works and the therapy is floundering.

In terms of specifics I often use a tape-recorder together with pictures that I have drawn of the characters. With some children I tape the initial story in advance of the session, while with other children it is taped in their presence, depending upon which format is likely to be more interesting to them. I simply introduce the technique with the statement that I made up or I am going to make up a story and would like the child to listen to it. Typically, as the story progresses, the child makes comments about its content and shows particular interest in certain aspects of the story or certain characters within the story. I then use the child's comments to elaborate upon the present story and/or to develop possible material for future stories. With some children I ask what they thought of the story and my questions are geared toward important therapy issues.

If after the first story or discussion the child is not very responsive, I typically introduce a second story the following week and encourage the child to participate and to do such things as use the tape recorder, draw pictures of the characters, or use puppets representing the characters as ways of increasing his or her involvement and enjoyment in the task. Most often these particular strategies are all that are required to engage the child. Of course, as with any therapy strategy, the clinician must be sensitive to the child's particular resistance and style so that the Creative Characters technique does not become intrusive, thereby intensifying defenses and weakening the alliance.

2. While the Creative Characters technique relies heavily on fantasy and language, I borrow from Santostefano's (1970) theory and research in recognizing the significance of the action modality especially in relation to fantasy and language; thus, when it is clinically appropriate I encourage stories not only to be told verbally but to be acted out in some fashion, such as in the form of a play. I have found that when a child physically enacts a story it often enhances fantasy production and helps to elaborate the particular themes. This clinical impression is supported by such research as that done by Saltz and his colleagues (1977). Saltz found that the addition of physical enactment of fantasy themes for preschool children promoted cognitive development, impulse regulation, and fantasy production. Not surprising to developmental theorists, Saltz's findings support the notion that sensory motor or action experiences lay the foundation for later higher level cognitive processes. In terms of cognitive functioning, the Creative Characters technique is capable of providing children who have cognitive problems (e.g., attentional deficits) with a medium through which to attend, represent and resolve conflicts in an articulated and focused rather than diffuse manner (this feature of the technique is discussed in greater detail later in the chapter).

3. Obviously the Creative Characters technique relies heavily on the use of displacement and metaphor. Through displacement it is typically easier for a child to communicate, at least initially. The degree of displacement used by the therapist is dependent upon the child, the nature of the conflict, and the level of resistance. In using displacement I attempt to build into the stories certain characters whose presence will permit me to facilitate the therapy work and articulate the therapy issues. These characters include:

(a) A representation of the child as well as different aspects of the child's conflict. For example, if a child is struggling with issues related to dependence and independence, one of the characters in the story should also be confronted with such issues, or in some cases each side of the conflict can be represented by a different character. To articulate the different issues I often select relevant names to give particular characters so that I might call a character representing a child's anger "Angry Bill Tornado" or a character representing a child's feelings of deprivation "Judy Hunger." By having these specific characters and names, I find that I can continually refer to them and thereby make specific conflicts and conflict areas more concrete. Such specificity facilitates the therapy work.

(b) A representation of the therapist such as a Wise Owl, a Teacher, a Wise Old Person or even a Detective. If such a character is not included, it becomes more difficult for the therapist to elaborate upon the story or offer comments and interpretations without these comments and interpretations seeming to be intrusive or artificial. A therapist characterization provides a natural format for the child's therapist to explore and gain an increased understanding of the child's problems, and to communicate through the story the dynamics of the child's struggle as well as more adaptive ways of handling and resolving this struggle.

(c) A moderator in the form of, for example, a newscaster who can within the natural boundaries of the story interview the different characters to elucidate the issues. Typically, this news commentator can summarize the therapy themes session after session, and can clarify issues as a means of enhancing the therapy. Children often enjoy such a character in the stories and will frequently switch roles so that they too can do the interviewing and the reporting. A tape recorder comes in very handy when such a character is included.

4. While Creative Characters relies on displacement, the goal of the technique is to generalize what is learned in the story with its problem-solving strategies to outside real-life situations. Guided by this goal the therapist might, when it seems appropriate, point out similarities be-

tween the child's behavior and that of particular characters in the story. Comparisons may also be drawn to similarities in dynamics. Creative Characters can then be used as a kind of behavior rehearsal, a testing ground for problem solving and mastery; that is, as characters in the story overcome their particular problem, the child can be encouraged to think about and imagine the characters when encountering the same or similar difficulties. For example, if a character in the Creative Characters technique overcomes feelings of being devastated when he or she loses at a game and no longer has to cheat to avoid such a situation, the patient can be encouraged to imagine the particular character when faced with a similar situation outside the treatment. Such a use of imagery and behavior rehearsal has been found to be a useful therapeutic strategy with a number of children (e.g., Lazarus and Abramovitz 1962).

Clinical Examples

I have selected several examples to illustrate the Creative Characters technique. Cases were chosen that illustrate problems faced by many children seen by child therapists. The nature of the technique makes it applicable though to almost any theme a child presents.

Case 1: "I'm Afraid to Try"

Many children whom I have seen in therapy have as a major presenting symptom the fear of trying different activities. Most often these children possess low self-esteem and view themselves as relatively incompetent and unable to succeed. They often feel that they cannot do well and thus use avoidance so as not to expose themselves to possible failure. One such child was Timmy, age 9, with a history of a seizure disorder since the age of 4 and many developmental deviations. Timmy's behavior was characterized by "I won't do it." Timmy's parents and teacher often reported that he would say "no" when given a new task to perform. In therapy Timmy was often quiet and reticent and when he did play, there was not very much focus to his material. Play might take the form of darts being shot wildly or paper being scribbled upon. His attention was limited at best. I decided to use the Creative Characters technique, both as a way of articulating Timmy's fears of failure as well as a strategy to help him settle down, attend, and focus in the treatment hour. I hoped to address both cognitive and affective functioning.

Timmy had mentioned to me that he had seen a circus on TV and liked the elephant act. Therefore, I introduced the character called "Johnny Scared, the Young Elephant" who wanted to be in an act in the circus which required that Johnny would have to learn to walk on two feet with the other elephants. At the beginning of one session, I told Timmy that I was going to play Johnny Scared, the Young Elephant and that I would have to learn how to walk on two feet and that could be very difficult. Timmy looked relatively amused as I made believe I was trying to walk on two feet but kept falling over (a behavior similar to Timmy's when he had seizures). Every time I fell over I would moan, "I can't take it any more and I'm going to quit. I'll never learn to stand on my own two feet." After saying this I often crawled on all four "feet" behind the chair in my office and said I would never try anything else again, it's too hard. Timmy became quite interested in this story and at my suggestion he played the animal trainer who was going to help Johnny Scared, the Young Elephant. Timmy proceeded to give me directions about walking on two feet, but at the beginning I continued to fall over and moaned and groaned and threatened to quit. However, Timmy, as the animal trainer, continued to encourage me. As Johnny Scared, the Young Elephant, I verbalized many of Timmy's own concerns.

In subsequent sessions Timmy played the role of Johnny while I played the animal trainer, and I also introduced the role of a newspaperman who was covering the circus and was going to write a story about Johnny Scared, the Young Elephant. As Johnny Scared, I told the reporter how I had never been able to do things very well and how I always wanted to quit but that quitting didn't help, and I would be teased by the other elephants if I did. This Creative Characters theme lasted for many sessions and eventually I made comparisons between Johnny Scared and Timmy's own behavior at school, especially in relation to Timmy's use of avoidance. Timmy was able to tolerate hearing and discussing these comparisons and soon his teacher reported that Timmy was trying more things at school and had even written in his book, "Don't Quit." This was a significant saying since as part of the Johnny Scared theme we had once hung a sign saying "Don't Quit." In one of the final weeks of this Creative Characters story Timmy and I changed Johnny Scared's name to Johnny Brave.

Case 2: "I'm Going to Explode"

Child therapists often face children who have significant problems in the area of impulse regulation and control. Such children act before they think and rarely give any thought to the consequences of their behavior. In the Creative Characters game I have represented this problem through such characters as racing cars that have poor brakes and have to be helped by mechanics, or taught to drive more safely by traffic officers, or by volcanoes that throw lava all over the place and have to learn to control their explosions. Of course, there are a number of other characters that can be used in addition to racing cars and volcanoes.

One example of a volcano character occurred with Billy, a 7-year-old boy who was referred because of continually hitting other children in unprovoked ways. The expression of anger was a major problem for Billy, but he would not talk about or represent this difficulty in the therapy situation. From my evaluation I had some clue that the seemingly unprovoked attacks were related to feelings of deprivation as well as feelings of being intruded upon. During one of the sessions, I took out some Play-doh, mixed some colors, and made a "volcano." Billy pitched in by taking the red Play-doh and putting it at the top of the volcano and over the sides and called it the lava. At my request Billy named the volcano, calling it Volly the Volcano. I then made up a story about Volly, and it concerned Volly never wanting anyone to step on him or to take food from the trees and gardens on his slope. In my story Volly spit out lava anytime someone stepped on him. This of course made the townspeople very angry and they were ready to use bombs to blow Volly up. As the story developed I introduced the character of Doctor Safety who was a volcano expert. Doctor Safety went to speak to Volly and actually empathized with Volly's position that he was angry at people for stepping all over him and taking his food. But Doctor Safety also wondered whether or not Volly might be lonely and sad at times because he would not let any people near him. Soon, Volly, some townspeople and Doctor Safety sat down to discuss the issue, and a settlement was reached whereby townspeople could come and sit on Volly but only a certain number at a time and only with Volly's permission.

In addition, Billy had Volly say that he would never shoot any more lava out, but Doctor Safety said that was unrealistic since the lava had to go somewhere and they decided that the lava could go to a place where no people lived on the other side of Volly (this of course had to do with the issue of redirecting the anger). However, in the story, as in most Creative Characters stories, solutions did not come about magically; for instance, for a number of sessions Billy had the townspeople breaking the rules with too many people walking on Volly and the latter becoming angry and spitting out lava. We also added at this point the character of a newsperson from a major TV station who interviewed a number of the concerned parties. Billy became increasingly involved in the material and began to draw pictures that he put up in my office of Volly, the newsperson, and the townspeople. As Volly's problem became more settled, I asked Billy whether or not people could sometimes feel like volcanoes, and Billy was able to answer yes and actually give a couple of examples when he had erupted at school. We spoke about this and we then set up a plan with the help of the school counselor and Billy's parents that involved Billy going to speak to the counselor when he became upset at school. Billy demonstrated growth in his capacity to control his anger and, as importantly, in his understanding of what the outbursts represented.

Case 3: "Why Aren't You Living Together?"

Our society has many children whose parents are separated or divorced and quite often we see such children in our clinical practice. It is not always easy for such children to discuss the feelings and thoughts they have related to their parents' divorce or separation. Many children feel torn in terms of loyalty, feel responsible for their parents being apart, or for not being able to bring them together, and entertain magical fantasies about their parents getting back together. With a number of such children I have found it helpful to introduce the Creative Characters technique to assist them with the stress they experience because of their parents' marital problems.

Lisa, age 6, was referred to me following her parents' separation and a brief hospitalization of her mother for depression and an overdose of sleeping pills. Initially, Lisa was very stressed and would not talk about what was happening. If I attempted any discussion she would become agitated and she frequently ran out of my office. She was having difficulty in school and at home and was struggling with many feelings of confusion and anger. In an attempt to focus these feelings, prior to one of our sessions I drew pictures of a chick called Chicky Worried talking to a dog called Doctor Sam. I also tape-recorded a story that Lisa was able to listen to about a rooster and a hen who loved each other, got married, and had a beautiful chick called Chicky. In my story the rooster and hen started to fight after a few years and eventually the rooster went to live on another farm. Chicky became very upset, did not know whom she wanted to live with, could not concentrate in school, and was plainly miserable. Obviously, I attempted to capture Lisa's predicament in the character of Chicky. Doctor Sam, a kind old dog, came and spoke to Chicky, and eventually Lisa (through the Chicky character) shared with him several worries, including her anger at both parents, especially at mother because of the hospitalization, her sense that she should be able to bring them together, and her unhappiness that she was not able to do so.

I was encouraged with how this Creative Characters story with its very direct displacement helped to bind Lisa's anxiety and permitted her to discuss some very emotionally charged issues, which only the session before prompted her to run out of the room. During the next few weeks, Lisa became very involved with the story and used the tape recorder to elaborate upon it. At first her stories were rather magical with the rooster and hen getting back together and everyone living happily ever after. However, with continued therapy the ending soon became more realistic. The Chicky Worried character came up throughout the treatment as an appropriate displacement, but eventually Lisa could translate Chicky's problems into her own situation. I should note that a year and a half later, at termination time, Lisa reflected about how difficult it had been for her to discuss her feelings with me and how she had run out of the office, but that talking about Chicky Worried helped her stay in the room.

Case 4: "Who Asked for a Baby?"

Another issue child therapists encounter is the universal problem of sibling rivalry. A number of children I have treated have harbored much resentment toward a younger sibling who is perceived to be the favorite one. Many times the intensity of the feelings and consequent strong defenses make such feelings somewhat inaccessible for work within the treatment session. Yet, with some children it becomes important to help articulate the issues of sibling rivalry and its many ramifications. I have used several different characters to represent sibling rivalry, but one of my favorites concerns the characterization of a kangaroo and its pouch.

Larry, age 9, was referred to me for intermittent soiling, oppositional behavior at home, hitting a younger sister, and often refusing to do any school work although he was extremely intelligent. A major dynamic related to his sister who was 5½ years old and actually favored by his parents. While there would at times be outbursts of anger toward his sister, Larry could not discuss these feelings of anger nor the experience of deprivation that was also associated with his younger sibling. I felt sibling rivalry was an important issue to confront in therapy so I taped a play about a boy kangaroo called Cuddly Kangaroo who loved being in his mother's pouch as they went everywhere together. However, soon Cutie Kangaroo was born and mother had room in her pouch for only one offspring, so Cuddly had to leave and he was very upset and angry. As with most other children, Larry quickly picked up on this story and helped me to tape record additional scenarios. In addition, we acted out stories by hopping around the office as kangaroos.

Larry's material about Cuddly focused on anger and it took such forms as having the mother kangaroo's pouch start to rip so that Cutie could not stay in it, of Cuddly showing anger by defecating on Kangarooland (Playdoh was squeezed onto a map of Kangarooland), of Cuddly refusing to go to school, of fires in the forest that endangered everyone, and of hunters hunting Cutie. To facilitate a solution to this solution, we developed a character of Old Man Kangaroo who befriended Cuddly and spoke to him on a number of occasions. Old Man Kangaroo verbalized Cuddly's feelings and he also spoke to Cuddly's parents to let them know how Cuddly felt. Old Man Kangaroo helped Cuddly to put out some of the fires in the forest. He asked the hunters to leave and he helped Cuddly feel more comfortable about growing up. He also arranged tournaments among different kangaroos including Cuddly as a more appropriate latency age expression of aggression and competition. The theme of Cuddly lasted over many months and eventually comparisons could be drawn between Larry and Cuddly. As Cuddly was being helped, Larry's soiling stopped, he became more manageable at home and less aggressive toward his sister. In addition, his teacher reported that his school work production increased markedly. There was much evidence that Larry was solidifying the gains from therapy and, in part, the character of Cuddly was responsible for Larry's progress.

Discussion

These clinical cases illustrate the efficacy of having structured material introduced in the treatment sessions by the child therapist. The particular technique outlined in this chapter, Creative Characters, provides one possible format through which the therapist can articulate and help the child resolve the focal issues in the therapy. I believe that the effectiveness of the Creative Characters technique is predicated on several of the following interrelated variables:

Displacement

Obviously the use of displacement and metaphor permits the distance that many children require in order to discuss, struggle with, understand, and master emotional conflicts. Even in those cases where it seems apparent that the child is immediately aware of the similarities between the predicament or challenges faced by the characters and his or her own situation, this awareness need not prevent the child from actively participating in and elaborating upon the stories. The story and its characters represent a relatively safe turf from which the child, strengthened by the nourishment provided and knowledge gained in this turf, can slowly venture as he or she confronts problems in "real life." As I implied earlier the therapist must be sensitive in insuring that the displacement truly represents a safe area, lest the child retreat even more. Therapeutic acumen is involved in selecting when and with what content a technique such as Creative Characters is used.

Binding Anxiety

Closely tied to the role of displacement in Creative Characters, but deserving separate mention, is the contribution this technique makes to binding anxiety; this contribution is especially critical for a child such as Lisa whose anxiety is overwhelming and disorganizing. The Creative Characters story, by providing focused and concrete representations of the child's emotional turmoil, counteracts and renders more manageable the child's diffuse, panic-like anxiety. The story is similar to an anchor that helps to moor a boat; once the boat is secured, repairs can be made. In therapy the story and its characters help to bind the child's anxiety and then can be used to elaborate and resolve conflict. While some child therapists may be wary of introducing structured material or tasks into the treatment process, viewing such an action as intrusive, perhaps anxiety provoking, and possibly robbing the child of certain therapeutic experiences, I believe that if handled appropriately a strategy like Creative Characters can lessen intense anxiety and facilitate the therapy endeavor.

Cognitive Focusing

While the efficacy of the Creative Characters technique can be understood, in part, in terms of such variables as displacement, symbolic representation, and the binding of anxiety, another related dimension that requires highlighting is the positive impact of this technique on cognitive functioning. A number of children seen by child therapists have significant cognitive problems often manifested by distractibility, limited attention span, poor memory, and difficulties remaining focused on any topic or material. Such children initially require much external support in therapy to help them to focus and attend so that they can develop the cognitive skills necessary to assist them to master their problems.

I believe the Creative Characters technique with the therapist's assistance can provide such support and strengthen cognitive processes in several ways. First, since children typically find the format and characters of this technique very interesting, they become increasingly motivated to focus on the stories, thereby slowly improving their capacity to attend and to sustain attention. Second, the nature of the technique encourages the child and the therapist over a period of time to contribute to delineating and then elaborating selected aspects of the personalities of the various characters; this is manifested, for example, as the feelings and beliefs of the characters become more realistic and more complex and there is movement away from simplistic explanations of behavior and simplistic solutions to problems. Consequently, the elaboration that transpires in the continued creation of the stories promotes the child's ability to focus upon and understand his or her own feelings and thoughts in more sophisticated, more integrated and less fragmented ways. In essence, elaborations of the stories and the characters require as well as foster improved cognitive skills and assist in the development of the child's observing ego.

As is apparent, the Creative Characters technique embraces both affective and cognitive functioning, helping each domain to advance and to nourish development in the other. To address both cognition and affect in therapy is very important since, as many clinicians and theorists have come to realize, the two domains are inextricably interwoven so that deficits in one adversely affect the functioning of the other (e.g., Mahoney 1977, Santostefano 1977). This intimate relation was certainly evident in the case of Timmy in which the Creative Characters technique served both to enhance cognitive functioning and resolve emotional conflict.

Mastery and Competence

I have used the Creative Characters technique with many children, and I have become increasingly impressed by the enthusiasm and satisfaction that most children show for the stories and characters. I believe that this enthusiasm and fun finds its roots in the experiences of a sense of mastery and competence, experiences that are critical to emotional well-being and self-esteem (White 1959). Many of our child patients enter therapy with feelings of incompetence, convinced that they have little, if any, ability to make things better or to determine what happens to their own lives. On some level they frequently feel trapped and helpless, and passive in the sense of lacking confidence to master situations (other than through certain maladaptive, self-defeating coping maneuvers).

I believe that Creative Characters enlists these children in a more active solution to their problems; it fosters a problem-solving atmosphere in which they become significant participants and it offers hope against the prevailing attitude of defeatism. In the stories they move back and forth from the role of the therapist to the characters representing themselves, actively being the helper as well as the one being helped, learning to observe and understand feelings and thoughts, and testing out solutions in therapy that can later be implemented outside the therapist's office. For instance, no words can adequately describe how Timmy felt as he helped Johnny Scared, the Young Elephant, walk on his own two feet or while playing Johnny, the ego pleasure he experienced in succeeding to learn to walk. The sense of mastery and competence that can be gained from the Creative Characters stories is a critical dimension of its effectiveness as a therapeutic strategy.

Most likely, other variables in addition to the ones addressed in this chapter have contributed to the efficacy of the Creative Characters technique, but those considered above seem to be most important.

In closing, I wish to emphasize again that structured approaches to child therapy are becoming widespread and it is my impression that a number of structured techniques, employed sensitively by the clinician, offer much promise in the treatment of emotional and cognitive disorders in children.

References

Berg-Cross, G., and Berg-Cross, L. (1976). Bibliotherapy for young children. *Journal of Clinical Child Psychology* 5:35–38.

Fassler, J. (1972a). *The Boy with a Problem.* New York: Behavioral Publications.

_____ (1972b). *Don't Worry, Dear.* New York: Behavioral Publications.

Gardner, R. (1971). *Therapeutic Communication with Children: The Mutual Storytelling Technique.* New York: Science House.

_____ (1972). *Dr. Gardner's Stories about the Real World.* Englewood Cliffs, NJ: Prentice-Hall.

_____ (1975). *Psychotherapeutic Approaches to the Resistant Child.* New York: Jason Aronson.

Gittleman, M. (1965). Behavior rehearsal as a technique in child treatment. *Journal of Child Psychology and Psychiatry* 6:251–255.

Goldings, C. R. (1968). Some new trends in children's literature from the perspective of the child psychiatrist. *Journal of Child Psychiatry* 7:377–397.

Goldings, C. R., and Goldings, H. J. (1972). Books in the playroom: a dimension of child psychiatric technique. *Journal of Child Psychiatry* 11:52–65.

Goldings, H. J. (1974). Focus on feelings: mental health books for the modern child. *Journal of Child Psychiatry* 13:374–377.

Halpern, W., and Kissel, S. (1976). *Human Resources for Troubled Children.* New York: Wiley, Interscience.

Lazarus, A., and Abramovitz, A. (1962). The use of "emotive imagery" in the treatment of children's phobias. *Journal of Mental Science* 108:191–195.

Mahoney, M. J. (1977). Reflections on the cognitive-learning trend in psychotherapy. *American Psychologist* 32:5–13.

Marcus, I. (1966). Costume play therapy. *Journal of Child Psychiatry* 5:441–451.

McKinney, F. (1975). Explorations in bibliotherapy: personal involvement in short stories and cases. *Psychotherapy: Theory, Research and Practice* 12:110–117.

Meichenbaum, D., and Goodman, J. (1971). Training impulsive children to talk to themselves: a means of developing self-control. *Journal of Abnormal Psychology* 77:115–126.

Minuchin, S., Chamberlain, P., and Graubard, P. (1967). A project to teach learning skills to disturbed delinquent children. *American Journal of Orthopsychiatry* 37:558–567.

Morgan, S. (1976). Bibliotherapy: a broader concept. *Journal of Clinical Child Psychology* 5:39–42.

Nickerson, E. (1973). Recent trends and innovation in play therapy. *International Journal of Child Psychotherapy* 2:53–70.

_____ (1975). Bibliotherapy: a therapeutic medium for helping children. *Psychotherapy: Theory, Research and Practice* 12:258–261.

Proskauer, S. (1969). Some technical issues in time-limited psychotherapy with children. *Journal of Child Psychiatry* 8:154–169.

_____ (1971). Focused time-limited psychotherapy with children. *Journal of Child Psychiatry* 10:619–639.

Prout, H. (1977). Behavioral intervention with hyperactive children: a review. *Journal of Learning Disabilities* 10:141–146.

Robertson, M., and Barford, F. (1970). Story-making in psychotherapy with a chronically ill child. *Psychotherapy: Theory, Research and Practice* 7:104–107.

Saltz, E., Dixon, D., and Johnson, J. (1977). Training disadvantaged preschoolers on various fantasy activities: effects on cognitive functioning and impulse control. *Child Development* 48:367–380.

Santostefano, S. (1970). The assessment of motives in children. *Psychological Reports* 26:639–649.

_____ (1971). Beyond nosology: diagnosis from the viewpoint of development. In *Perspectives in Child Psychopathology*, ed. H. Rie. New York: Aldine-Atherton.

_____ (1975). MBD: Time to take a new look. *Medical Times* 103:82–92.

_____ (1977). New views of motivation and cognition in psychoanalytic theory: the horse (id) and rider (ego) revisited. *McLean Hospital Journal* 2:48–64.

Schachter, R. (1974). Kinetic psychotherapy in the treatment of children. *American Journal of Psychotherapy* 28:430–437.

White, R. (1959). Motivation reconsidered: the concept of competence. *Psychological Review* 66:297–333.

Winnicott, D. W. (1971). *Therapeutic Consultations in Child Psychiatry.* New York: Basic Books.

19

Role Playing

RICHARD L. LEVENSON, JR. AND JACK HERMAN

The goal of child psychotherapy is to help alleviate a child's difficulty in affective, cognitive, or behavioral areas that impede developmental adaptations. According to Dodds (1985), child psychotherapy "is designed to change the child in some way either to ease internal pain, change undesirable behavior or improve relationships between the child and other people who are important in the child's life" (p. 15). Interventions typically have ranged from the direct type, for example, analytic, behavioral, client-centered, and family therapies, to the indirect type, which include consultation and "parent counseling" (Dodds 1985), as well as other methods.

As in adult psychotherapy, the relationship between therapist and child is crucial in order to set the stage for the intervention to have a successful outcome. There must be a working alliance and the establishment of a supportive, nonjudgmental atmosphere with emphatic understanding, in which the child can feel respected, nonthreatened, and free to think, act (within limits), and say what he or she feels. There must be regularly scheduled sessions ranging from one to three sessions per week. Yet, psychotherapy with children differs from adult psychotherapy in that children do not possess the cognitive abilities to assimilate that which is heavily language oriented. Harter (1977) noted that, within Piaget's (1952) concept, the child is in the midst of a developmental shift from prelogical to logical thought. As Harter (1977) stated: "for it is this particular transition, and the gradual development and solidification of logical operations during the concrete operational period, that seem intimately related to the child's comprehension and construction of a logical system of *emotional* concepts that define the affective spheres of his/her life" (p. 421).

For this reason, play therapy techniques, as well as numerous other primarily nonlanguage-oriented methods were developed (e.g., A. Freud 1965, Klein 1975). The therapeutic playing out of inner experience, ideas, affects, and fantasies associated with life events seems to aid the child in becoming more aware of the feelings and thoughts, conflicts, and ego dysfunctions that may underlie problematic or disturbed behaviors and affects and that provides an opportunity for the child to revise and resolve psychological and psychosocial problems.

Reisman (1973) provided a brief, but excellent theoretical history of play therapy. Allen (1942) believed play therapy served to help the child become aware of his or her identity as an individual in relation to the therapist and the nature of their relationship. Moustakas (1953) reported that play therapy was "a progression [of] the child's expression of feelings" (p. 111). Anna Freud (1965) saw a similarity between play therapy and psychoanalysis and theorized that "there is movement from surface to depth, from the interpretation of unconscious impulses, wishes, and fears or id content" (in Reisman 1973, p. 111). Anna Freud believed that play therapy reduced anxiety and emotional (neurotic) disturbance by helping the child become more aware of unconscious conflicts and hidden material.

Waelder (1933) wrote an interesting and early paper on psychoanalytic play therapy with a special emphasis on the repetition theme. Of course, Sigmund Freud (1920) was the first to posit that some forms of play are repetitious acts, possibly to gain mastery over some particular event that was anxiety producing or frustrating, by reversal of roles from passive to active. Erikson (1950) described play as a form of hallucinatory mastery over life experiences that induced feelings of anxiety and helplessness. When children use repetition or repeat an act or game, they are, in a sense, working through, possibly undoing or redoing via displacement and symbolization, and thereby articulating, assimilating, and integrating that which is unconscious and connected to a special set of circumstances. These circumstances might range from separation anxiety to protection against unconscious wishes or feelings of dread or hostility, for example, in relation to a parent.

Some children have imaginary playmates or friends; others may act out roles or take the part of a significant person in their environment. Repetition or role reversal, however, does not seem to be a pathological set of behaviors or solutions to anxiety or conflictual issues, but rather is curative in that it serves to repair hurts and losses. It helps the child

separate and individuate by inculcating a sense of mastery and competence, by giving an "illusion of accomplishment" (J. L. Herman, personal
communication, February 23, 1987) and by contributing to the healthy
adaptation and resolution of the normally stressful or anxiety-producing
events that must occur during childhood.

It seems logical, then, that some forms of child psychotherapy
incorporate techniques involving repetition. An indirect example of this
is Gardner's Mutual Storytelling Techniques (1971). Gardner's method
involves encouraging the child to tell a story into a tape recorder.
According to Schaefer and Millman (1977), "the child is asked to be the
guest of honor on a make-believe television program in which stories are
to be told" (p. 38). The therapist then tells a parallel story; but after a
psychoanalytic fashion, "healthier adaptations and resolutions of conflicts are introduced" (p. 38). Gardner's method is essentially a projective
technique in which, with a minimum of structure, the child is asked to
make up a story that is apprehended psychodynamically by the therapist
and then relayed back to the child with more adaptive solutions. We
know that in the process the child is going to construct a story based on
her construction of herself in relation to the world and her characteristic
adaptive or maladaptive ways of emotional problem solving.

The issue of Gardner's technique is that, while it may be a useful
diagnostic device, it may be questionable (from a psychoanalytic standpoint) as a therapeutic technique. The psychoanalytic concept of therapy
relies on creating a therapeutic climate that promotes natural, evolving,
moment-to-moment, spontaneous self-expression through play and verbalization with a *minimum* of structuring and interference by the therapist. The therapist aims to enable the patient to express himself *in his own
way*, in a stream of consciousness fashion, whether via verbalization or
play, or both. The therapist's job is to help the patient expand on
whatever the patient initiated, not to introduce anything new. Introducing an artificial task for the child patient, extraneous to what might be
on the child's mind at the moment, is to distract the child from whatever
he or she might be immediately experiencing and expressing. It is
important to stay within the immediate experience and not disrupt an
ongoing experiential process that might bear fruit if followed.

The therapist attempts to follow and expand on whatever the child
has introduced rather than distract the child by suggesting a game or a
make-believe television show, even when a child may be resisting. In the
latter case, the therapist attempts to follow the resistance and verbalize
what it might mean, rather than to introduce a device to try to bypass it.
The therapist acknowledges, clarifies, and interprets his or her under-

standing of the defensive reasons for the resistance, rather than trying to distract the child by introducing a new activity. The child's attention must be in the realm of everyday experience or occurrences so that there will be some connection between therapeutic interpretations and the child's incorporation of a corrective emotional experience.

The technique of role-playing has had a long history in various psychotherapeutic approaches. Traditionally, role-playing has been used by gestalt psychotherapists and in behavioral methodologies for reasons ranging from increasing emotional awareness to expanding repertoires of behaviors. Social psychological theorists such as McGuire (1961) and his "inoculation theory" have sought methods of cognitive-behavioral rehearsal to increase the individual's ability to deal with new and unfamiliar situations. Moreno (1969) utilized psychodrama, a psychotherapeutic technique of structuring, or partially structuring a real or hypothetical life situation, which the patient, along with assistants, is encouraged to dramatize in an improvisational manner while the therapist directs and comments upon the action. Perhaps the most important effort to utilize role-playing in psychotherapy was put forth by George Kelly within his Psychology of Personal Constructs. Kelly (1955) defined fixed-role therapy as "a sheer creative process in which therapist and client conjoin their talents" (p. 380). Rychlak (1973) reported that prior to fixed-role therapy the client is asked to write a self-descriptive sketch of his own character, which the therapist then rewrites in a role "based upon what the client has said of himself," but in contrasting themes, a role that the client knows he or she can act within as "experimental fantasy" (p. 496). Fixed-role therapy is then carried out for as many as eight sessions during which the client gains insight into the way he or she normally construes events and others, and thereafter he or she may decide to incorporate new behaviors and/or affective changes.

Within a social learning paradigm, Gottman, Gonso, and Shuler (1976) used modeling, role-playing, and behavioral rehearsal to improve social interactions among "isolated children." LaGreca (1983) discussed the efficacy of "role-play assessments" that serve to give the clinician insight into a child's repertoire of behaviors in contrived versus "structured observation formats." The contrived format is of particular interest here in that the patient is "asked to respond to a 'pretend' situation as if the situation were really occurring" (p. 121). Kendall and Braswell (1985), in their work with impulsive children, stated that "one reason for even including role-play tasks is to heighten the child's level of emotional involvement and arousal" (p. 135). Kendall and Braswell (1985), like LaGreca (1983), also reported that "hypothetical problem situations" which are role-played should be practiced prior to "real problem situations" (p. 136).

Gresham (1986) routinely uses role-playing when remediating social skills deficits in children. He reported that "behavioral role play tests or performances in analogue situations have essentially become the hallmark of assessment in social skills research" (p. 161). Among the advantages of using role-playing is that the technique depicts "actual behavioral enactment of a skill rather than a rating or perception of that skill" (p. 161). Irwin (1983) reported that role-playing and pretending may be used as a diagnostic technique in order to discern "the child's ability to present and solve a problem, tolerance for frustration, capacity for language . . . the ability to talk about and reflect on the experience including a discussion of feelings about the product which has just been created" (p. 164).

Irwin also highlighted that role-playing gives insight into the quality of the child's ability to relate with his or her therapist.

More recently, research has focused on using role play as a direct therapeutic intervention. Goldstein and Glick (1987) reported that successful interventions occurred from the use of role play within their program for "anger control" for adolescents who are "chronically delinquent" (p. 13). Goldstein and Glick's intervention is based, in part, on the premise that these youngsters often demonstrate "impulsiveness and overreliance on aggressive means for goal attainment . . . and characteristically reason at more egocentric, concrete, and in a sense, more primitive levels of moral reasoning" (p. 13). The program for anger control includes the role-playing of situations that have led previously to inappropriate expressions of anger. Role plays focus upon achieving insight into underlying cognitive and affective issues that are triggered either internally or externally. Trainers use modeling, clear descriptions of conflict situations, and behavioral rehearsal with repetitive demonstrations of appropriate behaviors that lead to nonaggressive, positive outcomes.

In child psychotherapy, we are not so much interested in using role play for the traditional uses of learning and rehearsal per se, but rather for its experiential value in promoting an internal corrective emotional experience, in which repressed affects can be integrated with cognitions of the self. We contend that what has been called *catharsis* is really a form of integration and mastery since, in apparently discharging pent-up affects, the child patient is undoing via reversal of roles or identities situations that created feelings of helplessness, but now serve to create a sense of completeness and control. It is suggested that children may not be especially insightful, but are willing to directly examine problematic areas in their emotional life. As noted, the necessary cognitive, language-based structures may not be sufficiently mature to allow for direct verbal intervention. Children, especially troubled children, lack the capacity for psychosynthesis, that is, the integration of intellectual and affective data. For these reasons, the technique of role-playing in child psychotherapy is seen as a valuable aid in reducing psychopathology and increasing awareness, understanding, and mastery in children and adolescents.

Preliminary reasons for the positive potential of this method are straightforward. First, it is simple to employ and involves the child in direct, everyday experiences in which they have interacted. Second, although it is a verbal technique and requires some sophistication in language use and comprehension, it taps the stream of consciousness and underlying conflictual material by allowing the child to use repetition as a tool toward mastery over an event that stimulated unresolved issues or conflicts. Unlike Gardner's (1971) Storytelling Technique, role-playing with children allows for direct participation and discussion in an area of conflict, and, through controlled therapeutic guidance, an implicit insightful experience might be achieved.

Role-playing in child psychotherapy may be utilized in any number of ways. Simply, it may be of use to help the angry child, for example, become aware of possible dysphoric feelings. The child may be enlisted in a role in which one can reexperience an upsetting conversation or event, one that centers around significant relationships or strong, disturbing affects or thoughts that perhaps are related to referral questions as to why the child was initially brought to therapy. Here is a typical example:

> *Brief Background:* This child, S., a 9.6-year-old boy, was referred for outpatient psychodiagnostic evaluation, after which an interview was conducted for about 30 minutes. He was referred for evaluation as he had expressed suicidal ideation, but would not discuss this. The following are verbatim excerpts of parts of a session, about 10 minutes into the interview.

> *Therapist:* The previous doctor who talked with you, S., let me know you have had thoughts of hurting yourself. Have you had thoughts like that lately?
> *Child:* (removing eye contact) No, not for over a year. Now I feel better because I can talk to my mommy more.
> *Therapist:* S., when you have had these thoughts, what are you doing at the time. I mean, where are you when you think like that?

Child: They happen when I go to the store for my mommy.

Therapist: What happens when you go to the store—do other boys or people bother you? Does something happen to make you afraid?

Child: No. (becoming anxious, restless, and distracted)

Therapist: S., let's try something here. I'm going to play a game with you. I'll be your mommy and you be you.

Child: Okay.

Therapist: (playing the role of the mother) S., I'm sending you down to the store again.

Child: I don't want to go.

Therapist: You have to. Get me a quart of milk, some eggs, and a loaf of bread.

Child: But mommy, I don't want to go again. That makes six times today—I won't go again.

(Note: At this time, the therapist is struck by S.'s revelations of the "sixth" time and stops the role play.)

Therapist: Okay, let's stop here S. You said six times? Why does your mommy send you to the store so many times? Does this happen a lot?

Child: It happens when I'm home, on weekends and nights. I don't like it.

Therapist: When do you have thoughts of hurting yourself?

Child: Sometimes when I'm outside or when I'm walking down those stairs. We live on the fourth floor. I just say that I'm going to jump in front of a car or off a roof.

Therapist: You know, it must make you feel very upset to have to go up and down those stairs so many times a day. I wonder if you ever feel angry about having to do that?

Child: I feel upset, but I'm not angry. I just don't want to go to the store so many times.

This information clearly demonstrates that valuable information may be obtained by both the therapist and child patient. The therapist has gained awareness of the typical situations in which these disturbing thoughts occurred, and the child has begun the process of catharsis. The child has also been given an opportunity to indirectly express his true feelings and knows consciously what is happening, but feels less threatened because he is acting within a role.

After this information is obtained, another role play takes place, but this time the therapist may use role reversal and play the child, while the child models the therapist role character. It is within this second role play that the therapist must reformulate, interpret, and provide clear and simple language so that the child may incorporate what he is hearing into the beginning of a corrective emotional experience. Here the therapist clearly models what he perceives the child to be feeling. Such an example follows:

> *Therapist:* S., let's play another game. This time I'll be you, and you play your mother.
>
> *Child:* Okay, I'll do it.
>
> *Therapist:* Okay, you tell me to go to the store, and we'll play act again.
>
> *Child:* S., go to the store and get me some cupcakes, some soda, some cigarettes, and some pie.
>
> *Therapist:* But, mommy, please, I don't want to go to the store again. You made me go five times already today.
>
> *Child:* You go or else!
>
> *Therapist:* Please, mommy, sometimes when I go I feel awful, like sad. I don't ever get to do what I want to do.
>
> *Child:* You better go!
>
> *Therapist:* Mommy, just listen. When I go to the store, I feel upset and sad. Sometimes, I might feel angry, too, but I also feel tired, because I'm little and I have to carry those big bags up to the fourth floor. Couldn't you go? Why do I always have to go?
>
> *Child:* Well, I guess I could go sometimes.
>
> *Therapist:* Maybe if I told you sometimes I'm very angry, you'd know I don't want to go.
>
> *Child:* Yes, from now on, you and I will both go, but I'll go more.
>
> *Therapist:* Good, but I also want you to know that I sometimes feel sad or angry at other times too—maybe we could talk about that, too.
>
> *Child:* Okay.
>
> *Therapist:* (concluding role play) Okay, S., let's stop here. Do you think you let me know how you feel?
>
> *Child:* I guess so, but I never talked about that before. I'm nervous. (starts to move around the room)
>
> *Therapist:* S., let's see if maybe we could just play now. What would you like to do?
>
> (Session continues.)

There is precedent within the literature for using role play as a psychotherapeutic technique with children. Smith (1977) found that role-playing had a significant impact upon the behavior of children. Aggressive children exposed to counterattitudinal measures became less aggressive after role-playing than those children who were "adult informed" (p. 400b). Sarnoff (1976) reports of a case in which, during displaced fantasy play, the therapist acted out the role of a slave boy and used this opportunity to help make the child more aware of his anger. Although displaced fantasy play utilizes imaginary characters, role-playing relies on the child's real experience with significant others, such as parents, siblings, friends, and teachers. Even if the child cannot say "I," a role play may be created in which children play the parts of others with whom they interact. Sarnoff (1976) stated that

> Once fantasy play has been established, it can be used as a means for working through conflicts and complexes. It is frequently wise for a therapist to approach a fantasy in terms of its affects. Often a child who cannot otherwise express his feelings can talk of them when speaking for a third person. There is an organizing and focusing effect that results from the experience of talking about a fantasy and affect in organized fashion with the therapist. [p. 199]

Harter (1977) employed role-playing in the cognitive-behaviorally oriented psychotherapy of a 6-year-old girl. Harter believed that, following a Piagetian model, a child whose cognitive skills are a function of the concrete operations stage "cannot yet think about his/her own thinking" (p. 425). Even if logical thought is present, it is probable that

> the conceptualization of an emotional network of concepts may lag considerably behind the application of logical principle . . . thus it is not surprising that children in the seven to ten year old range are still struggling with emotional concepts and are still subject to the kind of unidimensional all-or-none thinking that has been the focus of this (work). [p. 425]

Harter believed that children of the latency stage have extreme difficulty expressing contradictory emotions or "polarized feelings that seem incompatible" (p. 425). In her case study, Harter utilized role-playing to model feelings for a girl who was depressed and exhibiting lack of success in school, but would not express herself through standard play materials. Harter reported that her attempts to deal indirectly with the child's feelings were consistently hampered, especially during a game in which the child role played her teacher, while Harter played the role of the child. Harter, in this role, had typically remained passive, modeling the child's behaviors and feelings, until one session when she spoke up and told the child what it felt like to be frustrated in school and to feel upset. Within several sessions, the child began to assimilate this type of communication of feelings through discussion as well as blackboard drawings. Harter (1977) interpreted her success to the child's being able to concretize her "powerful but conflictual feelings," and the drawings they did "provided a concrete visualizable symbol to which we could attach real experiences" (p. 428).

Perhaps the most interesting and detailed description of the technique of role-playing within child psychotherapy was provided by Halberstadt-Freud (1975). Halberstadt-Freud conducted psychoanalytic psychotherapy with a 4-year-old girl, Lara, for a period of 4 years. Lara's traumatic history included the divorce of her parents, two hospitalizations for eye surgery, and suicide attempts by her mother. Her verbal expressiveness was meager and limited to one- or two-word responses; her level of play was extremely limited in that "she assembles the play-material and piles it in a big heap without taking pleasure in this activity" and gives no expression of affect, neither "pleasure or of pain" (pp. 164–165).

As Lara's ability to interact with standard play materials was inadequate, Halberstadt-Freud employed two types of role play as a therapeutic technique. First, standard role play with the child and therapist alternating roles was used. During this type of role play, Halberstadt-Freud took note of the actions of Lara as indicators of what she was feeling. Then, these actions were discussed and further developed within role-playing, but they were not interpreted directly. According to Halberstadt-Freud, "interpretation follows only later when reconstruction has taken place . . . besides voicing the thoughts and feelings of the [therapist's] part he also accompanies it with clarification and interpretation wherever he sees fit" (p. 167). Second, role-playing can be further removed if it is played out through dolls. Halberstadt-Freud stated that "feelings most defended against and defenses hardest to point out can thus be visualized and verbalized in an unobtrusive way" (p. 168).

In the case of Lara, Halberstadt-Freud reported that her depression improved in 3 months as she "gradually expressed more feelings, both positive and negative," and, at the end of treatment, Lara was doing well in school, able to form relationships, and work through her difficult, early stages to be able to develop a "good and stable sense of self" (p. 175). Halberstadt-Freud further stated that employing role play as a technique was valuable because, in the case of Lara, "direct interpretation of defense and content would lead to shame, withdrawal, and denial . . . though very direct in dealing with feelings, this technique is indirect as

regards ego participation or conscious awareness of the hitherto unconscious" (p. 175).

In summary, it has been shown that role-playing, a psychotherapeutic technique used with adult patients in numerous psychotherapy
models, may be a useful technique in the psychotherapy of children and
adolescents. Role-playing may be used in psychodynamic psychotherapy
as a prerequisite to clarification and interpretation, and by cognitive-
behaviorally oriented psychotherapists who may need an action-
oriented method of increasing the power of a talking, reality-oriented
intervention. Role-playing may be used with children whose emotional
difficulties may manifest themselves in depression, hyperkinesis, or
phobic reactions, for example, to dealing verbally with affects or feelings
behind conditions of enuresis, aggressiveness, impulsiveness, and interpersonal difficulties. It is a significant and powerful technique for the
child and adolescent psychotherapist.

Yet, role-playing is not only a valuable technique within the therapist's repertoire; it provides much information that can enlighten the
therapist as to the background of the child. First, role-playing gives the
therapist an opportunity to view how the child construes his or her world;
what impact the world has had on the child; and how the child moves
toward, against, or away from it (after Horney 1945). Second, insight into
how the child is treated by significant others (parents, siblings, peers, etc.)
and the quality of those interactions may be noted. Lastly, role-playing is
a nonthreatening technique in which most any child will become engaged, even those who may be guarded, suspicious, phobic, or dysphoric. Perhaps the most vital function role-playing may serve is to immediately and unequivocally provide a direct, child-centered view of the
feelings and/or affects one may be experiencing. Dramatic improvement
may be seen in the matter of weeks, or months, when role-playing is
employed, as the psychotherapist may quickly focus on specific issues or
affective domains in which the child is experiencing some difficulty or
conflict.

We have used role-playing with children and have found it to be a
valuable technique and an exciting experience in that it increases rapport and gives the child a sense of being understood, cared for, and
respected. Role-playing may be employed in a variety of settings, for
example, during child psychotherapy, or prior to or after a diagnostic
evaluation. Future clinical research should assess the efficacy of role-
playing within the psychotherapy or with difficult children, such as the
silent child. Perhaps these children need to be shown, indeed, that they
are waiting to be helped into helping themselves.

References

Allen, F. H. (1942). *Psychotherapy with Children.* New York: Norton.

Dodds, J. B. (1985). *A Child Psychotherapy Primer.* New York: Human Sciences.

Erickson, E. H. (1950). *Childhood and Society.* New York: Norton.

Freud, A. (1965). *Normality and Pathology in Childhood.* New York: International Universities Press.

Freud, S. (1920). *Beyond the Pleasure Principle.* New York: Norton, 1961.

Gardner, R. A. (1971). The mutual storytelling technique in the treatment of anger inhibition problems. *International Journal of Child Psychoanalysis* 1:34–64.

Goldstein, A. P., and Glick, B. (1987). *Aggression Replacement Training: A Comprehensive Intervention for Aggressive Youth.* Champaign, IL: Research Press.

Gottman, J. M., Gonso, J., and Shuler, P. (1976). Teaching social skills to isolated children. *Journal of Abnormal Psychology* 4:179–197.

Gresham, F. M. (1986). Conceptual issues in the assessment of social competence in children. In *Children's Social Behavior: Developmental, Assessment, and Modification,* ed. P. S. Strain, M. J. Guralnick, and H. M. Walker. Orlando, FL: Academic.

Halberstadt-Freud, I. (1975). Technical variations in the psychoanalytic treatment of a pre-school child. *Israel Annals of Psychiatry and Related Disciplines* 13:162–176.

Harter, S. (1977). A cognitive-developmental approach to children's expression of conflicting feelings and a technique to facilitate such expression in play therapy. *Journal of Consulting and Clinical Psychology* 45:417–432.

Horney, K. (1945). *Our Inner Conflicts.* New York: Norton.

Irwin, E. C. (1983). The diagnostic and therapeutic use of pretend play. In *Handbook of Play Therapy,* ed. C. E. Schaefer and K. J. O'Connor. New York: Wiley.

Kelly, G. A. (1955). *The Psychology of Personal Constructs.* Vol. 2: *Clinical Diagnosis and Psychotherapy.* New York: Norton.

Kendall, P. C., and Braswell, L. (1985). *Cognitive Behavioral Therapy for Impulsive Children.* New York: Guilford.

Klein, M. (1975). *The Psycho-analysis of Children.* New York: The Free Press.

La Greca, A. M. (1983). Interviewing and behavioral observations. In *Handbook of Clinical Child Psychology,* ed. C. E. Walker and M. C. Roberts. New York: Wiley.

McGuire, W. J. (1961). The effectiveness of supportive and refutational defenses in immunizing and restoring beliefs against persuasion. *Sociometry* 24:184–197.

Moreno, J. (1969). *Psychodrama.* New York: Beacon House.

Moustakas, C. E. (1953). *Children in Play Therapy.* New York: McGraw Hill.

Piaget, J. (1952). *The Origins of Intelligence.* New York: Norton.

Reisman, J. M. (1973). *Principles of Psychotherapy with Children.* New York: Wiley.

Rychlak, J. F. (1973). *Introduction to Personality and Psychotherapy: A Theory-construction Approach.* Boston: Houghton Mifflin.

Sarnoff, C. (1976). *Latency.* New York: Jason Aronson.

Schaefer, C. E., and Millman, H. L. (1977). *Therapies for Children.* San Francisco: Jossey-Bass.

Smith, C. D. (1977). Counter attitudinal role-playing and attitude change in children. *Dissertation Abstracts International* 39:400–B.

Waelder, R. (1933). The psychoanalytic theory of play. *Psychoanalytic Quarterly* 2:208–224.

20

Relaxation Training for Children

ARLENE S. KOEPPEN

Children experience some degree of tension at one time or another in the elementary grades. This tension can range from an "uptight" feeling right before an unprepared-for oral book report to a generalized tension and worry throughout the day. Some children experience discomfort during specific subject matter periods, others when beginning a new task, while others become upset after a correction from the teacher. Pressure to succeed, to always be right, to be liked, to have approval, or to cope with family problems can produce tension in a child.

School counselors are often called on to work with children whose academic or social development is hampered by similar kinds of pressures and they deal with these problems in a variety of ways. Some provide individual or group counseling to improve poor self-concept or poor peer relations or to reduce acting-out behavior. Some consult with a child's teacher to bring about change in the educational setting or provide remedial instruction for diagnosed learning disabilities. Some counselors seek the parents' help in alleviating the problem. Others use various methods and combinations of methods to involve the home and school, as well as the child, in bringing about positive change.

A potentially significant contribution to the counselor's repertoire of skills in this area is the use of relaxation techniques. These techniques are often used as one method of preparing an individual for dealing with anxiety-producing material, but they can be an end in themselves. Lazarus (1971) and Carkhuff (1969) have published guides for conducting relaxation sessions. Woody (1971) has provided a review of literature citing studies using systematic desensitization, with relaxation as the first step. Further cases are cited by Krumholtz and Thoresen (1969) and

Lazarus (1971). Lazarus has also recorded his relaxation material on tape. Most of the published materials on relaxation seem most applicable to adolescents and adults, and no intentions are stated regarding the application of these models to children. While the use of these models with children is not proscribed, such an extension is not readily apparent. A script written just for children could conceivably enhance the process of helping children learn to relax.

Relaxation exercises designed especially for children can help them to become aware of the feelings of body tension and provide skills to reduce it. Children can be taught how to reduce their muscle tension, and this seems to reduce anxiety as well. There was one boy whose arms and legs seemed like perpetual motion machines, yet he showed no awareness of this manifest tension. He mentioned that his parents were considering "putting me on some kind of pills to help me pay attention better." Though he denied any feelings of tension, he agreed to try a few relaxation exercises. He worked hard on the exercises but said he didn't feel any different afterward. Five minutes later his puzzled expression became a grin as he said, "It worked!"

Relaxation training can take place during individual or group counseling sessions, in physical education classes, or in a regular classroom setting. Once children develop the skills, they can relax without instructions from a trainer and thereby implement a higher degree of self-control. If successful mastery of relaxation skills works like successful mastery of academic tasks, then perhaps a case could be made for improved self-concept as well.

In training children to relax various muscle groups, it is not necessary that they be able to identify and locate them. The use of the child's fantasy can be incorporated into the instructions in such a manner that the appropriate muscle groups will automatically be used. Some precedent for the use of fantasy in a similar context was set by Lazarus and Abramovitz (1962). The use of fantasy also serves to attract and maintain a child's interest. One child told his counselor that the exercises stopped the butterflies in his stomach. The butterfly imagery expressed a real feeling for him; it has been replaced by the feelings connoted by a lazy cat.

It has been noted that although children will agree that they want to learn how to relax, they don't want to practice their newly acquired skills under the watchful eyes of their classmates. Fortunately, several muscle groups can be relaxed without much gross motor activity, and practice can go unnoticed. It pleases some children to perform these exercises in class and relax themselves without drawing the attention of those around them. It seemed important to one little girl that the exercises be "our secret that we won't tell the other kids." The effects of this type of training can extend beyond the classroom. A fourth-grade boy said that he used the exercises to help him get to sleep at night.

Below is a relaxation script designed for and used successfully with children in the intermediate grades. This script is similar in design to those used with adults (Carkhuff 1969, Lazarus 1971) but is intended to be more appealing to children. It is likely that the script is equally appropriate for children in the primary grades. Counselors are encouraged to experiment with it and to revise and extend it to include specific interests of children and incorporate other muscle groups. Eight muscle groups are included here. Other exercises can be developed to work with the upper thighs, upper arms, and different muscles around the face and neck as well as the flexing muscles in the feet and extending muscles in the hands.

In working with this script it is recommended that no more than fifteen minutes be devoted to the exercises at any one time and that no more than three muscle groups be introduced at one time. In the initial training sessions, the children are learning a new concept and new material. Two or three short sessions per week will help to establish these new behaviors. Aside from theoretical considerations, it is just too hard for some children to keep their eyes closed for more than fifteen minutes. Later sessions serve more to maintain the skills and provide a foundation for work in other areas. This type of session can follow a weekly pattern with ten or fifteen minutes devoted to relaxation, and the remainder of the time can be spent on other things.

It should be noted that many of the instructions should be repeated many more times than are indicated in the script and that such repetitions have been intentionally deleted. Each child or group of children is unique. Timing and pacing must follow the individual pattern created in the specific situation. One word of caution requires consideration: Children tend to get into this type of experience as much or more than adults and they are likely to be a bit disoriented if the session ends abruptly. Preparing children to leave the relaxed state is just as important as proper introduction and timing.

A Relaxation Training Script

Introduction

Today we're going to do some special kinds of exercises called *relaxation exercises.* These exercises help you learn how to relax when you're feeling uptight and help you get rid of those butterflies-in-your-stomach kinds of feelings. They're also kind of neat, because you can do some of them in the classroom without anybody noticing.

In order for you to get the best feelings from these exercises, there are some rules you must follow. First, you must do exactly what I say, even if it seems kind of silly. Second, you must try hard to do what I say. Third, you must pay attention to your body. Throughout these exercises, pay attention to how your muscles feel when they are tight and when they are loose and relaxed. And, fourth, you must practice. The more you practice the more relaxed you can get. Does anyone have any questions?

Are you ready to begin? Okay. First, get as comfortable as you can in your chair. Sit back, get both feet on the floor, and just let your arms hang loose. That's fine. Now close your eyes and don't open them until I say to. Remember to follow my instructions very carefully, try hard, and pay attention to your body. Here we go.

Hands and Arms

Pretend you have a whole lemon in your left hand. Now squeeze it hard. Try to squeeze all the juice out. Feel the tightness in your hand and arm as you squeeze. Now drop the lemon. Notice how your muscles feel when they are relaxed. Take another lemon and squeeze it. Try to squeeze this one harder than you did the first one. That's right. Real hard. Now drop your lemon and relax. See how much better your hand and arm feel when they are relaxed. Once again, take a lemon in your left hand and squeeze all the juice out. Don't leave a single drop. Squeeze hard. Good. Now relax and let the lemon fall from your hand. (Repeat the process for the right hand and arm.)

Arms and Shoulders

Pretend you are a furry, lazy cat. You want to stretch. Stretch your arms out in front of you. Raise them up high over your head. Way back. Feel the pull in your shoulders. Stretch higher. Now just let your arms drop back to your sides. Okay, kittens, let's stretch again. Stretch your arms out in front of you. Raise them over your head. Pull them back, way back. Pull hard. Now let them drop quickly. Good. Notice how your shoulders feel more relaxed. This time let's have a great big stretch. Try to touch the ceiling. Stretch your arms way out in front of you. Raise them way up high over your head. Push them way, way back. Notice the tension and pull in your arms and shoulders. Hold tight, now. Great. Let them drop very quickly and feel how good it is to be relaxed. It feels good and warm and lazy.

Shoulder and Neck

Now pretend you are a turtle. You're sitting out on a rock by a nice peaceful pond, just relaxing in the warm sun. It feels nice and warm and safe here. Oh-oh! You sense danger. Pull your head into your house. Try to pull your shoulders up to your ears and push your head down into your shoulders. Hold in tight. It isn't easy to be a turtle in a shell. The danger is past now. You can come out into the warm sunshine, and, once again, you can relax and feel the warm sunshine. Watch out now! More danger, Hurry, pull your head back into your house and hold it tight. You have to be closed in tight to protect yourself. Okay, you can relax now. Bring your head out and let your shoulders relax. Notice how much better it feels to be relaxed than to be all tight. One more time, now. Danger! Pull your head in. Push your shoulders way up to your ears and hold tight. Don't let even a tiny piece of your head show outside your shell. Hold it. Feel the tenseness in your neck and shoulders. Okay. You can come out now. It's safe again. Relax and feel comfortable in your safety. There's no more danger. Nothing to worry about. Nothing to be afraid of. You feel good.

Jaw

You have a giant jawbreaker bubble gum in your mouth. It's very hard to chew. Bite down on it. Hard! Let your neck muscles help you. Now relax. Just let your jaw hang loose. Notice how good it feels just to let your jaw drop. Okay, let's tackle that jawbreaker again now. Bite down. Hard. Try to squeeze it out between your teeth. That's good. You're really tearing that gum up. Now relax again. Just let your jaw drop off your face. It feels so good just to let go and not have to fight that bubble gum. Okay, one more time. We're really going to tear it up this time. Bite down. Hard as you can. Harder. Oh, you're really working hard. Good. Now relax. Try to relax your whole body. You've beaten the bubble gum. Let yourself go as loose as you can.

Face and Nose

Here comes a pesky old fly. He has landed on your nose. Try to get him off without using your hands. That's right, wrinkle up your nose. Make as many wrinkles in your nose as you can. Scrunch your nose up real hard. Good. You've chased him away. Now you can relax your nose. Oops, here he comes back again. Right back in the middle of your nose. Wrinkle up your nose again. Shoo him off. Wrinkle it up hard. Hold it just as tight as you can. Okay, he flew away. You can relax your face. Notice that when you scrunch up your nose that your cheeks and your mouth and your forehead and your eyes all help you, and they get tight, too. So when you relax your nose, your whole face relaxes too, and that feels good. Oh-oh! This time that old fly has come back, but this time he's on your forehead. Make lots of wrinkles. Try to catch him between all those wrinkles. Hold it tight, now. Okay, you can let go. He's gone for good. Now you can just relax. Let your face go smooth, no wrinkles anywhere. Your face feels nice and smooth and relaxed.

Stomach

Hey! Here comes a cute baby elephant. But he's not watching where he's going. He doesn't see you lying there in the grass, and he's about to step on your stomach. Don't move. You don't have time to get out of the way. Just get ready for him. Make your stomach very hard. Tighten up your stomach muscles real tight. Hold it. It looks like he is going the other way. You can relax now. Let your stomach go soft. Let it be as relaxed as you can. That feels so much better, Oops, he's coming this way again. Get ready. Tighten up your stomach. Real hard. If he steps on you when your stomach is hard, it won't hurt. Make your stomach into a rock. Okay, he's moving away again. You can relax now. Kind of settle down, get comfortable, and relax. Notice the difference between a tight stomach and a relaxed one. That's how we want it to feel—nice and loose and relaxed. You won't believe this, but this time he's really coming your way and no turning around. He's headed straight for you. Tighten up. Tighten hard. Here he comes. This is really it. You've got to hold on tight. He's stepping on you. He's stepped over you. Now he's gone for good. You can relax completely. You're safe. Everything is okay, and you can feel nice and relaxed.

This time imagine that you want to squeeze through a narrow fence and the boards have splinters on them. You'll have to make yourself very skinny if you're going to make it through. Suck your stomach in. Try to squeeze it up against your backbone. Try to be as skinny as you can. You've got to get through. Now relax. You don't have to be skinny now. Just relax and feel your stomach being warm and loose. Okay, let's try to get through that fence now. Squeeze up your stomach. Make it touch your backbone. Get it real small and tight. Get as skinny as you can. Hold tight, now. You've got to squeeze through. You got through that skinny little fence and no splinters. You can relax now. Settle back and let your stomach come back out where it belongs. You can feel really good now. You've done fine.

Legs and Feet

Now pretend that you are standing barefoot in a big, fat mud puddle. Squish your toes down deep into the mud. Try to get your feet down to the bottom of the mud puddle. You'll probably need your legs to help you push. Push down, spread your toes apart, and feel the mud squish up between your toes. Now step out of the mud puddle. Relax your feet. Let your toes go loose and feel how nice that is. It feels good to be relaxed. Back into the mud puddle. Squish your toes down. Let your leg muscles help push your feet down. Push your feet. Hard. Try to squeeze that mud puddle dry. Okay. Come back out now. Relax your feet, relax your legs, relax your toes. It feels so good to be relaxed. No tenseness anywhere. You feel kind of warm and tingly.

Conclusion

Stay as relaxed as you can. Let your whole body go limp and feel all your muscles relaxed. In a few minutes I will ask you to open your eyes, and that will be the end of this session. As you go through the day remember how good it feels to be relaxed. Sometimes you have to make yourself tighter before you can be relaxed, just as we did in these exercises. Practice these exercises every day to get more and more relaxed. A good time to practice is at night, after you have gone to bed and the lights are out and you won't be disturbed. It will help you get to sleep. Then, when you are a really good relaxer, you can help yourself relax here at school. Just remember the elephant, or the jawbreaker, or the mud puddle, and you can do our exercises and nobody will know. Today is a good day, and you are ready to go back to class feeling very relaxed. You've worked hard in here, and it feels good to work hard. Very slowly, now, open your eyes and wiggle your muscles around a little. Very good. You've done a good job. You're going to be a super relaxer.

References

Carkhuff, R. R. (1969). *Helping and Human Relations,* vol. I. New York: Holt, Rinehart & Winston.

Krumholtz, J. D., and Thoresen, C. E. (1969). *Behavioral Counseling: Cases and Techniques.* New York: Holt, Rinehart & Winston.

Lazarus, A. A. (1971). *Behavior Therapy and Beyond.* New York: McGraw-Hill.

Lazarus, A. A., and Abramovitz, A. (1962). The use of emotive imagery in the treatment of children's phobias. *Journal of Mental Science* 108:191–195.

Woody, R. H. (1971). *Psychobehavioral Counseling and Therapy: Integrating Behavioral and Insight Techniques.* New York: Appleton-Century-Crofts.

PART V
Board Games

21

Checkers

RICHARD A. GARDNER

It is important to state at the outset that I consider the game of checkers to be relatively low in therapeutic efficiency when one compares it to the wide variety of other therapeutic games generally utilized in child psychotherapy. My main reason for taking this position is that the game's potential for eliciting fantasy is low and therefore, it is not likely that the therapist will learn as much about unconscious processes as he or she would from games that more directly elicit projective material. The more structure and rules a game has, the less the likelihood that such material will emerge. Conversely, the closer the game resembles a "blank screen" the more likely the therapist will obtain material derived from unconscious processes. This drawback notwithstanding, the game has a definite place in the child psychotherapist's armamentarium. The game of chess, however, is of far lower psychotherapeutic value. Whereas a game of checkers can generally be completed within 10 to 15 minutes, the game of chess rarely can and usually goes beyond the standard 45 to 50 minute session. Continuing in the next session is impractical because the likelihood of all the pieces being in the same place at the time of the next session is extremely small. Furthermore, playing a 10- to 15-minute game of low therapeutic efficiency still leaves a significant portion of the session available for more highly efficient therapeutic modalities. Playing chess does not provide this opportunity.

The author's search of the literature has revealed very little on this subject. Other than articles by Loomis (1964, 1976), Levinson (1976), and the author (Gardner 1969), only occasional references to it were found—and then in the context of discussions of other aspects of play therapy.

This is not surprising in that its low therapeutic efficacy does not lend the game to extensive discussions of its psychotherapeutic value.

Description of the Game

Because the vast majority of readers are probably familiar with the game of checkers, a detailed description is not warranted. The game is well known throughout the western world and has been popular for thousands of years. It was played in the days of the pharaohs and is mentioned in the works of Homer and Plato. Basically, the game consists of a board of 64 squares, 32 black interspaced with 32 red. One player is supplied with 12 red checkers and the other with 12 black checkers. The players place their checkers on the black squares only, in the first three rows. Accordingly, because there are eight rows, the two center rows remain unoccupied at the onset of play. The checkers may only be moved diagonally along the black squares. The initial aim is to progressively advance one's checkers to the row closest to the opponent in order to obtain a king (a double checker). Regular checkers can only proceed in the forward direction one space at a time, in the direction toward the opponent. Kings, however, may move in any direction. The primary aim of the game is to jump an opponent's piece and remove it from the board. Jumping can only be accomplished when an opponent's piece is on the contiguous black diagonal square and the square beyond the opponent's piece is unoccupied. The player then jumps over the opponent's piece and removes it from the board. If the player is in a position to jump, then the rules require that the jump be made even if such jump then exposes the player to significant retaliation by the opponent, for example, a responding double or triple jump. The game ends when one player has been completely depleted of playing pieces.

Case Illustrations

The game can be of both diagnostic and therapeutic value. The manner in which the player plays the game and the comments made during the course of the game can provide the therapist with material of diagnostic value. In addition, the therapist's responses and the interchanges that evolve from the players' behavior and statements can be therapeutic. However, it is important for the reader to appreciate that much of the time may be spent in interchanges and activities that are of little, if any, therapeutic value. I will focus here on the potentially diagnostic and therapeutic material that may emerge.

Self-Esteem Problems

Insecure children will sometimes hesitate to begin playing the game because of the fear that they may lose. Instead, they may suggest a game of pure chance in which there is less likelihood of humiliation. Such a child may ask, "Are you good?" in the hope that the therapist will be a poor player and thereby increase the child's chances of winning. They may insist on going first each time, again in the hope of reducing the likelihood of losing. In the course of play such children may frequently interrupt the game to count the checkers in order to determine who is winning. Children with feelings of low self-worth are typically "sore losers." Sore losers are usually children with profound feelings of inadequacy whose need for winning to compensate for their feelings of low self-worth is exaggerated. They will often play a hard game, put all their energies into it, and moan at every loss or disadvantage. It is as if their whole worth as human beings depends on the outcome of the game. The therapist, however, should not fall into the trap of invariably allowing these children to win. The world will not be so benevolent and the child is not being provided with a reality experience. Allowing such children to win tends to perpetuate the use of the sore loser reaction as a way of manipulating others into letting them win. (Many children appreciate at some level that the adult is doing this.) Parents and therapists may so indulge the child, but peers are rarely going to do so.

Such a child, when playing with great tension and fear of losing, might be told, "You think that my whole opinion of you is based on the outcome of this game. That's just not so. My opinion of someone is based on many things and most of these things are much more important than whether or not the person wins or loses at checkers. What do you think about that?" My hope here is that the child will then engage in a discussion of my comments. But even if this overture is not successful (commonly the case with most children) the child's actually having the experience that the therapist does not laugh at or humiliate him or her for losing can be a corrective emotional experience. Alexander and French (1946) emphasized this important aspect of the therapeutic process.

Self-esteem must, at least in part, be based on *actual* competence, not delusional or fantasized competence (Gardner 1973b). It is common practice on the part of parents and teachers to attempt to enhance children's feelings of self-worth by praising them in an abstract way, for example, "What a nice (kind, good) boy you are" and "What a lovely girl." Such comments are often meaningless. Because they do not direct their attention to some specific quality or area of competence they are not likely to be successful in enhancing feelings of self-worth. And, if the child senses that he or she is being "buttered-up" this may lower self-worth—especially in the sensitive child who appreciates that the adult is utilizing these gratuitous compliments because of the fact that the praiser cannot think of anything genuine to praise. Far more effective compliments are: "What a beautiful model boat you built," "Good catch!" and so on. These focus on the actual qualities and accomplishments that are proof of the child's capabilities. In the game of checkers one can accomplish this with such comments as, "That was a very clever move," "Gee, I fell right into your trap," "Boy, you really had me sweating there for a while."

Related to the issue of competence is that of competition. In fact, it is very difficult to separate entirely the two issues. One cannot truly assess one's competence without measuring it against the competence of others. And this comparison process inevitably introduces an element of competition. There are those who believe that all competition is psychologically detrimental and ultimately ego-debasing, both for the winner and the loser. I am not in agreement. I believe that one must differentiate between healthy and unhealthy competition. In healthy competition there is respect for one's opponent and the aim is to win but not to degrade and humiliate one's adversary. In unhealthy competition these undesirable factors may become predominant. If not for healthy competition, we might all still be living in caves. Unhealthy competition, however, has resulted in much grief in the world and has resulted in many people suffering significant pain, torture, and even murder. Winning a hard-fought game of checkers—in a benevolently competitive way—can provide the child with an increased sense of self-worth.

Holmes (1964) emphasizes this point. He describes the fiasco that resulted in the physical education program of his adolescent residential treatment center when rivalry and scorekeeping were eliminated when games were played. The boys refused to attend. However, when a vigorous program of training and competition was instituted, Holmes reports,

The boys left the gymnasium perspiring, panting, and bone-weary. They complained lavishly and in chorus. They were bright-eyed, square-shouldered, and flushed with pride in the aftermath of battle. The boys follow a year-round schedule of coaching in tackle football with full equipment, basketball, boxing, baseball, and track. Each of these endeavors requires many consecutive weeks of monotonous drill, all without a prospect of immediate reward. When they have acquired sufficient skill and strength to qualify for competition, the boys are forthwith subjected to the 'threat' of winning and losing. The approach has provided them with an earned and well-deserved sense of masculine accomplishment. [pp. 319–321)

A number of years ago, the author had an experience while playing checkers with a child that demonstrates some important points related to competition, winning, and ego-enhancement. While playing checkers with a 5-year-old boy, he exhibited what I thought was an exaggerated investment in whether or not he was winning. In order to help alter what I considered to be an inappropriate attitude, I said to him, "Andy, the important thing is how much fun you have while playing, not whether you win the game." To this he replied, "No, you're wrong, the *important* thing is whether you win the game!" The boy was for the most part right. We pay lip service to comments such as mine, but who of us would enjoy tennis, bridge, or chess were there no winner. My revised advice to him would be, "There are two important things: how much you enjoy playing the game and whether you win; both can be fun."

The issue of competition and the therapeutic benefit of winning leads necessarily to the question of whether the therapist should let the child win. This may be a dilemma. If the therapist plays honestly and wins most games, this can be antitherapeutic in that the child may be humiliated and deprived of the feeling of accomplishment associated with winning. If the therapist purposely loses, the child may benefit from the gratifications of winning, but the therapist is being dishonest with the patient, and the child may sense this and lose trust in him or her. Although the author is a strong proponent of being honest with children (generally it is a *sine qua non* of therapy), this is one of the situations in which the author considers falsification of the truth to be justified. He allows the child to win or lose depending on what is therapeutically indicated at that time for that particular patient. He has not found his patients to have basically lost trust in him over this duplicity, probably because there is so much openness and honesty in compensation, and possibly because winning and losing is usually so balanced that the child does not become suspicious. Such duplicity, used sparingly and with discretion, serves to enhance the children's self-esteem and makes them feel worthwhile and competent.

The child with feelings of low self-worth may try to change the rules in the middle of the game in order to improve his or her chances of winning. For example, the rules of the game are that one *must* jump if one is in the position to do so. Insecure children may recognize that complying with this rule will place them in a particularly disadvantageous position and may then refuse to jump. To such a child, I will generally say, "Look, this game is no fun if we don't play by the rules. If you want to continue playing with me you're going to have to follow the rules. I'm sure that if you tried to change the rules in the middle of the game with your friends, they probably wouldn't want to play with you again." My response here is based on the assumption that if the child were to be allowed to change the rules, the sense of ego-enhancement that might then come from winning would be compromised by the knowledge that the success was not honestly attained. Furthermore, some useful information is provided the child regarding peer relationships. My hope here is that if I am heard, my advice will improve the child's relationships and thereby enhance feelings of self-worth. However, after making this comment I might add, "If you want to make up special rules for the next game, rules that apply to both of us, I'll be glad to try them. But remember, once we agree to the rules at the beginning of the game, they can't be changed in the middle of the game."

One should observe whether the child is having fun while playing the game. Pleasure enhances self-esteem and serves as a universal antidote to many psychogenic problems. It has been said that "pleasure is the food of the ego." I am in full agreement with this statement. While one is having fun, one is less likely to be dwelling on one's psychogenic problems. With joking and laughing even further therapeutic benefit may be derived from the game. If, however, the child is not deriving pleasure from the game, it behooves the therapist to attempt to ascertain why. And such failure to enjoy it may be the result of a variety of psychogenic problems, some of which will be discussed later.

Psychotherapy, like all forms of treatment, has both advantages and disadvantages—as well as potential risks. One of the risks of psychotherapy is that the patient may compare himself or herself unfavorably with the therapist and this can lower feelings of self-worth. After all, a central element in the therapeutic process is the therapist's pointing out the patient's errors. No matter how sensitively this is done, and no matter how much benevolence there may be in the therapist's communication in this area, there is no question that a game of one-upmanship is being played. Accordingly, there is an intrinsic ego-debasing factor in the psychotherapeutic process, the benefits to be derived by the patient notwithstanding. In classical psychoanalysis especially there is this risk. The analyst strictly refrains from revealing his or her deficiencies to the patient and this cannot but ultimately be an ego-debasing factor in the treatment. Accordingly, when the therapist can reveal a deficiency in a noncontrived way in the course of treatment it can lessen the influence of this ego-lowering element in treatment. The way in which a therapist lost this opportunity, while playing a game of checkers with a child, is demonstrated well in the following illustration.

Case Illustration

The child made a poor move, to which the therapist responded: "Are you sure you want to do that?" The boy looked up slightly irritated, thought a moment and then replied: "I did it and don't want to change it." The child's manner and facial expression communicated his attitude: "I made the mistake and I'm man enough to accept the consequences." This was, indeed a mature and healthy response on the boy's part but, unfortunately, the therapist did not take full advantage of the further therapeutic opportunities this incident provided. Had he said, "You're right. I'm sorry I treated you like a baby. Good for you for stopping me," he would have accomplished a number of things: Such a comment would have revealed that the therapist, too, is fallible and that would have helped the patient see him as a human being, with both assets and liabilities. It would have thereby served to lessen the chances of the unrealistic idolization of the therapist that so often occurs in treatment. It would have further communicated that the therapist was mature enough to admit his errors and that such admission enhances one's manliness rather than detracts from it. In the identification with the therapist that inevitably takes place in successful treatment, the child would have been exposed to these healthier attitudes for incorporation. Lastly, the suggested comment would have reinforced the patient's mature reaction, thereby increasing the likelihood that it would become ingrained in his personality and be utilized in the future.

The actual experience of having engaged in an activity which has been mutually enjoyable is ego enhancing to the patient. This is not only related to the pleasure the child has derived from the game but because the child has been instrumental in providing the therapist with some pleasure as well. The child thereby feels needed, useful, and wanted. Such feelings are often minimal or even lacking in many children who are in treatment and experiencing them can be ego enhancing. Furthermore, the child may have learned some better playing techniques from the therapist that have have improved his or her game. The utilization of this knowledge in games with peers may be salutary, especially with regard to the enhanced feelings of self-worth that it provides.

Passive-Dependency

Passive-dependent children tend to be very compliant in many areas of their lives and this tendency is likely to reveal itself when playing checkers. Such children are likely to comply with the therapist's decisions with regard to the ground rules necessary prior to the game. For example, if asked which color checker he or she wants, the child may respond, "It doesn't matter, you take whichever one you want." Of course, the fear of engendering resentment in the therapist for insisting on a particular color may be operative in this response. Whether it be this or other psychodynamic factors that are operative in this response, the net result is that the patient is anxious to please.

Although strict adherence to the rules of the game require jumping when one has the opportunity, many children do not follow this rule when playing with peers. Most play according to one of three rules pertaining to whether one has to jump: (1) a player must jump if he or she is in a position to do so, (2) the player himself or herself can decide when in such a position, and (3) if the player fails to jump and could have done so, the opponent may remove from the board the checker that has failed to make the jump. The therapist does well to discuss with the child before the beginning of the game exactly which rule he or she is used to playing with. To assume that the child has played with the traditional rule may result in an "argument" as the game gets under way. Accordingly, at the outset, I generally ask children which of the rules they follow and may inform them of the traditional rule if they are not familiar with it. In each case, we make a decision regarding which rule should be followed. This, of course, is dependent on the clinical situation. With passive children, however, the child is very reluctant to make the decision and prefers that the therapist decide which of the three rules to follow. Again, one often sees a fear element here with regard to stating the preference.

Egocentricism

Some children are egocentric in compensation for feelings of low self-worth. Others, however, are egocentric because they may have been indulged by overprotective parents. On the other hand, others may be egocentric on a neurodevelopmental level, and this is especially true for children with neurologically based learning disabilities (to be discussed in a later section). These children have little capacity for putting themselves in the position of other people and "want what they want when they want it." They often do not seem to be affected by the negative effects of their narcissism. Rejections and even punishments often do not get them to appreciate that their self-serving attitudes are alienating. When with friends, they are reluctant to share, even when their friends leave the home because of their selfishness.

When playing the game of checkers, such a child might insist that his or her version of the rules is the correct one and be very unreceptive to playing even one game with another rule. Such children will often not wait their turn and become very impatient when the therapist pauses to think about his or her next move. Therapists do well not to allow themselves to be rushed by such children and may even feign contemplation in order to give them some lessons in self-restraint and respect for the rights of others. Of course, children playing with great levels of tension and anxiety may also exhibit impatience that may appear to be egocentricism. Impulsive children, as well, may also appear egocentric.

By careful observation of the egocentric child's play, one may observe other manifestations of his or her narcissism. The child may focus only on his or her own pieces without thinking about the opponent's position. Such a child then easily falls into traps. The mechanism by which the child focuses on his or her own pieces only, to the exclusion of the therapist's, is probably analogous to social situations in which the child does not place himself or herself in another person's position. Such a child might be helped to become more socially aware by such comments as, "Watch out for my king," "You fell right into my trap," and "If you had moved there, you could have had a double jump." These comments, of course, not only help the child improve his or her game but, more importantly for the purposes of this problem, can increase these children's motivation to project themselves into other people's positions.

Withdrawn, Autistic, and Schizophrenic Children

These children have little capacity for pleasure, whether it be while playing checkers or engaging in other activities in life. They have little joy in winning and little disappointment when they lose. In the course of the game they may be distracted by their fantasies. Schizoid children, or those who prefer their fantasy world to that of reality, may obsess at the end of the game about how it might have been otherwise, for example, "If I had moved there, then I would have gotten a double jump," or "If the checkers had been like this, then I would have won." To this, the therapist should respond in such a way that the child is directly confronted with reality: "Yes it's true that if your checkers had been that way, you might have won. But, they weren't. Maybe in the next game you'll be able to beat me by doing that."

Suspicious or paranoid children play cautiously and defensively. Paranoid children may project their anger onto their therapists and fear retaliation for its expression. Accordingly, such a child may be afraid to win in anticipation of the therapist's hostile reaction. This may be expressed in such comments as, "Don't be mad at me if I win." They may hug their pieces to the sides and rear of the board and may spend long periods of time deliberating in order to avoid being jumped or trapped.

The child whose schizoid behavior is the result of environmental more than constitutional/genetic factors is likely to have come from a chaotic and unpredictable home. In such households, there is little structure and the disorganization so engendered in the child may reveal itself in the game of checkers. He or she does not follow the rules and follows no plan of attack during play. The therapist's insistence that the rules be adhered to can be therapeutic in that it provides the child with the living experience that if the rules are not followed then he or she will be deprived of the gratification of playing the game. Of course, if the child gets little pleasure from the game anyway, this deterrent will not prove significantly effective. In addition, the therapist's own commitment to an organized lifestyle can serve as a model in contrast to that of the child's parents and relatives.

Antisocial Behavior Disorder

Children with antisocial behavior may exhibit their symptoms in the game. Such children will often play an aggressive and serious game with great interest in winning. They will respond with glee at every advantage and then rub salt into the therapist's wounds if they do win. Hostility displaced from other sources becomes vented on the therapist. When losing, they may not hesitate to pick up the board and disrupt the whole game. Of course, this can be seen in other children such as neurologically impaired children with impulsivity or children with low self-esteem who cannot tolerate losing. In the extreme, such children have no hesitation trying to destroy the game itself—so great may be their rage.

Antisocial children often exhibit manifestations of associated impairments in superego development. This may manifest itself in their cheating during the game. The therapist does well to point this out to the child and not permit it. In such situations, I may make comments like, "Look, this game is no fun if you're going to cheat. If you want to play with me, you'll have to play it straight. I'm sure your friends feel the same way." The child here is being provided with a living experience that the therapist will not tolerate the antisocial behavior. Of course, if the child is willing to go further into the reasons why he or she is exhibiting such behavior, I am receptive to doing so. However, my experience has been that these children (like most children in therapy) are not particularly interested in gaining insight into the unconscious roots of their problems, in the hope that such revelations might bring about a reduction of their symptoms. And antisocial children, especially, because their symptoms are ego-syntonic, are even less motivated for such self-inquiry.

Obsessive-Compulsivity

Obsessive-compulsive children may be so wrapped up in their doubting, indecisiveness, and procrastination that they find it difficult to enjoy themselves. They may become concerned with whether the checkers touch the marginal lines of the squares and are often concerned as to whether the crown side of the checker faces upward on the kings and the noncrown side of the checker faces downward for the unkinged checkers. Whereas Freud considered unresolved, oedipal, especially sexual, problems to be central to the development of obsessive-compulsive symptoms, my experience has been that repressed anger is more often involved in the development of such symptomatology. Accordingly, I make attempts to lessen guilt over anger in the course of my work with these children. If, for example, I suspect that the child may be angry over the fact that I have won a game and is too inhibited to express such anger, I will make comments designed to reduce such inhibition, for example, "I can't imagine that you're not even a little bit angry over the fact that I have now won three games in a row. Most kids certainly would be. I know that I would be." "I think the main difference between you and other kids is this. Other kids who get angry show it; you get angry and don't show it." "What do you think would happen if you told me how angry you were?"

Neurologically Based Learning Disabilities

Children with neurologically based learning disabilities may exhibit many manifestations of their disorder—both the primary organic and the secondary psychogenic—in the course of playing the game. Elsewhere (Gardner 1973a, 1973c, 1974, 1975b, 1975c, 1979a, 1979c) the author has described in detail both the organic and the psychogenic manifestations of children with this class of disorders. For the sake of brevity, I will refer to these children as NBLD (neurologically based learning disabilities) children.

Although in the age group when most children are well acquainted with the game, NBLD children may not know how to play. This may be due to either intellectual impairment or lack of exposure. Because they tend to withdraw from others in an attempt to hide their deficits, many of these children often deprive themselves of development in areas of basic physiologic and neurologic competence. Accordingly, such a child might intellectually be capable of playing the game but might not display aptitude because of withdrawal. Such children might be ashamed to admit their ignorance of the game when invited to play and may anxiously suggest another activity. When one attempts to teach such children the game, their difficulty in understanding and following the rules, in remembering what has been learned, and in appreciating many of the concepts can make such teaching an arduous task.

Prior to play, the author generally lets the child set up the board and the checkers. These children may place the board with the central fold at 90 degrees to its normal position or put the checkers in the wrong squares. They may try to set up four rows instead of three, then run out of checkers, and then become frustrated and confused.

Characteristically, NBLD children play a sloppy game. They do not place checkers in the centers of the squares due to coordination, motor, and/or perceptual deficiencies. They often forget whether it is their own or their opponent's turn, especially if there has been a long thinking lapse between moves. In such pauses, they may ask what the opponent's last move was or even who made the last move. Such children have to be repeatedly reminded of the rules because they tend to forget them, for example, only kings can go backwards or it was decided at the beginning that one must jump if one is in a position to. They may continue to move their checkers directly ahead rather than diagonally and jump over two instead of one checker. They may even jump over their own pieces. They may have trouble differentiating between the powers of kings and the regular checkers, although they usually understand that it is preferable to have kings.

These children, because of their marked feelings of inadequacy and hypersensitivity to defeat, will often react badly to losing. And because of their impulsivity they are often unable to restrain their disappointment and angry reactions. They may mess up the board, turn it over, and even fling the checkers at the therapist. The normal child, when putting away the checkers, usually places them in the box in a symmetrical fashion, forming piles of equal height. When these children attempt to do this, they often have difficulties. The piles are of different heights and they have trouble forming a symmetrical pattern.

The following game of checkers was the first one played with a 12-year-old NBLD child with an IQ of about 80. It illustrates both the neurophysiological as well as the psychogenic pathological reactions that can be observed when these children play checkers.

Case Illustration

The patient was first asked if he would like to play a game of checkers. He replied, "OK, but I'm afraid I'll beat you." The comment revealed his feelings of inadequacy which he handled with compensatory bravado and projection onto the therapist of the retaliatory anger he would feel in himself if he were the loser. The author replied, "I usually don't take the game so seriously that I get angry if I lose. It's only a game, it doesn't mean the end of the world to me if I lose."

The patient chose red and tried to set up his checkers in four rows instead of three. Running out of checkers, he looked puzzled, removed them completely and tried again with the same results. I then set up mine, and after a few glances at my side of the board, he was successful on his third try. Suspecting that there might be much embarrassing tutoring later on, I let him learn this "without" me.

When asked about what rules he follows with regard to jumping, he said that the way he plays one doesn't have to jump. I agreed to play that way.

When I asked him who would go first, he replied, "Smoke before fire, so I go first." This comment, in the setting in which it was made, revealed many of his defects in conceptualization. The normal mnemonic that many children use to determine which color goes first is, "Fire before smoke." This refers to the colors red and black, and because fire precedes smoke, red goes first. The fact that the patient said, "Smoke before fire" revealed that he was not forming a visual image of the fire with the subsequent smoke, but was reiterating what he had heard. Furthermore, his rote repetition was also incorrectly recalled. Even if he were not thinking logically about the temporal sequence of smoke and fire, he still might have related smoke to black and fire to red. Had he done this, then by his statement "smoke before fire," blacks would have gone first. But because he had chosen red, it was obvious that his decision to go first had no relationship at all, on any level, to his comment.

Within a few moves, he was in a position to jump me and he asked if he had to jump. He had already forgotten the jumping rule we had agreed on. He made a number of errors commonly made by the NBLD child. He moved his own checkers backwards in the face of an attack and had to be reminded repeatedly that only kings can move backwards. He tried to jump his own checkers on a few occasions, did not see double jumps but only single ones, and often forgot to take my piece off the board after he had jumped it.

During play, he repeated, "If I beat you, I know you'll be a sore loser." Then he would reassure himself about his projected aggression: "You'll take it like a man," that is, "You'll repress your rage, you won't get angry at me the way I would with you if you won." The patient was again told that I didn't think the game so important that I judged myself or other people totally on whether or not they were good checker players.

At one point, the patient made an excellent blocking move. When I asked why he had so moved, he gave the wrong reason for the right move. He kept score by counting the number of checkers each of us had taken off the board and failed to take into account whether the pieces on the board were kings or not. When his checkers reached my side, he did not ask for a king, and when given kings, he did not move them to attack me from the rear.

In spite of all of this, the patient "won" the game, at which point he burst into gales of laughter. "I slaughtered you. . . . You can't win them all, old man . . . (guffaws). . . . Now, who's an expert at this game . . . (more cackling). . . . The expert beats them all . . . (further horse-laughs). . . ." Besides the compensatory ego enhancing mechanisms displayed here, the hostile element was also obvious. In this case, I represented his mother whom he unconsciously did wish to slaughter, because of her having sent him to a hospital for three years.

After some further chest thumping, the patient put the checkers back in the box. The piles were not of equal height and although this was finally accomplished, his attempts to form a symmetrical pattern of reds on one side and blacks on the other were unsuccessful.

Summary and Conclusions

When playing games with children, adults do far better for themselves and the children if they select a game that is enjoyable to both. When an adult finds a game tedious, but continues to play through obligation, the child is deprived of many of the benefits to be derived from the experience. The child usually senses the adult's boredom and lack of interest through the latter's impatience and easy irritability, and so the game can become a trying and oppressive ordeal. In child psychotherapy, it is especially important to make every attempt to engage in activities that are interesting and enjoyable to the therapist as well as the child. Checkers, which is a game that can be played with pleasure by both child and adult, is in this category.

After the first few games, however, much of the game's diagnostic value is gone but the therapeutic benefits can continue indefinitely. However, the therapist may find his or her enjoyment and interest lagging, especially after the game has exhausted its potential for diagnostic information. One way of stimulating ongoing interest in the therapist is to let the child get far ahead, then, when the therapist has only one or two checkers left, to the child's eight or nine, to play as diligently as one can. A variation that may also enhance the child's pleasure is to play "opposite checkers." In this variation one tries to get jumped and the "winner" is the one who is first depleted of all checkers.

Strupp (1975), one of the more sober evaluators of psychoanalytic psychotherapy, believes that a central element in the efficacy of psychoanalytic treatment is its capacity to teach individuals how to live more effectively and efficiently. When one handles life situations and problems in a better way, one is less likely to have to resort to neurotic adaptations. In a way, checkers can teach lessons in better living. One is responsible for one's fate and suffers the consequences of one's actions. Whether a person wins or loses is in part determined by one's own acts. If one plans ahead and is appropriately cautious, then one does better than if one sits back and leaves things to chance. The lesson of being master of one's fate is present in most skill games. However, one is not completely master; one must reckon too with others in the world with whom we must compromise, avert, deal with head on, and at times succumb to. All these lessons can be learned in microcosm in a relatively painless way in the game of checkers.

Checkers can also be used for decompression purposes at the end of a particularly tension-laden session. Although there may be little specific psychotherapeutic value derived from the game per se at that point, it does have the benefit of lessening tension. Finally, I consider it important to reiterate to the reader that checkers is a game of relatively low psychotherapeutic benefit. Accordingly, it should be used sparingly in the psychotherapeutic process. The author generally will use it only near the end of the session, after most of the time has been devoted to what he considers to be more highly efficient therapeutic activities. The reader who is interested in the author's views regarding what these are might refer to his publications in this area (1975a, 1979b). There are therapists who will spend many sessions completely devoted to playing checkers. I consider this to be a "cop out " for the therapist in that it is a relatively easy way to spend the session and it is a "rip off" for the patient and his or her family.

References

Alexander, F., and French, T. (1946). The principle of corrective emotional experience. In *Psychoanalytic Therapy: Principles and Application* pp. 66–70. New York: Ronald.

Gardner, R. A. (1969). The game of checkers as a diagnostic and therapeutic tool in child psychotherapy. *Acta Paedopsychiatrica,* 36:142–152.

_____ (1973a). *MBD: The Family Book about Minimal Brain Disfunction.* New York: Jason Aronson.

_____ (1973b). *Understanding Children: A Parents' Guide to Child Rearing.* Cresskill, NJ: Creative Therapeutics.

_____ (1973c). Psychotherapy of the psychogenic problems secondary to minimal brain disfunction. *International Journal of Child Psychotherapy,* 2:224–256.

_____ (1974). Psychotherapy of minimal brain disfunction. In *Current Psychiatric Therapies,* ed. J. Masserman, vol. 14, pp. 15–21. New York: Grune and Stratton.

_____ (1975a). *Psychotherapeutic Approaches to the Resistant Child.* New York: Jason Aronson.

_____ (1975b). Psychotherapy in minimal brain disfunction. In *Current Psychiatric Therapies,* ed. J. Masserman, vol. 15, pp. 25–38. New York: Grune and Stratton.

_____ (1975c). Techniques for involving the child with MBD in meaningful psychotherapy. *Journal of Learning Disabilities,* 8:16–26.

_____ (1979a). *The Objective Diagnosis of Minimal Brain Disfunction.* Cresskill, NJ: Creative Therapeutics.

_____ (1979b). Helping children cooperate in therapy. In *Basic Handbook of Child Psychiatry,* ed. J. Noshpitz, vol. 3, pp. 414–433. New York: Basic Books.

_____ (1979c). Psychogenic difficulties secondary to MBD. In *Basic Handbook of Child Psychiatry,* ed. J. Noshpitz, vol. 3, pp. 614–628. New York: Basic Books.

Holmes, D. J. (1964). *The Adolescent in Psychotherapy.* Boston: Little, Brown.

Levinson, B. M. (1976). Use of checkers in therapy. In *The Therapeutic Use of Child's Play,* ed. C. Schaefer, pp. 283–284. New York: Jason Aronson.

Loomis, E. A. (1964). The use of checkers in handling certain resistances in child therapy and child analysis. In *Child Psychotherapy,* ed. M. R. Haworth, pp. 407–411. New York: Basic Books.

_____ (1976). Use of checkers in handling resistance. In *The Therapeutic Use of Child's Play,* ed. C. Schaefer, pp. 385–390. New York: Jason Aronson.

Strupp, H. H. (1975). Psychoanalysis, "focal psychotherapy" and the nature of the therapeutic influence. *Archives of General Psychiatry,* 32:127–135.

22

Chess

WILLIAM H. SMITH

It is common practice in psychiatric hospitals to employ activities such as sports, games, and creative arts in treatment programs. How the therapeutic role of such activities is regarded, however, hinges on how the treatment process in general is conceptualized (Key et al. 1958). One widespread, highly influential view (Menninger 1948) emphasizes the role of activities in the expression and/or rechanneling of drive energies. In this view, the potential benefits that warrant the inclusion of these activities in a treatment program are that competition is an outlet for the instinctive aggressive drive and the act of creating serves the erotic, constructive, or creative drive. Another point of view (Llorens and Johnson 1966), one less anchored in the early, drive-oriented psychoanalytic theory, regards activities as enhancing adaptive functioning through the practice and mastery of ego skills: "These include physical and motor performance skills as well as skill in psychological, social and interpersonal interaction" (p. 179). Still another point of view (Barnard 1954) places most weight on *inter*personal rather than *intra*personal considerations: "Even more important than the specific activity is the emotional atmosphere in which the activity is carried on, and the relationships created between the patient and the therapist who guides the activity" (p. 22).

The thesis I shall advance here is that in evaluating activities for use in treatment, each activity should be regarded as a complex, multifaceted event—no dimension should either be ignored or attended to exclusively. The selection of activities that will further (or at least be compatible with) treatment aims can best proceed from a broad, thorough analysis of their characteristic elements. A framework or matrix within which such an appraisal of activities could be made would facilitate clinical decisions regarding the potential benefits or disadvantages of a given activity for a particular patient. I propose the following framework for such analysis. Descriptions should be made of: (1) the formal aspects, such as materials and space required; (2) the physical and intellectual prerequisites for participants; (3) the interpersonal aspects; (4) the opportunity afforded for gratification of needs and discharge of drive energies; and (5) the task demand from a cognitive, affective, and motoric-muscular standpoint. I do not intend to suggest that these considerations are independent of one another, only that for purposes of analysis they may profitably be separated. As a demonstration of this framework, I present an analysis of the game of chess.

Formal Aspects

Chess is a table or board game. Two players sit opposite one another across a game board upon which are thirty-two chess pieces, sixteen for each player. Each piece has a value commensurate with its freedom of movement and its consequent power to capture the opponent's pieces—except the king whose movements are limited but whose importance is paramount. The rules of the game are easily obtainable and need not be presented here. Suffice it to say that the object of the game is to direct the pieces according to their prescribed moves in a fashion designed to capture and remove the opponent's pieces until an opportunity is created to put the opponent's king in a position of capture—the checkmate.

All that is necessary beyond the pieces, the board, and the two players are two chairs, a table, and a lighted room sufficiently quiet to allow the players to concentrate.

Physical and Intellectual Prerequisites

No physical activity is required except that necessary to move pieces around the board without upsetting the others. Seeing the board and the pieces is, of course, necessary unless the set has been especially adapted for the blind. Exceptional intelligence is not required to play the game; however, a high level of intelligence (at least of a certain sort) is necessary for one to become an expert player. Most people can learn the basic elements of the game within a few hours' instruction. There is evidence that once acquired, the ability to play chess is not lost in psychosis (Fine 1956) and that patients described as schizophrenic can be taught to play (Pakenham-Walsh 1949).

Interpersonal Aspects

The interpersonal aspects of the game can occur on two levels—the cooperation and competition between the opponents, and the symbolic representation of human events through the characters and actions of the pieces. Beginning with the two players' agreement to begin the game, the entire activity is one of interdependency. Each player must await the move of the other before his own move, and each move must be calculated with regard to the opponent's preceding move. There must exist, then, an interpenetration of minds, with each player continually wondering what the opponent is thinking.

It is often said that there is no element of chance in chess. While this remark may seem an overstatement when applied to the play of novices, there is, even then, no doubt about where responsibility for the move lies. With no plausible latitude for rationalization or excuse, a loss is undeniably a loss, and a victory a victory; the responsibility for the outcome rests squarely on the players. In some activities, such as bowling, a player's performance can be assessed in absolute terms, that is, his score is not contingent on his opponent's performance. In chess, however, a move is good only in terms of the threat it poses to the opponent, and a move is poor only in terms of the opportunities it presents to the opponent. The competitive aspect of the game is clear; the point is to defeat the opponent. Chess is exclusively an intellectual contest and, as such, is particularly provocative for those whose intellectual performance is a source of self-esteem. Only improved performance in a rematch can attenuate the sting of defeat; and in each game the players face anew the prospect of losing, winning, or tying, for the game is not over until one of these outcomes is clear.

Since the interaction between players may be almost exclusively nonverbal, those who have difficulty talking to others may keep verbal interaction to a minimum while actually interacting quite closely, in the sense described above. When the two players are a therapist and his patient, as Fleming and Strong (1943) demonstrated, chess can be a valuable avenue of communication and even a primary therapeutic medium. Depending upon the skill and training of the therapist, the game can become an opportunity for interpretation of some of the patient's conflict areas, those manifested in his style of play and in the ways he experiences playing, winning, and losing.

A great deal has been written about the symbolic aspects of the game.[1] For example, Coriat (1941) said that

The unconscious symbolic oedipal nature of the game lies in the fact that the game is essentially a reanimation of the player's family conflict resulting from the Oedipus complex. The protection of the

---

[1] See Fine (1956) for a good summary of these ideas.

Queen from loss is for the purpose of retaining her as long as possible to attack the King. Whatever the character traits of the player or his rationalized conscious attitude during the game, the unconscious primary purpose is the same, a reenactment of the fundamental Oedipus conflict. [p. 35]

The basis for the assumption about the symbolic oedipal nature of the game lies in the fact that the destruction of the king is the aim of the game. The prohibitions against this father murder are nicely observed in the fact that the king is never actually captured and removed from the board. While this interpretation of the nature of the game has been "confirmed" by clinical observations of chess players, it seems possible that the symbolic significance of the activity may vary from player to player, though perhaps with this as the richest possibility. Indeed, Menninger et al. (1963) wrote, "In every chess game there are trillions of possible moves and there are almost as many combinations of symbolic gratifications for the players" (p. 143).

Gratification of Needs and Discharge of Drive Energies

Many writers (Coriat 1941, Fine 1956, Jones 1951) have emphasized the rich oedipal symbolism of the game as the major source of gratification, seeing it as touching upon conflicts around aggression, narcissism, homosexuality, and masturbation.[2] Narcissistic gratification may be derived through demonstration of intellectual prowess and through identification with the king. The mastery of a complex skill (or at least the improvement of one's ability to perform a difficult intellectual task) may also be a source of gratification. Since the game is generally considered a pastime of the intellectually gifted, some measure of social regard may be reaped, even though quite spuriously, from association with the game.

The discharge of energies in the game occurs in highly sublimated form, that is, far removed from direct drive expression. Fine (1956) states, "in the chess player . . . the ego is strong: it is capable of tolerating a great deal of libidinal stimulation, it can renounce primitive gratification with original objects and it can neutralize the drive energies to a high degree" (p. 28). To the extent that the game is a symbolic reenactment of an internal struggle, some gratification may be afforded by the projection of this painful struggle onto substituted inanimate objects, through partial

---

[2]This view of the game may partly account for the fact that it tends to be more attractive to men than to women.

drive expression via symbolic enactment and some degree of mastery over the conflict. The principal avenues of gratification in chess, therefore, are intellectual-narcissistic and highly sublimated aggressive ones.

Task Demand from a Cognitive, Affective, and Motoric-Muscular Standpoint

Since chess requires a minimum of physical involvement, strength, dexterity, coordination, and the like are of little relevance in this activity. The most salient aspect of chess is its emphasis upon intellectual processes. The rules of the game are strict, and the nature of play complex. Therefore, a standard of reality via rules is set forth against which numerous task demands emerge.

Although unflagging vigilance need not be rigidly maintained, concentration must be sufficient to allow the player not only to take careful note of the opponent's moves and strategy but also to pursue a series of mental trial actions—"if–then" propositions that will guide his decisions (e.g., if I move my pawn here, he will move his bishop there; if I then move my knight here, he will have to defend his queen with either his bishop or his knight, etc.). Each action must be preceded by thought and the consequences of each move carefully weighed. The player must be alert to what the opponent hopes to achieve by each of his moves and must plan each of his own moves accordingly; no information may be disregarded. A number of separate elements (e.g., values and positions of various pieces) must be appraised and coordinated in a systematic, organized way. Flexibility, that is, continual reevaluation of the situation, is also critical, for a plan will need to be modified or abandoned according to those changes introduced by the opponent's responses.

While the emphasis is upon logical and systematic thought, the thought must eventuate in action, but no action should be made impulsively or carelessly. No move should be made without benefit of prior thought. A player must maintain control over any affective stirring that might prove disruptive to judgment or attention.

Chess is an anxiety-provoking game. To quote Karl Menninger (1942): "Whatever else it is, chess is not a relaxing game. Playing chess is a very intense and exciting experience which only one who has gotten well into it can fully appreciate" (p. 81). Anxiety may be mobilized around winning or losing or symbolic aspects of the game. A constant threat may be posed by the fear that what is symbolic may become real, depending on the intactness of the players' ego defenses, but some reassurance is no doubt gained by the fact that it is, after all, only a game.

The necessity for constant thought also helps bind anxiety. In summary, the exercise of intellectual processes not only in executing the play of the game itself but also in controlling the affective potentialities attendant to the game's real and symbolic aspects can be said to be the principal adaptive challenge posed by chess.

Discussion

Finding that chess serves certain intrapsychic and interpersonal purposes for some persons does not, of course, mean it will do so for everyone. For that matter, the issue of whether adaptive capacities can be strengthened through exercise or practice is by no means an established fact (Reider 1967). While it is inviting and even somewhat compelling to assume that such capacities as persistence in the face of frustration or careful, meticulous planning and execution of a project would generalize to areas of life other than those in which they are practiced, this is an empirical issue that is far from conclusively established.

However, case history reports (Fleming and Strong 1943, Slap 1957) have indicated that for *some* patients chess may be a powerful treatment tool. Fine (1956) suggested that for one expert player chess actually warded off a psychosis for a time. He also quoted a prison psychologist as saying that prisoners who learned chess during their incarceration were less likely to be recidivists, since they appeared to have learned better ways of handling their aggression.

While my purpose in analyzing the game of chess was not to promote the use of chess in treatment, some comments about its application might illustrate the potential use of such an analysis. As part of a program of reinstating orderly, logical, goal-directed thinking, playing chess might be encouraged for those suffering a breakdown of ideational defenses. To foster the interposition of thought between impulse and action, the careful weighing of consequences before acting, it might be encouraged for people whose difficulties include impulsivity. Someone for whom verbal communication is too anxiety provoking could use chess as a vehicle for establishing an interacting relationship. Encouraging the expression of aggression in controlled, socially appropriate ways, that is, to offer chess as an avenue of sublimation, might also prove helpful for those whose aggressive impulses are not well controlled. The game might be discouraged for those whose narcissistic valuation of themselves and/or their intellect is a problem. Also to be discouraged from playing might be those who tend to have difficulty relating to others in other than intellectually pretentious or competitive ways. These few examples show how once the various elements of an activity are spelled out, it can be recommended or discouraged for use in a treatment situation, depending on the treatment goals for the given patient.[3]

A treatment team, having analyses comparable to the one presented here for all the activities at its disposal, could prescribe a combination of activities coordinated to serve complex treatment aims. For example, one activity might be included in a patient's schedule principally because it allowed him to experience self-esteem building gratification in completing projects that eventuate in a product (such as ceramics, woodworking, etc.), another because it promoted careful thought and control over impulsivity (such as chess, radio repair, etc.), and another because it involved cooperation with a number of peers (such as a drama group, patient newspaper, etc.). Prevailing treatment philosophies and theoretical persuasions ultimately guide the use of any activity: the characteristics of the patient that are deemed important to modify, the point at which an activity is introduced into a treatment process and for what specific purpose, and so forth. By the same token, activities comprise only a portion of a therapeutic milieu and may play a much larger role in the treatment process for some patients than for others. However, for whatever uses activities are put in a treatment program and with whatever treatment philosophy prevails, the outline offered here for analyzing the elements of the activities employed may prove helpful, since it offers a comprehensive view of any activity.

References

Barnard, R. (1954). Milieu therapy. *Menninger Quarterly* 8:20–24.

Coriat, I. H. (1941). The unconscious motives of interest in chess. *Psychoanalytic Review* 28:30–36.

Fine, R. (1956). Psychoanalytic observations on chess and chess masters. *Psychoanalysis,* Vol. 4, Monograph 1.

Fleming, J., and Strong, S. M. (1943). Observations on the use of chess in the therapy of an adolescent boy. *Psychoanalytic Review* 30:399–416.

Jones, E. (1951). The problem of Paul Morphy: a contribution to the psychology of chess. In *Essays in Applied Psychoanalysis.* Vol. 1: *Miscellaneous Essays.* pp. 165–196. London: Hogarth.

Key, E. W., et al. (1958). *Project 52: A Study in Adjunctive Therapies Coordination.* Topeka, KS: Washburn University.

---

[3]In offering this framework for analysis of the intrinsic qualities of activities, I have not touched upon the personal characteristics of the treatment personnel or the relationship established between staff personnel and patient. This omission is by no means a tacit implication that such relationships are not important; it is only that such considerations are not the focus of this chapter.

Llorens, L. A., and Johnson, P. A. (1966). Occupational therapy in an ego-oriented milieu. *American Journal of Occupational Therapy* 20:178–181.

Menninger, K. (1942). Chess. *Bulletin of the Menninger Clinic* 6:80–83.

Menninger, K., et al. (1963). *The Vital Balance: The Life Process in Mental Health and Illness.* New York: Viking.

Menninger, W. C. (1948). Recreation and mental health. *Recreation* 42:340–346.

Pakenham-Walsh, R. (1949). Chess as a form of recreational therapy. *Journal of Mental Science* 95:203–204.

Reider, N. (1967). Preanalytic and psychoanalytic theory of play and games. In *Motivations in Play, Games and Sports,* ed. R. Slovenko and J. A. Knight, pp. 13–38. Springfield, IL: Charles C Thomas.

Slap, J. W. (1957). Some clinical and theoretical remarks on chess. *Journal of Hillside Hospital* 6:150–155.

PART VI

Electronic Techniques in Play Therapy

23

Nintendo Games

JAMES E. GARDNER

Therapists working with children have long used a variety of activities in sessions with their young patients. Rather surprisingly, however, despite the appeal of games and their seemingly obvious rightness when working with children, there is no mention of formal game use in the early literature on play therapy (Schaefer and Reid 1986).

Play seems to have been introduced into child psychotherapy by clinicians such as Anna Freud (1928), Klein (1932), and Axline (1947). The purposes of play ranged from the enhancement of interest in the therapy session to the promotion of fantasy expression and ventilation of feeling. Loomis (1957) discussed the game of checkers and its use in therapy with children. Subsequently, the literature on games in therapy and games for therapy has proliferated (Berg 1982, Burks 1978, Gardner 1973a,b, Oden 1976, Schaefer and Reid 1986, Zakich 1975). Computer and computer-type games such as Nintendo, Atari, and Sega have been added to the inventory of traditional card and board games.

Nintendo, a game system that plays on a regular television set with arcade quality-type graphics, has been found to be an excellent ice-breaker and rapport-builder. Many children are surprised that a grown-up (the therapist, in this case) has a computer game player and can play the games well. The interaction over the games serves to provide enjoyment and to place therapist and child on a common ground—the territory of computer games.

As with any game, however, and perhaps with almost any activity, the interaction over the games can branch out into questions of sportsmanship, fairness, cooperation, rivalry, the nature of winning and losing and how one conducts oneself under the different circumstances, and the nature and meaning of competition. Not only do the games provide excellent behavioral observation opportunities for the therapist, they also provide innumerable chances for the therapist to model selected appropriate game-playing behaviors while reinforcing same on the part of the child.

Many of the games provide excellent opportunities for the therapist to observe: (a) the child's repertoire of problem-solving strategies (e.g., Legend of Zelda); (b) the child's ability to perceive and recall subtle cues as well as foresee consequences of behavior and act on past consequences (e.g., Super Mario Brothers); (c) eye–hand coordination (almost all the games involve this but, especially, games such as Duck Hunt for younger children and Gradius, Mach Rider, and others for older children); (d) the release of aggression and control of same (e.g., Kung Fu); (e) the ability to develop appropriate methods of dealing with the joys of victory and frustrations of defeat in a more sports-oriented arena (e.g., Techmo Baseball and Football, Basketball, Soccer, etc.); (f) the satisfaction of cognitive activity in the involvement of the recall of bits of basic information (e.g., Jeopardy); and (g) the enjoyment of mutually coordinating one's activities with another in a spirit of cooperation (e.g., Gyromite).

Four Brief Case Presentations

The use of the Nintendo games discussed as follows is considered only a part of the child's therapy, an adjunct to the program. Other aspects of the therapy such as the relationship between child and therapist, story telling, restructuring of home contingencies, ventilation through drawing or doll play, and direct or indirect interpretations of the child's behavior were used with each child. However, for the children noted in the following, and for many other children, the Nintendo games were, perhaps, the most useful factors in the child's improvement in therapy.

Case Examples

D. is a 5-year-old only child who was referred for fighting and generally disruptive behavior in his kindergarten classroom. His diagnostic visits indicated intact conceptual-perceptual systems and no indication of attention deficit disorder.

Parents reported probable abuse in the form of excessive punishment by a housekeeper some eighteen months before; this situation lasted for half a year or more before the housekeeper left.

Subsequent to the housekeeper leaving, D. fearfully confided to his parents the physical and verbal punishments that had been visited on him. D. was very angry at the housekeeper and his parents for allowing her to come into the house and for not protecting him. He was also resistant to any new housekeepers or baby sitters, manifesting extreme anger when parents left home to go to work or out in the evening.

By the time D. was referred to therapy, the situation at home and at school was turbulent. The therapist moved to structure the situation at home and assist the parents toward becoming: (a) more consistent in dealing with D.'s anger and separation fears, (b) less guilty and consequently less easy for D. to manipulate, (c) able to perceive ways in which their busy work schedules could better accommodate the responsibilities of parenting a little boy.

In various sessions with D. the therapist (T.) used art-, play-, and talk-therapy initially but the child's disruptive behavior at home and school continued. D. was assisted in ventilating his feelings of anger and betrayal using toy people, storytelling techniques, acceptance of his feelings, and direct interpretation of his behavior. D. could and did discuss his anger toward the housekeeper and his parents but his disruptive behavior continued at school with parents and teacher reporting much out-of-control behavior on D.'s part.

In the fourth session, D. was introduced to Nintendo using the Super Mario Brothers game. He played the game enthusiastically, but because of his strong propensity to rush ahead pell-mell, reflective of his generally disturbed state of mind, D.'s man, Mario, continued to fall off cliffs, get bumped off walls, and fall into holes. When this happened, D. filled the air with curses, he cried, and often hurled the controls to the floor. Upon such behavior, T. turned off the Nintendo until D. regained control and could assure T. that he could play more calmly. D. was then allowed to resume his game though, usually, the same cycle would repeat itself within minutes.

T. continued this pattern with D. through the next two sessions (D. was being seen on a once-per-week basis), adding generalizing statements to the contingency interactions. Such statements were of two kinds: (1) if–then statements for the moment (e.g., If you throw the controls, it's cool off time) and (2) generalizing statements (e.g., If you behave like this at school, you will be benched and other kids will not want to be your friend, etc.).

Concomitantly, T. modeled "in control" behavior as he played the game using Luigi, Mario's brother. Playing in control, Luigi could stay on the board a long time and reach many higher levels. T. used a thinking-out-loud procedure to demonstrate to D. how and what the strategies were, what to remember, when to jump, and so on. T. would indicate to D. that he was going to yield the board so that D. could play again, also suggesting that D. try to play in a more controlled manner. The concept of *In Control Behavior* became central.

The process of ventilating anger through assertive play while remaining in control seemed important in D.'s situation. D. apparently learned that controlled, nonangry play was more effective for the game and, by extension, in the home and in the classroom. During play, T. provided various comments in an attempt to generalize from the office-setting to home and school (e.g., "In control helps and works well; out of control causes all sorts of problems with Mario or with mom, or with teachers"; etc.).

By the tenth session, D.'s behavior was markedly improved in all areas. He manifested good self-control with peers on the playground and in class and was entirely appropriate in the home setting.

C., a 10-year-old girl manifesting deep feelings of insecurity and separation anxiety, with these apparently secondary to background problems involving hospitalization of family members and being left alone, was introduced to talk, play, art, and Nintendo therapy over the ten months of her eventually successful treatment (parent conferences were used to assist parents in reducing inadvertent reinforcement for fearful behavior on C.'s part). All aspects of C.'s therapy seemed about equally important, but the Nintendo games used served to underline two of C.'s major fears: being called on to answer questions in school and being left alone in the world.

The game of Jeopardy, played as seen on television except players type in their responses, seemed useful to C. with respect to her school fears. C. played this game against T. for a portion of virtually every one of her first ten sessions. In these initial sessions, C. usually would not even hazard a guess to the questions for which answers, using the Jeopardy format, had to be provided.

T. found that if he provided the correct responses, C. would accept these as her own. From this base of responding, C. was then encouraged to try her own response, with T. often providing hints or prompts. Finally, C. provided her own response without T.'s help. At this point, C. had begun attending school regularly and her teacher observed that she was interacting in class and asking and answering questions as she had never done before.

Another portion of C.'s session was spent playing Zelda, an adventure game. In the initial sessions featuring Zelda, C. manifested great timidity about moving about the Overworld, and even more inhibition with respect to exploring the levels of the Underworld. Her anxiety caused her to approach the game with rigidity and C. often repeated her mistakes, seeming not to perceive what was necessary for her to help her character, Link, move about the world of the game board.

Play stopped frequently as we discussed how fears sometimes kept us from exploring new things and freely going about enjoying ourselves in the world around us. Discussions often focused on how Link must feel since he is alone on the game board surrounded by hostile others; how he must continually think and fight, generalizing these thoughts first to other children throughout the world, then to those in C.'s school, then herself.

C. soon mastered the world of Zelda, almost concomitantly with mastering Jeopardy and finding it easier to attend and socialize at school. She soon found that her fears of going to friends' houses for sleepovers, going to movies with friends, riding her bike in the neighborhood, were greatly diminished. The fears soon were gone and C. could function once again in a normal manner.

J. was 7 years old when referred for therapy because of extreme fearfulness, severe facial and speech-sound tics, sleep disturbance, and major problems in his relationships with peers, parents, and younger brother. He has now been in therapy for a year and a half, and the frequency of visits has been reduced from two times to once per week. J. is very bright, manifesting a phenomenal memory (e.g., memorizing all of the lyrics for various musicals, all the parts of certain plays, etc.). However, his brightness and awareness often seemed to work against him since J.'s fearfulness increased as a function of what he read in newspapers and/or heard or saw on television news and his precocity tended to be annoying to many peers.

The first few months of therapy with J. involved working through his high need to control the situation by insisting that all activities be carried out in an order prescribed by him (as he did at home and, as often as possible, at school and in social situations). We played Candyland, Chutes & Ladders, then drew pictures. Any attempt at deviating from these activities or this sequence caused J. to decrease participation to the point of immobility and increase facial and speech tics.

In an attempt to introduce new and more variable activities into the sessions, T. one day stated that, while J. was drawing, T. was going to play Mario Brothers on Nintendo. The first three sessions in which this happened found J. remaining at the drawing table, almost studiously avoiding T. and the new activity in which T. was engaged. J.'s mother reported a heightened agitation and anger at home during this week and a half.

In the fourth session following the introduction of Mario Brothers, when T. moved across the room and turned on the Nintendo set, J. followed and stood beside T.'s chair observing the game. As J. watched, T. talked about the game and demonstrated how Mario, then Luigi, could be made to jump ditches, find magic mushrooms which made them larger and flowers which gave them "firepower" and, finally, defeat a dragon and save the princess. I also demonstrated "losing" a character (e.g., into a pit, burned by a dragon, bumped by a Meanie, etc.) and showed how the character could be made to appear again so that all was not lost.

The following session found J. requesting the Mario Brothers games instead of any other activity. However, J. would not play the game and insisted that he would rather watch T. play, stating that he was not sure that he could do the game. Approximately fifteen minutes into the session, T. asked J. to hold the control paddle with the game on Pause (no action) while T. went for a glass of water. J. did so. Upon returning, T. asked J. to continue to hold the paddle while T. placed his fingers over J.'s and together they played the game. T. gradually withdrew his hands and, thus, his direct assistance to J. on the game while J. began, awkwardly and seemingly fearfully, to play.

J. was playing Mario Brothers eagerly within weeks. Although a top-flight player would see much room for improvement in J.'s game, the real improvement from T.'s standpoint was that J. had moved from his rigid pattern, was playing a game which required flexibility (among other things), and was meeting the various trials and tribulations of the game with enjoyment and courage.

At this point, J.'s parents and classroom teacher noted his heightened interaction with peers, a reduction of tics, and a reduction of his generalized fearful behaviors. The game had seemingly "jumpstarted" J., catching his imagination and showing him that he could handle the world of Mario and Luigi and, perhaps by extension, much of his own world, as well.

It is not suggested that the use of these computer games was anything more than an adjunct to the psychological improvement of the four emotionally disturbed children previously described. However, in these and many other cases such games have proved to be a very important therapeutic tool. In this it is recognized that, theoretically, one can use almost any material to teach almost any topic or to help almost any child, given sufficient imagination (and luck) on the part of the teacher or therapist.

What may be possible in theory, however, may not be feasible in practice. Therefore, therapists, who have so little direct or real influence over the thoughts and feelings of their child patients (as opposed, say, to the very real control or influence, at least at the overt behavioral level, which can be exerted by parents and teachers) more or less need all the help they can get.

Traditionally, as previously indicated, this help has often come in the form of games, drawings, stories, and other activities in which therapist and child-patient engaged. It is likely that most child therapists offer play and playfulness in equal amounts. Add these ingredients with sensitivity, intelligence, training, and experience and the features of good child therapy begin to emerge. Add the use of the games of the day, which is to say in-office arcade type games (whether Nintendo, Sega, Apple, IBM, etc.) and the innovative therapist appears to have a good chance of being useful with many types of children's problems.

With children, at least, one's clinical techniques tend to change as a function of the trends of the times, though one's goals remain the same (i.e., to be useful to a frightened, hurt, or angry child and his/her family). Slower-paced activities such as playing checkers or chess, building models, or telling or reading stories together seems, with many youngsters, difficult terrain over which to establish a relationship. The apparent advantages of the quieter activities may be outweighed by the disadvantages of the lack of interest of the child and, worse, the child's perception of the counselor as old fashioned. Such a perception is more serious than it might at first appear because the therapist, to be helpful, needs to be seen as knowledgeable and reasonably "with it" (not "cool") as well as trustworthy, kind, and true.

References

Axline, V. (1947). *Play Therapy*. Boston: Houghton-Mifflin.
Berg, B. (1982). *The Changing Family Game*. Dayton, OH: University of Dayton Press.

Burks, H. F. (1978). *Psychological Meanings of the Imagine! Game.* Huntington Beach, CA: Arden.

Freud, A. (1928). *Introduction to the Technique of Child Analysis.* Trans. L. P. Clark. New York: Nervous and Mental Disease Publishing.

Gardner, R. A. (1973a). *The Talking, Feeling, Doing Game.* Cresskill, NJ: Creative Therapeutics.

——— (1973b). *Understanding Children.* New York: Jason Aronson.

Klein, M. (1932). *The Psycho-Analysis of Children.* London: Hogarth.

Loomis, E. A. (1957). The use of checkers in handling certain resistances in child therapy and child analysis. *Journal of the American Psychoanalytical Association* 5:130–135.

Oden, T. (1976). *The Transactional Analysis Game.* New York: Harper & Row.

Schaefer, C. E., and Reid, S. E., eds. (1986). *Game Play.* New York: Wiley.

Zalick, R. (1975). *The Ungame.* Anaheim, CA: The Ungame Co.

24

High Tech Play Therapy

RICHARD G. JOHNSON

The microcomputer is making many changes in our world including how our children play. Arcade games and their home computer versions engage our children's attention because they are different from traditional toys. Most toys are passive. They may be manipulated and moved about, but they don't respond or, at best, have limited responses. The fascination of the computer for children is that it does respond and does so in complex and interesting ways. How might these new "toys" be used in play therapy? Can counselors and psychologists capitalize on the interest children have in computers?

This chapter describes the use of a microcomputer in play therapy with children between 9 and 12 years old in a learning clinic operated by the College of Education of Michigan State University. The clinic provides diagnostic, tutorial, and counseling services to school children in the vicinity of the University and furnishes a setting for training and research for the College of Education.

Play Therapy

Play therapy has been one method used in counseling children in the clinic. This approach has been used to develop a diagnostic understanding of the child and to establish a working relationship as discussed by Amster (1943). It has also been used to help children to deal with anxiety experiences and, as Obernbreit (1980) suggests, to allow children to experiment with ideas, behaviors, and feelings in a safe environment. Finally, play therapy as outlined by Landreth (1983) has been employed to encourage children to express feelings and to desensitize them to past events that produce unpleasant emotional responses.

Children have difficulty expressing their thoughts and feelings. They can often express themselves more easily in action than in words. Play is their natural and comfortable medium of expression. Children are more likely to express themselves openly and honestly through play, which allows the expression of feelings, the exploration of relationships, and the disclosing of wishes. As play is the language of the child, it provides a medium for building the working relationship between the counselor and child that is essential in counseling (Harter 1983, Landreth 1983). Dolls, puppets, cars and trucks, a doll house, and paints and other drawing materials have all been used in the clinic. Recently, in addition to these traditional play things, a computer has been employed. The computer is an Apple IIe that was purchased primarily to be used in the instructional programs in math and reading.

Turtle Graphics

Counselors in the clinic first began using the computer with individual children by showing them how to use turtle graphics in LOGO, a computer language well suited for young children as well as adults. LOGO's turtle graphics allow the user to draw interesting figures and designs on the screen by directing a small triangular object called the turtle. As the turtle is directed to move across the screen, it leaves a line. Directions to move and turn are accomplished simply by typing commands like "FD 50" and "RT 90" to indicate moving 50 units forward and then turning 90 degrees to the right. A few minutes of instruction and children are able to draw squares, circles, and other geometric figures and combine them into complex designs in several colors. The introduction of this computer software has been well received by the children and counselors. It has been used initially to help children feel at ease and to begin communicating with the counselor. It has enhanced the children's motivation to come to the clinic. Telling their friends that they are going to the university to work on the computer gives them an acceptable reason for not being available to play with friends after school on certain days.

Painting with the Computer

The initial experience with turtle graphics was so positive that other ways of using the computer were sought. Perhaps the most promising was the use of a graphics pad that allows children to draw in color on the screen by moving their fingers across the smooth surface of the pad as they would in fingerpainting. Of course, there are no paints. The pad attached to the computer translates the pressure of the fingers to marks on the screen in any color chosen by the user. The particular device used was the *Power Pad* with *Leo's 'lectric Paintbrush* software, both developed by Chalk Board, Inc. There are other graphics tablets on the market priced as this one was at approximately one hundred dollars including the pad and software.

The child can select from six colors in addition to black and white by a touch of the finger on a small circle of color on the pad. Other features allow objects drawn to be moved to different parts of the picture or objects to be repeated. For example, one tree can be drawn, then repeated several times to produce a forest. The pictures drawn can be saved on disk and then be returned to the screen at a later time.

Computer Art Therapy

The counseling techniques used with this graphic arts medium were taken from Nickerson (1983) and Winnicott (1971) who describe the use of art in play therapy. The child is invited each session to draw a picture. When finished, he or she is asked to tell a story about it. The counselor asks questions like, "What's happening in your picture?" and "What will happen next?" Through "understanding a child's drawings, we can better understand the child who created them" (Sheniak 1981, p. 53). Another technique is to help children to associate colors with feelings, for example, red for anger and black for sadness. They are then asked to paint how they feel using colors, not trying to represent how they look but to portray their mood now or at some particular event in their life. A third technique used is Winnicott's Squiggle Technique (1971) in which the counselor makes a squiggle, a line with a few curves in it, and the child is asked to make a picture using the line. When finished, the child makes up a story about the picture and the counselor asks questions.

Computer art is a way of enhancing communication between the child and the counselor and offers a projective assessment tool as well as a medium for looking at new ways of perceiving self and exploring new and more adequate coping behaviors.

The initial phase in play therapy using the computer as an art medium is diagnostic and relationship building. The child is given a great deal of freedom about what to draw and what colors to choose. The counselor encourages the child to talk about the drawings but does not direct or make interpretations. When the relationship between the counselor and child has been established, interpretations are made, but indirectly at first. The counselor has a character from the child's story make the observation. The counselor might say, for example, "The boy in your story thinks that no one likes him." This indirect approach is taken so that the child's defenses will not be alerted. Later the counselor may attempt to associate the child with a character in the story by saying, "You're a bit like the boy in this story." The counselor can then be more direct by saying, "I know someone who thinks that no one likes him," and then describe the child. At this stage, the child knows that the counselor is talking about him and the counselor can be even more direct. This gradual approach to discussing the child's feelings or concerns in play therapy has been described by Harter (1983).

Coping mechanisms can be identified in the stories that accompany the pictures and are then discussed. Alternative ways to cope can be developed and tried out in the story. The child is asked to relate his or her own experiences to those situations in the story. The trying out of alternative coping strategies in the child's story is a behavioral rehearsal for the child in dealing with the same problems in real life.

Play can be a means of identifying and dealing with hostility toward parents or siblings as it was with one child in the clinic who, in his stories involving his family, had his mother always in precarious positions, on the roof or hanging from the gutter of the roof about to fall. In the discussions of these stories, the child revealed some strong negative feelings about his mother. When such emotions are discovered, the counselor helps make the child aware of them and helps the child learn how to deal with those feelings. The child may also be helped to see the relationship through the eyes of the other person by having the child tell the story from the other person's perspective.

The counselor helps the child learn ways to deal with the anger-producing situation by asking questions like, "How could you tell the other person how you feel?," "What could you do so as not to feel so bad?," "How might you prevent this from happening again?" If no suggestions are made, the counselor offers some and has the child try them out in the story or in a role-played enactment of the problem situation with the counselor.

These discussions begin with the drawing and the story told about it and then move to focus on the child's life. This transition is achieved by first asking the child how the story characters might better handle the situation and then how the child might handle similar situations in his or her life.

Feeling Paintings

The graphic pad and computer have been especially useful in helping children identify and discuss feelings. The counselor asks the child to identify feelings associated with each color and to draw how he or she felt in emotional situations. As the child draws, the counselor may ask if other feelings might also be present and if so, suggest that other colors be used to represent these feelings.

The discussion about such a drawing can lead to identifying those situations that produce negative feelings, the frequency and intensity of those emotions, and the kinds of feelings that the child would like to have. The child can be asked to "paint" happy feelings and describe the kinds of things that bring these kinds of feelings.

A feelings painting can be used each counseling session to monitor progress. The child is asked to draw feelings that summarize the week or summarize the week's experiences in the problem situations. The painting should include the negative feelings as well as the positive ones in proportion to their occurrence during the week. As the feelings painting is discussed, it is modified if necessary. Finally, the picture is saved on disk so that the sequence of paintings can later be reviewed to note progress using this subjective technique.

Children are sometimes troubled by strong negative emotions— guilt, fear, and grief are examples. Through art, subjects that a child may consider prohibited can be expressed and feelings can be released (Shenick 1981). Art therapy using conventional media or computer art can be helpful in desensitizing them to the emotion provoking stimuli. One 11-year-old boy was referred to the clinic because his mother reported that since her husband's death two years earlier, the boy had become overly dependent upon her. He would become "ill" when she occasionally went out in the evening without him. The boy had never cried over his father's sudden death nor did he talk about his father since that event. The mother also had difficulty dealing with her grief and had not been able to discuss the tragedy with her son.

After a few sessions of rapport building and free painting, the counselor asked the boy to choose colors and draw the saddest day of his life. He drew some black lines then a large black scribble. The counselor said that it appeared that he had been very sad and asked him what the occasion was that caused him to be so unhappy. The boy said that he had been sad when his pet bird had died. They discussed this for a while and then the counselor asked if there was another occasion when he had felt this sad. The boy then said that he had the same feeling, "only worse," when his father had died. In the discussion that followed, the boy also identified a feeling of anger in his reaction to his father's death. Red was added to his picture to represent this anger. As the discussion progressed, the boy finally let go and cried. The counselor assured him that it was quite a proper response. Feeling that the boy had been upset enough for that session, the counselor told him that they would leave that topic for then but that they would return to it again in future sessions. Over the next few sessions, they did return to the subject, and the boy was able to talk about the death much less emotionally and to discuss good times with his father without exhibiting any stress.

Not having had the opportunity to talk about the death because the topic was avoided by his mother and himself, the boy had no help in rationalizing the anger he felt or in allowing his pain to be expressed. The feeling paintings and a skillful counselor allowed this boy to express his feelings and deal with his grief.

Summary and Discussion

The microcomputer was employed as a creative medium in art therapy using a graphics pad and counseling approaches developed with more traditional art media. The children who had this opportunity as part of their counseling looked forward to their sessions, and our initial experiences with the computer have encouraged us to continue exploring its applications in counseling. Although the use of the computer hasn't added anything yet to the theory of play therapy or to basic approaches used, it does provide a play medium that captures children's interest and provides a novel way to do things that have customarily been done in art and play therapy. Perhaps with continued experimentation, a unique contribution of the computer in therapy may be identified. For now, in addition to its ease of use, the computer's major advantage is the interest it generates in children and in the counselors using it. The computer age is here; we might do well to learn what it has to offer counselors and psychologists.

References

Amster, F. (1943). Differential uses of play in treatment of young children. *American Journal of Orthopsychiatry* 13:62–68.

Harter, S. (1983). Cognitive-development considerations in the conduct of play therapy. In *Handbook of Play Therapy,* ed. C. E. Schaefer and K. J. O'Connor. New York: Wiley.

Landreth, G. L. (1983). Play therapy in elementary school settings. In *Handbook of Play Therapy,* ed. C. E. Schaefer and K. J. O'Connor. New York: Wiley.

Nickerson, E. T. (1983). Art as a play therapeutic medium. In *Handbook of Play Therapy,* ed. C. E. Schaefer and K. J. O'Connor. New York: Wiley.

Obernbreit, R. (1980). Art therapy: agent in education. *Pratt Institute Creative Arts Therapy Review* 1:59–66.

Shenick, D. (1981). Art as therapy. *School Arts* 81:7.

Winnicott, D. W. (1971). *Therapeutic Consultations in Child Psychiatry.* New York: Basic Books.

Credits

Chapter 3: "Structured Play Therapy," by Gove Hambridge, Jr. Reprinted from the *American Journal of Orthopsychiatry,* vol. 25, pp. 187–203. Copyright © 1955 by the American Orthopsychiatric Association Inc. Reproduced by permission.

Chapter 4: "The Use of Two Houses in Play Therapy," by Linda Kuhli. Reprinted from the *American Journal of Orthopsychiatry,* vol. 49, pp. 432–435. Copyright © 1979 by the American Orthopsychiatric Association Inc. Reproduced by permission.

Chapter 5: "Using Puppets for Assessment," by Eleanor C. Irwin. Originally published as "Puppets in Therapy: An Assessment Procedure," in the *American Journal of Psychotherapy,* vol. 39, pp. 389–400. Copyright © 1985 by the *American Journal of Psychotherapy.* Reprinted by permission of the Association for the Advancement of Psychotherapy.

Chapter 6: "Finger Puppets and Mask Making," by R. L. Jenkins and Erica Beckh. Originally published as "Finger Puppets and Mask Making as a Media for Work with Children." Reprinted from the *American Journal of Orthopsychiatry,* vol. 12, pp. 294–300. Copyright © 1942 by the American Orthopsychiatric Association Inc. Reproduced by permission.

Chapter 7: "Costume Play Therapy," by Irwin M. Marcus. Originally published as "Costume Play Therapy: The Exploration of a Method for Stimulating Imaginative Play in Older Children," in *Journal of the American Academy of Child and Adolescent Psychiatry,* vol. 5, pp. 441–452. Copyright © 1966. Reprinted by permission of Williams and Wilkins Publishers.

Chapter 8: "Use of the Telephone in Play Therapy," by Moshe H. Spero. Originally published as "Use of the Telephone in Child Play Therapy," in *Social Work,* January 1980, pp. 57–60. Copyright © 1980 by the National Association of Social Workers. Reprinted by permission of the National Association of Social Workers.

Chapter 9: "Block Play," by Robert J. Resnick. Originally published as "Block Playing as a Therapeutic Technique," in *Psychotherapy: Theory, Research and Practice,* vol. 13, pp. 170–172. Copyright © 1976 by the Division of Psychotherapy of the American Psychological Association. Reprinted with permission from the Division of Psychotherapy of the American Psychological Association.

Chapter 10: "Sandplay," by John Allan and Pat Berry. Reprinted from *Elementary School Guidance and Counseling,* vol. 21, pp. 300–306. Copyright © 1987 by the American Counseling Association. Reprinted by permission of the American Counseling Association.

Chapter 11: "Water Play," by Ruth E. Hartley, Lawrence K. Frank, and Robert M. Goldenson. Originally published as "The Benefits of Water Play" in *Understanding Children's Play,* by Ruth E. Hartley et al. Copyright © 1952 Columbia University Press, New York. Reprinted with the permission of the publisher.

Chapter 12: "The Use of Food in Therapy," by Mary R. Haworth and Mary Jane Kelly, from *Child Psychotherapy,* edited by Mary R. Haworth, pp. 330–337. Copyright © 1964 by Mary Haworth. Reprinted by permission of HarperCollins Publishers.

Chapter 13: "Mud and Clay," by Adolf G. Woltmann. Originally published as "Mud and Clay: Their Functions as Developmental Aids and as Media of Projection," in *Personality—Symposium of Topical Issues,* edited by W. Wolff, pp. 35–50. Copyright © 1950. Reprinted by permission of Grune and Stratton, Inc.

Chapter 14: "Finger Painting," by Jacob A. Arlow and Asja Kadis. Originally published as "Finger Painting in the Psychotherapy of Children." Reprinted from the *American Journal of Orthopsychiatry,* vol. 16, pp. 134—146. Copyright © 1946 by the American Orthopsychiatric Association, Inc. Reproduced by permission.

Chapter 15: "The Squiggle-Drawing Game," by Lawrence Claman. Originally published as "The Squiggle Drawing Game in Child Psychotherapy," in the *American Journal of Psychotherapy,* vol. 34, pp. 414–425.

Copyright © 1980 by the *American Journal of Psychotherapy*. Reprinted by permission of the Association for the Advancement of Psychotherapy.

Chapter 16: "The Emotional Barometer," by Suzanne Elliott. Originally published as "The Emotional Barometer: A Graphic Aid to Counseling," in *Elementary School and Guidance Counseling*, vol. 21, pp. 312–317. Copyright © 1987 by the American Counseling Association. Reprinted by permission of the American Counseling Association.

Chapter 17: "Mutual Storytelling," by Richard A. Gardner. Originally published as "Mutual Storytelling: A Technique in Child Psychotherapy" in *Acta Paedopsychiatrica*, vol. 38, pp. 253–262. Copyright © 1971. Reprinted by permission.

Chapter 18: "Creative Characters," by Robert Brooks. Originally published as "Creative Characters: A Technique in Child Therapy," in *Psychotherapy: Theory, Research and Practice*, vol. 18, pp. 131–139. Copyright © 1976 by the Division of Psychotherapy of the American Psychological Association. Reprinted with permission from the Division of Psychotherapy of the American Psychological Association.

Chapter 19: "Role Playing," by Richard L. Levenson, Jr. and Jack Herman. Originally published as "The Use of Role Playing as a Technique in the Psychotherapy of Children," in *Psychotherapy: Theory, Resesarch and Practice*, vol. 28, pp. 660–666. Copyright © 1991 by the Division of Psychotherapy of the American Psychological Association. Reprinted with permission from the Division of Psychotherapy of the American Psychological Association.

Chapter 20: "Relaxation Training," by Arlene S. Koeppen. Originally published as "Relaxation Training for Children," in *Elementary School Guidance and Counseling*, vol. 9, pp. 14—21. Copyright © 1974 by the American Counseling Association. Reprinted by permission of the American Counseling Association.

Chapter 21: "Checkers," by Richard A. Gardner. Originally published as "The Game of Checkers in Child Therapy," in *Game Play: Therapeutic Use of Childhood Games*, edited by C. E. Schaefer and S. Reid, pp. 215–232. Copyright © 1986 by John Wiley & Sons. Reprinted by permission of John Wiley & Sons.

Chapter 22: "Chess," by William H. Smith. Originally published as "An Approach to the Analysis of Activities: The Game of Chess," in *Bulletin of the Menninger Clinic,* vol. 39, pp. 93–100. Copyright © 1975. Reprinted by permission of the Division of Scientific Publications, the Menninger Clinic.

Chapter 23: "Nintendo Games," by James E. Gardner. Originally published as "Can the Mario Brothers Help? Nintendo Games as an Adjunct in Psychotherapy with Children," in *Psychotherapy: Theory, Research and Practice,* vol. 28, pp. 667–670. Copyright © 1991 by the Division of Psychotherapy of the American Psychological Association. Reprinted with permission from the Division of Psychotherapy of the American Psychological Association.

Index

About the Editors

Charles Schaefer, Ph.D., is Professor of Psychology and Director, Psychological Service Center, Fairleigh Dickinson University, Hackensack, New Jersey. Dr. Schaefer is the founder and Chairman of the Board of the Association for Play Therapy, a national organization that includes international membership. He is a Fellow of both the American Psychological Association and the American Orthopsychiatric Association. Among Dr. Schaefer's publications are the outstanding books *Handbook of Play Therapy* and *The Therapeutic Use of Child's Play*, which have become classics in the field. Dr. Schaefer maintains a private practice with children and their families in Hackensack, New Jersey.

Donna Cangelosi, Psy.D., is an instructor in child and adolescent psychotherapy at the New Jersey Institute for Psychoanalysis in Teaneck, New Jersey. She is a member of the Association for Play Therapy and the American Psychological Association. Co-editor of the book *The Playing Cure*, she has authored several chapters on psychodynamic treatment with children as well as the forthcoming book *Saying Goodbye in Child Psychotherapy*. Dr. Cangelosi has lectured throughout the country on topics related to separation, loss, and divorce issues in children; psychodynamic play therapy; and the ending phase of treatment. She maintains a private psychotherapy practice with children, adolescents, and adults in Teaneck